I Will Tell You the Mystery

I Will Tell You the Mystery

A Commentary for Preaching on the Book of Revelation

Ronald J. Allen

CASCADE *Books* · Eugene, Oregon

I WILL TELL YOU THE MYSTERY
A Commentary for Preaching on the Book of Revelation

Cascade Books
An Imprint of Wipf and Stock Publishers
199 W. 8th Ave., Suite 3
Eugene, OR 97401

www.wipfandstock.com

PAPERBACK ISBN: 978-1-4982-2591-5
HARDCOVER ISBN: 978-1-4982-2593-9
EBOOK ISBN: 978-1-4982-2592-2

Cataloguing-in-Publication data:

Names: Allen, Ronald J., author.

Title: I will tell you the mystery : a commentary for preaching on the book of Revelation. / by Ronald J. Allen.

Description: Eugene, OR: Cascade Books, 2019. | Includes bibliographical references.

Identifiers: ISBN 978-1-4982-2591-5 (paperback) | ISBN 978-1-4982-2593-9 (hardcover) | ISBN 978-1-4982-2592-2 (ebook)

Subjects: LCSH: Bible. Revelation—Commentaries.

Classification: LCC BS2825.53 A37 2019 (print) | LCC BS2825.53 (ebook)

Manufactured in the U.S.A.   06/07/19

For
Lilah Marie Allen
To whose father, Canaan, I dedicated an earlier book.
For both daughter and father
I pray for a new heaven and a new earth.

Contents

Preface

The title, *I Will Tell You the Mystery*, is adapted from Revelation 17:7. In Revelation 17:1–6, John pictures a human figure seated on a scarlet beast with seven heads and ten horns. In verse 7, an angel says, "I will tell you the mystery of the woman and of the beast."[1] In the following verses, the angel then explains the significance of the figure on the beast. The book of Revelation communicates through images, and this movement from reporting the image to explaining it encapsulates the call of the preacher. As the angel does in Revelation 17:1–18, a preacher needs to explain the images in relationship to God's purposes and help the congregation consider appropriate responses.

The introduction for preachers overviews the historical setting of the book of Revelation, its literary approach, and introduces the perspectives on theology and preaching that inform this commentary. The volume then follows the lines of a traditional biblical commentary, moving passage by passage. Ministers who preach from specific texts will find the commentary format handy as they can turn immediately to the text for the week.

I do repeat some of the interpretive perspectives from the introduction in the commentary itself. Under the pressure of moving sermon preparation along, preachers sometimes overlook the introductions to commentaries. Preachers often go immediately to the comments on the text and never pick up the commentator's "take" on the biblical material.

The distinctive focus of this commentary is on preaching.[2] Yet, because I am committed to the notion that the best preaching typically arises

1. All citations from Scripture are from the New Revised Standard Version.

2. Most commentaries focus on locating the otherness of the text in antiquity without giving significant attention to possible implications for today. Four significant commentators who think about the importance of the text for our world are Boesak in his *Comfort and Protest*, Boring in his *Revelation*, Reddish in his *Revelation*, and Rowland in his "Book of Revelation." Hermeneutical considerations are just below the surface in Blount, *Revelation*.

from particular contexts, this book suggests possible issues for preaching but does not offer fully developed sermons.

This book seeks (1) to help preachers recognize what the book of Revelation (with its apocalyptic theology) invited people in antiquity to believe and do, (2) to bring that viewpoint into conversation with contemporary revisionary theology, and (3) to help preachers help their congregation identify what it can genuinely believe and confidently do. My part of the contemporary conversation is informed by mutual critical correlation through process theology.[3]

In today's world—in the trap of so many kinds of empire—the book of Revelation can particularly help preachers identify phenomena that are similar to the idolatrous, unjust, exploitative, violent, and self-destroying qualities of the Roman Empire. Even more, they can help their congregations discern the presence and coming of a new heaven and a new earth with its love, peace, justice, mutuality, and abundance. Along the way, the commentary names theological points at which progressive preachers may disagree with aspects of the book of Revelation. Indeed, they may sometimes preach against a text.

For several years, I have put out every book with a prayer. I pray that this one will help preachers and listeners lean towards the kind of world described in Revelation 21 and 22: a new heaven and new earth.

---

3. By way of theological foreshadowing, I should say at the outset that I do not agree with John that God plans to destroy the present world and replace it with a new cosmos. I do believe God is always present offering possibilities of better worlds as human beings work with God, with one another, and with nature.

Abbreviations

Torah, Prophets, and Writings

Gen	Genesis	Isa	Isaiah
Exod	Exodus	Jer	Jeremiah
Lev	Leviticus	Lam	Lamentations
Num	Numbers	Ezek	Ezekiel
Deut	Deuteronomy	Dan	Daniel
Judg	Judges	Hos	Hosea
Ruth	Ruth	Joel	Joel
1–2 Sam	1–2 Samuel	Amos	Amos
1–2 Kgs	1–2 Kings	Obad	Obadiah
1–2 Chr	1–2 Chronicles	Jonah	Jonah
Ezra	Ezra	Mic	Mic
Neh	Nehemiah	Hab	Habakkuk
Job	Job	Zeph	Zephaniah
Ps/Pss	Psalms	Hag	Haggai
Prov	Proverbs	Zech	Zechariah
Eccl	Ecclesiastes	Mal	Malachi
Song	Song of Songs		

Gospels and Letters

Matt	Matthew	Col	Colossians
Mark	Mark	1–2 Thess	1–2 Thessalonians
Luke	Luke	1–2 Tim	1–2 Timothy
John	John	Titus	Titus
Acts	Acts	Phlm	Philemon
Rom	Romans	Heb	Hebrews
1–2 Cor	1–2 Corinthians	Jas	James
Gal	Galatians	1–2 Pet	1–2 Peter
Eph	Ephesians	1–2–3 John	1–2–3 John
Phil	Philippians	Rev	Revelation

Other Ancient Literature

Ant.	Josephus, *Antiquities*	3–4 Macc	3–4 Maccabees
B. Bat.	b. Baba Batra	1QM	War Scroll
2 Bar.	2 Baruch	1QS	Rule of the Community
Did.	Didache		
1 En.	1 Enoch	Sib. Or.	Sibylline Oracles
2 En.	2 Enoch	Sir	Sirach/Ecclesiasticus
1–2 Esd	1–2 Esdras	Wis	Wisdom of Solomon
Jub.	Jubilees	T. Dan	Testament of Daniel
Let. Aris.	Letter of Aristeas	T. Levi	Testament of Levi
1–2 Macc	1–2 Maccabees	T. Mos.	Testament of Moses

Introduction for Preachers

Every commentary on a biblical book contains an introduction that overviews authorship, date, circumstances of writing, purpose, literary style, and theological viewpoint. This introduction covers the same territory, but with an eye toward preaching. Along the way, I also note parallels and differences between life in the Roman Empire and life amid empires today, between John's apocalyptic theology and my own process thinking, and between the purposes of preaching in the book of Revelation in its ancient setting and possible purposes of preaching in conversation with that book today.

The Preacher in Conversation with the Book of Revelation

This book seeks to foster conversation with the book of Revelation. Because the word "conversation" comes up frequently in theological discourse today, I will note here that I use it to refer to a particular way of doing theology (mutual critical correlation) in concert with process theology.[1]

Most Preachers Seek a "Preachable X" in the Text

Most preachers assume that a biblical passage contains an authoritative word for today. As theologian Edward Farley puts it, a preacher presumes that each biblical passage has "a preachable X."[2] Through exegesis, theological

---

1. This perspective on preaching and theology is elaborated in several places—e.g., Allen and Allen, *Sermon without End*, as well as briefer discussions in my "Preaching as Mutual Critical Correlation" and "Preaching as Conversation." A seminal work is Allen, *Homiletic of All Believers*.

2. Farley, "Preaching the Bible," 76–77.

analysis, and hermeneutics, preachers seek to *identify* authoritative elements in the text and to *apply* them to today. Preachers build a bridge from then to now, making a correlation between then and now through direct application, an analogy, or a parallel function for the text.[3]

When preaching from the book of Revelation in this model, one searches for an instructive word in the text for the contemporary community. If a preacher encounters difficult exegetical, theological, or hermeneutical perspectives, a preacher continues to look for pathways that open the way to a more acceptable perspective. As Edward Farley vividly says, the preacher tries to "save" the text.[4]

A Conversational Approach: Listening to Others and Adapting Appropriately

By comparison, in conversational theology based on mutual critical correlation, preacher and congregation listen to the voice of the biblical text in dialogue with other voices from the tradition and the contemporary world. The preacher and the community search for what they can most deeply believe about God's purpose and how to respond appropriately. In real conversation, each participant is open to being changed by others. Hence, preachers cannot be committed in advance to the idea that they can make a positive correlation between the text and today.

In the conversational approach, a preacher does not presume that every word of every passage is authoritative. Through exegesis, a preacher seeks to identify what John asked the followers of Jesus in late-first-century Asia Minor to believe and do. The preacher brings the text into conversation with other sources of insight, such as wider Christian tradition, the preacher's deepest theological and ethical convictions, and how the preacher believes that God works in the universe. The preacher is then in a position to help the congregation consider what it can believe and do today. Such conversations typically arrive at one of three weigh stations.

1. The conversation may lead the preacher to embrace what the text asks listeners to believe and do, and to draw out implications for the present. This text can encourage the congregation to clarify and even enlarge its view of God's aims in the world and how to respond.

---

3. For the relationships of the Bible to preaching in historical and contemporary theological families, see my *Thinking Theologically.*

4. Farley, "Preaching the Bible," 78–79.

2. The conversation often leads to a mixed perspective: The preacher can embrace some elements of what the text asks listeners to believe and do, but must differ with other parts. I often find that I can agree with certain perspectives in a passage, but disagree with others. This conversation may yield a "preachable X" alongside some points of view that the congregation cannot embrace.

3. The conversation may lead a preacher to disagree with what a text assumes about God's purposes and actions, as well as human responses. The preacher must preach against the text. The conversation helps preacher and congregation move towards claiming what they most believe and need to do. Sometimes naming what we do not believe helps us clarify what we do believe.

All of these interpretive options are on the table when approaching individual texts in the book of Revelation. The book has much to offer the world today. However, as I point out more fully below, some of its claims about God's purposes and God's exercise of power are deeply troubling.

The Social Location of This Commentary

Social location has become a significant item in contemporary theology. My social location is that of a progressive, older, Eurocentric, heterosexual, middle-class male in the United States, a lifelong member of the Christian Church (Disciples of Christ), in the family of process theology. People in my social location usually benefit from contemporary forms of empire. I write this commentary in conversation with that group more than others because, with many interpreters, I see John the Revelator (in part) challenging Christian communities that are, in the prophet's view, in danger of accommodating too much to empire.

While I think John believed that the opportunity for repentance had passed for the empire itself, I also think John believed that congregations and individuals in the empire could still do so. I differ from John in this regard: I believe it is still possible for contemporary empires, as well as smaller communities and individuals, to turn away from empire orientation, and to join the movement to the new heaven and the new earth.

As I note below, the preacher may need to emphasize assurance for persons already making faithful and true witness and for congregations in social locations oppressed by such things as racism and sex and gender exclusion. Such communities may need assurance that God is at liberating work in solidarity with them more than they need the challenge discussed just above.

Many Ministers Today Hesitate to Preach from the Book of Revelation

I lead Bible studies on the book of Revelation in local congregations. Participants often comment, "I can't remember when we had a sermon or a study on this book." Despite the pertinence of some themes in the book of Revelation, I gather that a good many pastors in the historic churches are reluctant to preach or teach on it.

Some Ministers Struggle with How to Interpret This Book

I have asked some ministers, "Why this silence?" Some say that the book of Revelation is just too hard to understand. "It's just too bizarre." "It sounds like John was on a hallucinogen." "It is so confusing." Baffling, bewildering, cryptic, fearful, mystifying, obscure, puzzling, and unintelligible—these are words some ministers associate with the last book of the Bible. ·

I do not mean to be disrespectful, but I have to say that when ministers say such things, they show that they do not do their homework. To be sure, students in seminary are often exposed to little more critical interpretation of the Revelation than reading thirty pages in an introductory textbook and hearing thirty minutes of a survey lecture. However, broader training in exegesis gives ministers the skills to focus on this—and every—book in the Bible. Moreover, we now have an abundance of books and articles setting out responsible perspectives on the book of Revelation.

The Lectionary Minimizes the Book of Revelation

While preachers often say that the lectionary pushes them towards texts they would otherwise avoid, the opposite is the case with the book of Revelation. The Revised Common Lectionary assigns readings from the apocalypse to only eleven days in the three-year cycle. Moreover, some of the readings repeat from year to year. Indeed, the lectionary assigns only six distinct passages from the book of Revelation over the three-year cycle. Thus, the lectionary preacher can easily avoid preaching from the book of Revelation.[5]

Popular Apocalypticism Clouds Perception of the Book

Many preachers in historic churches are uneasy with popular portrayals of apocalypticism represented by the *Left Behind* series.[6] Contemporary media often leave the impression that Left Behindism is the *only* way to understand biblical apocalypticism. Many clergy in progressive churches have an insufficient grasp of the history and detail of Left Behindism (and its larger context in premillennialism) to engage it meaningfully, so they leave the subject in the closet.

Furthermore, nearly every congregation contains people who adhere to premillennialism. Some ministers are unwilling to risk getting crosswise with such members by offering alternative interpretations. As a pastor says, "Why should I risk setting off an exegetical firestorm when the congregation's food pantry is running low, and everybody will give food—regardless of what they think about the end-times?"

Compelling Reasons for Preaching on the Book of Revelation Today

Nevertheless, there are compelling reasons for preaching on the book of Revelation today. When approached with respect for differences of opinion, Revelation can be a gathering point for meaningful conversation.

---

5. Consultation on Common Texts, *Revised Common Lectionary*, 128.

6. Tim LaHaye and Jerry B. Jenkins created the *Left Behind* series of books and movies. The series gives narrative expression to the approach to eschatology known variously as premillennialism, Darbyism, chiliasm, millenarianism, or dispensationalism. This approach creates a timeline for the end of the present age of history by drawing on material throughout the Bible, especially the books of Isaiah, Ezekiel, Daniel, and Revelation. Premillennialists differ among themselves on many matters of detail. Efird offers a thumbnail approach to the history of Darbyism and various millennial approaches to the book of Revelation (and to wider apocalypticism) in his *Left Behind*. Farmer sketches four main approaches in the history of the interpretation of the book of Revelation in his commentary: preterist, historicist, futurist, and symbolic (*Revelation*, 3–6). His broad taxonomy of millenialisms is helpful: dispensational premillennialism, historical premillennialism, postmillennialism, and amillennialism (*Revelation*, 7–13). Reddish provides a superb comparison of views on the Millennium (*Revelation*, 391). Balmer places premillennialism in its larger cultural context in his concise *The Making of Evangelicalism*, esp. 27–40.

The Book is in the Bible

The book of Revelation is in the Bible. While churches subscribe to various perceptions of the nature, authority, function, and extent of the canon, virtually all Christian communities agree that interaction with the Bible is essential to helping communities come to clarity regarding what they most deeply believe about the nature of God, the divine purposes for the world, and how to respond in mission. The book of Revelation is part of the Christian family story. As in all families, we value different family members in different ways. I do not have to act like my great Uncle Hube, who had a little moonshine still in the Ozarks, in order to care about him. His life can still help me think about my choices for my own values and behavior.

The minister is called to see that teaching takes place in the congregation. Such teaching should help build up the congregation in ways consistent with the congregation's deepest and most theologically appropriate understandings of the divine purposes. To fail to offer interpretive help is to fail the ministerial calling.

A Credible Alternative to Popular Apocalypticism

Not helping a congregation make sense of the book of Revelation may leave the congregation at the whim of popular interpretive winds that can blow uncritically through the window of the church. How are congregants to make critical choices about interpretive routes if they do not know the routes and their strengths and weaknesses?

I usually lead Bible studies on Revelation in congregations with moderate to progressive theological leanings. When the Bible study group gathers in the church basement for the first time, a number of people are aware of *Left Behind* perspectives, but not others. Many members have vague, uncomfortable impressions of premillennialism, but cannot say why. Their theological intuition is, "I do not want to believe that God would do the violent things associated with popular end-time thinking." But they do not have exegetical and theological resources to go beyond their uneasiness.

Such folk are often relieved and empowered by learning about credible exegetical, theological, and hermeneutical alternatives for interpreting the book of Revelation. As several people have said, "In my heart, I wanted to believe something else, but I did not know it was possible. Now I do."

Empire Then and Now

The book of Revelation seeks to help its hearers struggle with such questions as "How shall we respond to the Roman empire? What does it mean for us to be faithful when confronted by the values and behaviors of the Roman empire?" While the western Roman empire collapsed in 476 CE, there are similar empires today. Per our discussion of five possible responses to empire below, contemporary congregations must deal with the question, "How do we respond to manifestations of empire today?"

Basic Questions of Authorship, Date, Location, Audience, and Purpose

The exegetical interpretation of the book of Revelation begins with the basic questions of who wrote it? When? Where? What kind of literature is it? And why? The Revelation provides more data on questions of authorship, location, audience, and purpose than do most other biblical materials. Indeed, John directly comments on these matters in Revelation 1:1-2, 9-11.

The Visionary: John, a Prophet

A person named John wrote the book of Revelation (Rev 1:1, 4, 9). While Christians have sometimes thought that this John was from the immediate circle of Jesus, or the John associated with the Fourth Gospel, neither seems likely. If the book of Revelation was written about 95 CE (as most critical scholars suppose), a John from Jesus' circle would have been almost impossibly old for the time. The literary style, language, and theology of the Gospel of John differ so dramatically from those of the book of Revelation that the two books could hardly come from the same quill.

John was an apocalyptic prophet (Rev 1:1-2; 22:6, 9). Prophets in the early church believed that they received messages from God concerning the present and the future. The prophets delivered the messages to the congregations. The messages were intended to help the community interpret events taking place around them in relationship to the destruction of the present age and the final manifestation of the realm of God. John was probably the ancient equivalent of a circuit rider, a prophet who traveled from congregation to congregation and whose route included the seven churches mentioned in Revelation 2:1—3:22.[7]

---

7. Hence, I typically refer to the congregations (plural) to whom John wrote.

Written about 95 CE in a Time of Idolatry, Exploitation, Injustice, and Violence

Most scholars today date the book of Revelation to about 95 CE, during the latter part of the rule of the emperor Domitian, who was on the throne from 81 to 96 CE. Domitian reigned during the middle of the so-called *Pax Romana*, the peace of Rome extending from 27 BCE to 180 CE.[8] The *Pax Romana* received its name from the fact that there were relatively few conflicts in the empire, in contrast to the almost-constant disturbances of the prior two centuries.[9] However, the relative military quiet inside the empire masked tensions that made everyday life difficult for most.[10] The book of Revelation presumes these tensions.

Tensions in the Roman Social World

Caesar and the Senate controlled the empire in collaboration with a network of associates and the wider span of elites. Some Caesars related collegially with the Senate, while others were more dictatorial. Transfers of power from one Caesar to another often took place by revolt, murder, and suicide. Violence at the apex of the social pyramid of the empire signaled that violence was a part of life in all areas of the empire.

Domitian was an efficient administrator. But he alienated the Senate by moving towards dictatorship while enforcing his will through brutality. The Roman government coerced the population with military force. I used to say that the Romans had soldiers at every crossroad in every village and city in the Mediterranean basin. That made a great line, but it was hyperbole. Nevertheless, the Roman army was large, and it used violence to enforce submission. The population paid for its own oppression through taxes, including feeding the army in the form of taxation on agricultural products.

8. Indeed, some Christians continue to speak uncritically of "the glory that was Rome."

9. The *Pax Romana* was sometimes known as the *pax imperium*, imperial peace. While the *Pax Romana* may have been a time of relative internal quiet for many places in the empire, violence did occur, as in the case of the Roman war against the Jews, which included the destruction of the temple (66–70 CE), the subsequent destabilization of many Jewish communities, and the mass suicide at Masada (73 CE). Rome actively repressed the Bar Kokhba revolt (132–35 CE).

10. Preachers who are not familiar with life in the Roman Empire and the different ways early Christian communities responded to the empire will find an accessible, highly quotable guide in Carter, *Roman Empire*.

Conflict often took place at the borders of the empire. Rome perceived a particular menace from the Parthians, just to the east of the empire. The tension of potential invasion and war was in the air.

Roman society was rigidly structured as a social pyramid in which the people in the lower 97 percent of the pyramid deferred to those in the apex. The Roman world did not have a large middle class. A patronage system dominated relationships in the empire with clients (from the lower strata of society) indebted in multiple ways to patrons (from the upper strata). About 15 percent of the population of the Roman Empire was typically enslaved, including as much as 40 percent of the population of Italy. Many people felt trapped in the social pyramid. Occasional persons in the lower strata could advance, but only by playing according to rules that benefitted people in the upper strata.

The upper classes owned most of the land and means of production, as well as most modes of transportation. Wages were low. Many people were impoverished, disempowered, and dependent. Many people lived day to day. Food shortages occurred often. Many households in the 97 percent were squeezed. Taxes could be as high as 20 to 40 percent. The differences in qualities of life between the upper and lower classes was stark. The wealthy typically lived on large spacious estates removed from the dense population areas where the struggling classes lived in squalor.

Similar dynamics operate in the world today.[11] Preachers sometimes casually identify the United States with an empire. However, a more nuanced view sees empire today in an international network of power relationships (economic, political, social) that largely serve the interests of the upper and middle classes.

The Imperial Cult

While the Roman Empire allowed diversity in religious practice, a fusion between imperial rule and religion developed. According to Roman mythology—especially in the upper classes—the empire was the child of the gods. Roman court theologians typically declared that the deities appointed the Caesars. The Caesars were closely associated with the divine beings, but were seldom considered fully divine while the Caesars were still alive. The Senate did declare many Caesars divinized after their deaths.

Domitian leaned towards claiming divine honors while still alive, but stopped short of naming himself a god. Yet his reign was so brutal that the

11. Jensen offers a brief and highly quotable picture of empire today, its threat, and positive steps forward in his *We Are All Apocalyptic Now.*

Senate refused to divinize him at death. On the contrary, after his assassination, the Senate voted officially to condemn his memory to oblivion.[12]

We sometimes speak in a casual way about the imperial religious cult that grew up around the Caesars. To the early twenty-first-century ear, the singular form of the word "cult" may suggest a uniform religious expression, whereas the imperial cult took many forms in different areas ranging from public services of worship in which the gods ordained and blessed the emperor; to places of worship for sacrifice to the gods in behalf of the emperor; to parades, birthday celebrations with religious overtones, and hymns and songs composed for the emperor. While there was little direct worship of the Caesars as gods, participants in the imperial cult often spoke of Caesar and the imperial household in terms that had traditionally been associated with gods and goddesses. In some temples, worshipers offered sacrifices to the image of the emperor.

For John, the imperial cult has two dimensions. The first is the religious institution itself. The second is as a wider symbol. To participate in the imperial cult was to accede to Rome—to the gods, Caesar, and the wider network of values and behaviors at the power center of the empire. Rome allowed individuals and households to worship traditional deities. But there was a social expectation, especially on the part of power brokers in the Roman system, that individuals and households *would* participate in the imperial cult.

There were significant religious centers associated with the emperor cult in several cities mentioned in the book of Revelation. Such a center was opened in behalf of Augustus (who was divinized after death) and the goddess Roma in Pergamum. In 89 CE, such a place was built for Domitian in Ephesus. Smyrna and Thyatira each had centers for imperial worship.

The famous Priene Calendar Inscription (9 CE) calls Augustus Caesar "son of God" and "savior" and refers to Caesar's proclamations as "gospel." Domitian was reported to have been called "lord and god." John, like some other writers of the Gospels and letters, expressly contrasts the nature and rule of the Caesars and the empire with that of God, Jesus, and the realm of God.

---

12. The extreme practice of *Damnatio Memoriae*, "condemnation of memory," could be a formal action, taken largely with reference to emperors and other elites, through which the Senate could seek to remove as much of the memory of the person as possible. It could involve removing the name of the condemned person from public places, seizing the property of the erased person, and rewriting the laws that she or he had established. The practice could also take place informally. Of course, the fact that we know quite a bit about these figures indicates that the practice of memory erasure was not completely successful.

The great classics scholar E. R. Dodds characterized life in the Roman Empire shortly after John as an "age of anxiety."[13] While Dodds focused on a time later than that of the Revelation, the description "age of anxiety" also applies to the reign of Domitian. Despite the *pax imperium*, the threat of chaos was never far away.

Those on the top of the social pyramid were anxious about turmoil from below. Those below feared the multiple forms of coercion from those above. The elites often acted aggressively, even viciously, to keep those below in their places. Droughts, floods, and other natural disasters could interrupt life.

Many churches today exhibit an informal union of church and state that is similar to the imperial cult. Such churches support the state (or political groups) without critical reflection. For example, some churches teach a version of manifest destiny or American exceptionalism, or engage in flag-waving. Many other churches, while less flagrant, assume that the church shares the values and behaviors of the dominant culture. However, occasional congregations, denominations, and movements contain people whose attitudes towards the state are more like those of John.

Possible Responses to Empire

At the time John spoke, people had to decide how to relate to the Roman Empire. Today, Christians (and others) must make similar decisions with regard to how to respond to contemporary forms of empire.

A Complication in Responding to Empire Today: The Structure of the New Jerusalem

A complicating factor enters the discussion of how to respond to empire, especially today. The Roman Empire assumed the social structure of a pyramid in which power was exercised from the top down and in which those in the upper reaches significantly determined the character of the lives of those in the lower regions.

One of my students, Leah Yen, notices that when we "pull back the curtain" on John's vision of the new Jerusalem, "we see that it reads like it was written by someone railing against empire who does not realize just

13. Dodds, *Pagan and Christian.*

how deeply empire has shaped that person's values and ways of seeing the world."[14] She comments:

> John, much like the Emperor, believes that enemies ought to be crushed outright. John, much like the Emperor, believes that the best manifestation of power is absolute territorial dominion. At no point does the author of the Book of Revelation question the correctness of the social pyramid or the predominant attitude of "It's good to have a monarchy." John adapts the oppressive pyramidal mentality. This just recycles the same structures of relationship with a new boss running things.

Leah Yen recognizes that the values of the realm of God (e.g., love, peace, justice, and abundance) are quite different from those of the realm of Caesar. But as long as the structure of relationships and exercise of power remains in the new Jerusalem as they were in the old earth, the vision of the peaceful new heaven and new earth will be only partially realized.

Commentators sometimes view John's notion of power as kinder and gentler by pointing to the fact that in the old age, conquering on the part of the Lamb and witnessing community takes place not by brute force, but by means of remaining faithful in the face of persecution and death. Moreover, whereas some apocalyptic theologians in John's time describe the final face-off between God and evil in visceral detail, John does little more than report that the Lamb captured the beast (19:11–17) and that God sent down fire to consume the dragon (20:7–11). However, when push comes to shove, the power of God simply overcomes the power of Satan. John does move in the direction of redefining power relationships when the prophet points out that the faithful reigning with God in the new heaven and new earth (22:5) takes the form of worship, which includes serving God's purposes (22:3b). Nevertheless, the basic hierarchical paradigm appears to be place.

When it comes to responding to empire today, I think not simply of replacing the empire of the world with an empire of God that is structurally much the same, but of a new Jerusalem, which is truly a *community* whose fundamental relational principle is mutuality, and in which all participants work together for common blessing. Process theology can conceive not only of a renewed world in this way, but one which honors the initiative of a God who exercises power by lure.

---

14. Yen, "Revelation 20:7–15." Translators sometimes point out that the expression "realm (*basileia*) of God" could be rendered "empire of God."

Five Possible Responses to Empire

I note now five major options for responding to empire then and now.

1. Full participation. People could fully embrace the empire, which meant embracing the emperor and the imperial cult. In the late first century, most members of the upper class took this path.

2. Minimal participation. People could do what they needed to survive, engaging the empire in necessary, practical, minimal ways, but not fully investing in the mythology of the Roman Empire.

3. Overthrow the empire through violence. A few people actively sought revolution to overthrow Rome. However, this action brought about swift and brutal Roman response.

4. Look to God for a new world. In my view, the book of Revelation and other apocalyptic writings fall into this category.[15] People committed to apocalypticism tried to make a faithful witness while minimizing cooperation with the empire.

5. Transform the empire by nonviolent means. This was not a common idea in the first century. Many Christians today—including me—think that Jesus and the early church practiced nonviolence. I think, however, that they did so within the apocalyptic framework and did not expect nonviolence to transform the empire. Today, many Christians look to nonviolent means to replace the injustice, exploitation, scarcity, and violence of empire with a mutual social world, similar to the one mentioned just above, and that is loving, peaceful, just, and abundant for all.

Of course, many congregations then (as now) contained individuals and groups who responded differently to empire. One of John's goals is to help the congregations become aware of their relationship with the empire, to analyze that relationship critically, and to respond appropriately. The preacher today, of course, needs to do the same in our early twenty-first-century, postmodern context.

Book of Revelation as Apocalyptic Theology

The book of Revelation is a work of apocalyptic eschatology. This end-time way of thinking, which became popular among Jewish writers in the last three centuries BCE, assumes that God is all-powerful and that all things

15. For development of the apocalyptic idea, see the next section.

take place either by initiation of God or by the permission of God. In fact, the underpinning of apocalyptic theology is that God is in control. It sees history divided into two eras—the present, evil age marked by Satan, the demons, idolatry, fractiousness, violence, exploitation, and scarcity, and a coming new world in which all things embody God's purposes of love, peace, justice, and abundance. God will end the present age and bring about a new world.

John adapts this viewpoint to the particular circumstances of the churches in the late-first-century Asia Minor. The book of Revelation, like many other documents in the Gospels and letters, sees God working through Jesus Christ to begin a partial transformation in the present, with the final completion coming in the future. Signs of both the condemnation of the evil present age and of the coming of the new world are already taking place. In the meantime, history is a conflict zone between God and Satan represented respectively by Jesus and the church and by Caesar and the empire.

John differs from some other apocalyptic works in that John does not describe the final apocalyptic events in detail. To oversimplify, John sees the great transition taking place in two stages. The first is the capture and punishment of the Roman Empire (also known as Babylon and the beast). God brings about this destruction through social forces in history. The second is the defeat and sentencing of the dragon (also known as the ancient serpent, the devil, and Satan). In both cases, John reports the occurrence of, but does not describe in detail, the climactic defeats (19:11–21; 20:7–10).

When referring to the Roman Empire, John has the imperial class especially in mind—Caesar, the official government at all levels, the imperial cult, the upper class, the army, and others who participate in (and benefit from) the Roman system. While many in the lower classes were not willing participants in the empire, they would share significantly in Rome's fate.

John wants hearers to believe that the Roman Empire not only operates according to the values and practices of the old age, but also embodies the rule of Satan (Rev 12:18). The prophet repeatedly excoriates Rome for idolatry, exploitation, injustice, and violence. In the first century, it was easy for people to become confused about which empire is trustworthy and lasting—the empire of Caesar or the realm of God—because the Roman Empire deceived the inhabitants of the world by imitating the realm of God.

The Roman Empire refused to repent of its violations of divine intentions. Consequently, a dramatic claim of the book of Revelation is that God is already working through social processes within and beyond the empire to destroy it. The social conditions and tensions within the empire, and between the empire and its rivals (e.g., the Parthians), are the beginning stages of its collapse. While John does not articulate a specific timeline of events leading to the great transition, the prophet believes the destruction of Rome is inevitable.

While the time for the empire to repent has passed, it is still possible for occasional individuals and communities to do so. Revelation 11:13 implies that some in the empire respond to the witness of the church. People "from every nation, from all tribes, and peoples and languages" are included in the vision of the eschatological community (7:9; cf. 5:9; 14:6).

Purposes of the Book of Revelation

Scholars take two different paths to the situation of John's congregation in relationship to the Roman Empire, and consequently, to the specific purposes of the Revelation. One long-standing school of thought sees the congregation undergoing persecution. John writes to encourage the congregation to endure. The writer assures the congregation that God will see them through the conflict and suffering which results from their witness. Yet, against this point of view, there is no evidence of widespread persecution taking place in Asia Minor at the time John wrote.

According to the other pathway—and the one that makes more sense to me—persecution had not begun on a large scale, but John anticipated that it would do so. Some in the congregations were faithful, so John writes to encourage them to continue with patient endurance. John believed that many people in the congregations were in danger of accommodating too much to Rome, particularly by participating in the imperial cult and in the network of attitudes, actions, and relationship it represented. Their danger was not withering in the face of persecution, but of acculturating to the degree that they would be complicit in the violations of the empire. Those who shared in the culture of Rome would also share in its condemnation and destruction.

From this point of view, the book of Revelation presents listeners with a choice. They can cooperate with the Roman Empire and share in its destruction, or they can remain faithful (or repent and become faithful) and be part of the community moving towards the new heaven and new earth. John urges the congregations to "come out" of the empire. As we develop further in connection with 18:4, "coming out" includes refusing to participate in the imperial cult and in the behaviors and relationships represented by that cult. It also certainly includes being willing to face social criticism from others and to risk possible legal consequences, including the possibility of martyrdom. Some scholars think it includes the possibility of losing current sources of income that assumed going along with the empire. One would have to find alternative employment.

When thinking hermeneutically, a starting point is that the situation of John's congregation in antiquity is similar to the situations of many congregations affiliated with Eurocentric culture in the United States today.[16] Many such congregations are so acculturated with conventional Eurocentric society that they are effectively chaplains passing the hand of blessing over things with empire qualities such as racism, nationalism, classicism, ethnocentrism, exploitation, violence, and other manifestations of injustice and brokenness.

The preacher can help the church recognize its complicity in empire, warn the church about the consequences of continued complicity, help the church think about how to "come out" of the contemporary Rome, and offer the church possibilities for recognizing and responding positively to the presence and purposes of the new heaven and the new earth.[17]

To be direct, I think very few congregations today are willing to repent altogether of collusion with latter-day Babylon or to take the radical steps of coming out in the way John envisions. That would involve constructing an alternative social world, including alternative means of making a living that are independent of empire, as well as refusing to engage in many legal requirements of citizenry. I think very few clergy are willing to do this. To be painfully honest, I am not ready to go this route.

However, I do think preachers can begin to raise these possibilities. When presented in increments that the congregation can manage, and when accompanied by pastoral support, ideas can develop over time. By way of example, not even a generation ago, uttering the word "homosexual"

---

16. Many racial and ethnic congregations today are in situations more like the situation of the congregations described in the first pathway to reconstruct the context of the congregations to whom John wrote. As minority communities, they are caught in the web of larger Eurocentric cultures which are at the heart of contemporary empires. Something similar can be said also of congregations whose ministries include people of Eurocentric origin but whose social locations are reminiscent of the first-century community to whom John sent the book of Revelation, e.g. LGBTQAI communities, immigrant congregations, feminist communities, communities in which poverty and unemployment are widespread, communities of the disabled, and many others. (While Eurocentric individuals and communities can be oppressed, even repressed Eurocentric communities typically enjoy some of the benefits of Eurocentric privilege.) Many such communities struggle against the larger forces of empire in ways the first pathway pictures. In such settings, the purposes of preaching include those of the first pathway above, namely assuring the congregation of the divine presence in the midst of their struggle and encouraging the congregation to remain faithful even when they are tempted to give up.

17. On "coming out," see Rev 18:4.

in public worship in many congregations caused a tension in the room that was palpable. After years of patient, pastoral discussion, many of those congregations are much more inclusive, and some are actively affirming. Something similar can happen with respect to the call to "come out."

At the same time, a pastor's eye is likely to notice some individuals and households in the heart of Eurocentrism who need assurance. For example, some congregations choose to stand for values and behaviors counter to empire. They often need assurance. Moving to the level of households and individuals, things like illness or addiction can leave people feeling under the heel of a despot. In such circumstances, it is pastorally appropriate to emphasize assurance.

From Resistance to "Yes We Can!"

Many progressive Christian communities summarize the responsibility of the church today as resisting empire and think of the church as a community of resistance. Progressive preachers love to find subversive elements in the Bible. To be sure, resistance is part of the vocation of the church today. Many biblical texts do contain an element of subversion. However, in my mind, resistance and subversion are only half the mission. Beyond that, preachers need to help the church imagine (and aim towards) the more positive construction of a world with the values of the new heaven and the new earth. One of the enduring—and motivating—images of Barak Obama's presidential campaign in 2008 was the vivid and empowering cry of "Yes We Can!"

The Book of Revelation Communicates Its Message through Images

Many people are bewildered by the book of Revelation because of its literary style. Most of the book is presented in the form of images that seem bizarre, even frightening, to many North American listeners. Even passages that appear to be straightforward (e.g., the letters to the seven churches) are shot through with references that are not immediately apparent to today's community.

Some interpreters in an earlier time thought that the book was written in a secret code to hide the message from the Romans. While that idea has been discredited, writing in a code does have some similarities to the approach of the apocalyptic writers, but with important differences. In a secret code, the writer assigns specific meanings to specific expressions to hide the code from outsiders. The listener with the key to the code can then decipher the meaning. John, like other end-time writers, created word pictures in theological symbolism (kin to theological code) in language drawn from the Torah, Prophets, and Writings, and from other apocalyptic literature. John uses the associations evoked by these pieces of literature to interpret the church's current situation in relationship with the Roman Empire and the broken old age. Traditional Jewish literature provided the basic keys to the associations in John's images. For example, the prophet uses the name Babylon—brutal enemy of Judah who sent the leaders of the community into exile 597–539 BCE—to interpret Rome as a latter-day version of that ancient empire (Rev 14:8; 16:9; 17:5; 18:2, 10, 21).

It is as if John drops a bucket into the well of traditional Jewish literature and brings up words, images, and stories. John assembles them into a vision. The listener combines the associations of the image's elements to grasp its meaning.

The Same Message Over and Over:
The Spiral Structure of Book of Revelation

After one of my classes had been working its way through the book of Revelation for several weeks, a student looked up from the pedagogical fog and asked, "Haven't we heard this theme before—at least twice?" The book of Revelation essentially articulates the aforementioned central point over and over, with some supplementary material and a sense of increasing intensity. An expanding spiral is a useful model for the structure of the Revelation. The book does envision the movement of time from the broken present to the eschatological future. As I say tirelessly in this commentary, John does not set out a timeline of specific events, but does see the conflict between God and Satan intensifying throughout history. The Revelation portrays these events in progressively more threatening tones in the movement from the opening of the seals to the coming of plagues to the pouring of the bowls until history reaches the climactic events of the defeat of the empire, the millennium, and the coming of the new heaven and the new earth.

The image of an expanding spiral catches both the forward movement and the widening and deepening of the eschatological conflict (the great ordeal, the tribulation). Because different parts of the book make similar points (albeit with different images), the commentary itself sometimes sounds repetitive. A preacher may, indeed, think, "Haven't I heard this theme before?" Of course, John never simply repeats themes. The prophet always adapts them from section to section, and a preacher wants to take account of the nuances of particularity in each case.

The Apocalyptic Theology of the Book of Revelation and the Process Theology of This Commentary

Conversational theology in the mode of mutual critical correlation involves interchange among different voices. The dialogue in this book involves two main voices: the voice of the apocalyptic theology and the voice of process theology. I will now sketch and compare the main lines of the two schools of thought, with emphasis on the categories that are most pertinent to interpreting the book of Revelation.[18] Because of the space limitations, I must oversimplify.

From passage to passage, in the commentary proper, I try to do several particular things. I identify what the apocalyptic John most truly wants listeners to believe when they receive the passage. From a process perspective, I compare John's theological convictions with my own process interpretation. I identify points of positive contact between John's theological worldview and my own. As necessary, I identify aspects of the text that are theologically troubling and attempt to pose more theologically appropriate ways of thinking.

God's Overarching Purpose

In apocalyptic theology, to use language from the book of Revelation, God's overarching purpose is to replace the "first things" (22:4; the present broken world permeated by empire) with a new age, represented symbolically as the new heaven and the new earth (21:9—22:5). In comparison, Clark M. Williamson describes God's overarching purpose as blessing—that is, *shalom* (peace) with oneself, God, all our neighbors, and nature.[19] Majorie Suchocki speaks of the divine purpose as "inclusive well-being."[20] Process thinkers

18. In my view, Williamson offers the best systematic theology for a neo-process perspective (in conversation with Tillich, post-Shoah theology, narrative theology, and feminist theology) *Way of Blessing, Way of Life*. Farmer, *Revelation*, comments on the book of Revelation in process perspective. Keller offers a provocative "feminist guide to the end of the world" in dialogue with apocalypticism and process in *Apocalypse Now and Then*. Her *God and Power* finds apocalypticism deeply influencing the current urge towards empire and offers a counter-proposal.

19. Williamson, *Way of Blessing, Way of Life*, 16.

20. Suchocki, *Fall to Violence*, 66.

do not imagine God replacing one cosmic world with one another. Rather, blessing (inclusive well-being) must take place within this world.

John describes the new heaven and the new earth in the rich symbolism of 21:9—22:5. As the commentary indicates, the qualities of this new Jerusalem are very much like the qualities of life envisioned for community in process thought. God seeks for all individuals and communities, in humankind and nature, to live together in love, in relationships of mutual support in which all act for the good of the other and for the good of the larger world. John imagines an external existence for all human beings beyond this world.

The Nature and Extent of Divine Power

Apocalyptic theology—like much traditional theology—sees God as all-powerful and, consequently, all things taking place either by God's initiation or God's permission. God can do what God wants to do when God wants to do it through the means that God chooses. God can intervene directly in history, or God can work through other means.

According to process conceptuality, God's power is limited. God has more power than any other entity, but God cannot intervene directly in history to do whatever God wants. God does not choose to limit God's power. The divine power is limited by God's nature.

A key point for process is that God exercises power not by brute force, but by lure—that is, by invitation. God invites members of the human family to participate with God and with other members of creation in the pathway that leads to blessing. God's desire to bless and power to lure is infinite. From a process point of view, the book of Revelation is a lure towards the kind of world envisioned in the New Jerusalem.

Process thinkers speak of God's nature having two parts—a constant part and an adaptable part. The constant is God's intention to bless everyone and everything. The adaptable part comes as God adapts the precise personal, social, and cosmic meanings of blessing according to the limitations and possibilities of each context. God ultimately seeks for all things to live in fullness of love, peace, justice, mutuality, and abundance. But, because God cannot rearrange historical circumstances by single direct acts, God offers as much blessing as is possible to each member of creation (human and beyond) in each situation. God seeks to lure participants in each context to fuller experiences of blessing.

The extent of blessing in particular situations typically depends on two things: the possibilities available in the context and how fully individuals respond to the lure in that context.

Judgment and Punishment

John imagines a distinct moment of final judgment in a cosmic setting, after which human existence continues forever. For the faithful, this life takes place in the new heaven and the new earth. For the disobedient, this life takes place in eternal torment in the lake of fire.

Process thought does not include such a singular moment of final judgment. The fact that God cannot directly punish those who cooperate with destructive purposes does not mean such decisions have no consequences. When we decide against God's aims of love, peace, justice, mutual support, and abundance, we invite the consequences on ourselves. God does not bring down the axe of judgement. Rather, we set in motion patterns of value and behavior that bring about pernicious results. These consequences may be dramatic, as when fraudulent lending practices disrupt the economy. Consequences may be immediate, or they may take place over generations. About 95 CE, John envisioned the destruction of the Roman Empire, but the empire in the west did not disintegrate until 476 CE.

In apocalypticism, the final judgment is final. That's it. In my thinking, God does not wish ill on people who act against God's desires. To be sure, God grieves such choices and suffers with their consequences. But, as a friend said, "God keeps offering new possibilities for blessing in ways possible in each context."

As noted earlier, John believed that God consigned unfaithful people to be "tormented day and night forever" in the lake of fire (20:7–15). While some process theologians believe that the totality of human experience takes place in this life, I join those thinkers who believe that a form of personal human consciousness does continue. While I do think it is important for people—including myself—to be fully aware of the consequences of the evil in which we have been complicit, I cannot imagine a God of unrelenting love seeking for this awareness to be the totality of consciousness forever. I pitch my tent in this regard with those who believe that ultimate existence takes place in a vast network of divine love.

Human Agency in Change

In line with other works in apocalyptic theology, the book of Revelation sees God as the agent who will bring about the change from old world to the new. John does not envision the church as an agent of social transformation to recreate the present broken world as the kind of community symbolically portrayed in Revelation 21:9—22:5. Yes, the prophet thinks the church can announce this change, critique the present brokenness, disengage from the values and behavior of Rome, point to signs of judgment and regeneration, and invite others to repent and become part of a community on the road to the New Jerusalem. People have agency in deciding whether to join or reject the movement towards the new age, but the church does not have a part in bringing it about.

By contrast, process theologians believe that human action, in partnership with divine presence, is necessary to transform the present world. Process thought places priority on God's grace and initiative: Without regard to human merit, God graciously seeks to lure the world towards blessing. But humankind and nature must participate with God for the divine purposes to come about.

The church does need to be theologically circumspect on this point. Some preachers and congregants leave the impression that if the church does not respond directly to God's possibilities for love, peace, justice, mutuality, and abundance, then these possibilities go unrealized. To be sure, the church can help optimize possibilities for blessing by participating with God. But the church is not the only community that can respond to God's lure. Whenever and wherever people and nature respond positively to the divine lure, they move toward possibilities for love, peace, justice, mutuality, and abundance. People respond to the divine lure, whether or not that lure is named. People can embrace it, reject it, or ponder it. We can respond consciously or unconsciously. We can respond with intellectual clarity or at the intuitive level of feeling.

Approaching Sermons on Texts from the Book of Revelation

By communicating its message through word-pictures, the book of Revelation is, par excellence, a case of imaginative theological expression. A creative preacher might be inspired by the imaginative mode of the Revelation to a sermon that communicates less through linear thought and more through imaginative association and feeling.[21]

Preachers do need to be clear about the purpose(s) of the sermon. They may organize the sermon around one bold purpose. But the situations of congregations are often complicated. A particular situation may call for more than one emphasis.

- To what degree does the situation of the congregation call for a sermon that urges the congregation to repent of its complicity in empire?

- To what degree does the situation of the congregation call for a sermon that encourages the congregation to gather the strength to continue to witness in the face of conflict?

- To what degree does the situation of the congregation call for assurance of the divine presence and promises?

A preacher cannot decide the purpose of a particular sermon in a particular congregation on the basis of a preaching help, a biblical commentary, or the memory of the moral exhortation of a seminary professor. The preacher listens to the text in congregational context in conversation with deep theological convictions.

The Puritan Plain Style for Preaching on the Book of Revelation

However, in view of the fact that many contemporary people have difficulty understanding the book of Revelation, I suggest a more explanatory approach for many sermons: the traditional Puritan Plain Style sermon, which includes introduction, statement of the direction of the sermon, exegesis, theological reflection, implications, and transition to further consideration:[22]

Introduction

> The preacher might invite the congregation into the sermon by naming feelings, questions, issues, and associations related to the book.

---

21. Examples of sermons engaging texts from the book of Revelation may be found in Rogers and Jeter, *Preaching Through the Apocalypse*, as well as in Jones and Sumney, *Preaching Apocalyptic Texts*.

22. The Puritan Plain Style is discussed in many places in the contemporary literature of preaching, among them my edited work, *Patterns of Preaching*, 7–13.

Statement of the Direction of the Sermon

> In a short paragraph, the preacher might explain how the sermon will unfold, perhaps as simply as, "I am now going to look at this text in its setting in the book of Revelation, think with you about what you really believe in relationship to this text, and consider possible implications for today."

Exegesis

1. The preacher might briefly overview the historical context and purpose of the book of Revelation.

2. The preacher might briefly place the passage in the literary unfolding of the book of Revelation.

3. The preacher might explain the elements of the passage, especially if the passage is a word-picture of the kind discussed above.[23]

Theological Reflection

1. The preacher might summarize what the text asked people to believe and do in its setting in the book of Revelation.

2. The preacher might engage the text in conversation with theology/theologies in the congregation and the preacher's own theology. What are points of similarity? Difference?

3. Out of the theological conversation of the second point, the preacher might summarize options for what people might believe and do today. Per discussion above, the preacher might embrace the theology of the text, have a mixed perspective (embracing aspects but not embracing other aspects), or disagree with the text.

4. I think preachers should typically voice their own perspective on what they believe and plan to do, but in a way that invites further conversation.

---

23. Here the sermon might move through the text word by word, image by image, verse by verse, or meaningful unit by meaningful unit. Preachers who use a big screen in worship might project an artistic rendering of the word-picture of the text, and then use a separate image for each element of the word-picture, supported by other slides that help interpret the picture as a whole and the individual elements. However, I hasten to note that I have yet to see an artist's rendering that does justice to what I see in my imagination when I hear descriptions directly from the book, especially when filled out with a little historical background.

Implications for Today

1. The preacher might help the congregation think about possible, practical implications for today for individuals and households.

2. The preacher might help the congregation think about possible, practical implications for today in the life of the congregation.

3. The preacher might help the congregation think about possible, practical implications for today in the world beyond the congregation.

Transition to Further Consideration[24]

> The speaking must stop, but the preacher does not want the congregation to conclude thinking about the sermon. The preacher shapes the ending of the sermon to invite the congregation to respond appropriately. Such responses range from encouraging the congregation to continue thinking about the topic to taking a concrete action.

As a conventional linear thinker, I find these steps easy to follow. However, there is no magic to this outline. A preacher could arrange these elements in different orders. For example, the preacher might begin with contemporary theological or social issues as the frame for approaching the text. Or the homily might begin with the preacher's own theology as a wall against which to bounce the ball of the theology of the text. The key is that the sermon must provide the congregation with the historical, literary and theological information they need to engage in a meaningful conversation with the text.[25]

Speak Respectfully and Represent Others Fairly

Moderate and progressive preachers sometimes speak dismissively about popular apocalypticism. However, civility and respect are basic requirements for speech in the Christian house. There is no place for making fun of viewpoints with which one disagrees. Moreover, congregants who are sympathetic to popular apocalypticism may simply tune out scornful speech on the preacher's part. The preacher thus loses the possibility for real conversation. To be sure, we need to name—and deal critically with—differences in

---

24. This part of the sermon is sometimes called the conclusion, but, of course, the last thing the preacher wants is for listeners to conclude thinking.

25. My *Patterns of Preaching* discusses thirty-four different approaches to shaping the sermon.

interpretation, but we need to do so in such a way as to respect the otherness of different points of view.

In some contexts, the preacher may find it beneficial to engage respectfully in direct comparison of elements of historical-critical understanding of the book of Revelation and popular apocalypticism. In such efforts, the preacher represents others in fair and informative ways. This is not the place for caricature. When listeners have a clear view of the interpretive landscape and where the various interpretive houses are located, listeners are often better able to identify what they really believe and why. This effort may involve explaining the big picture of premillennialism, as well as key ideas such as the dispensations, tribulation, the rapture, Armageddon, and the role of Israel.

Occasional interpreters emphasize what John did not do without putting forward a proportionate statement of what we can positively take away from conversation with the book of Revelation. For example, interpreters often stress that John did not lay out a detailed timeline of events leading to the end in the manner assumed by contemporary Darbyism. A church, however, cannot build an identity, faith, and mission on what it does not believe. Preachers need to help us move towards a faith that can support the patient endurance needed for witness with transformative potential, so necessary in the early twenty-first century.

Having considered the historical setting, literary genre, and purposes of the book of Revelation, as well as exegetical perspectives and theological proclivities, the time has come to look at the text itself. We move through the book of Revelation from start to finish, engaging in conversation regarding possible meaning for today along the way.

Revelation 1

Revealing the Ruler of Rulers

The beginning of the book of Revelation orients listeners to the nature of the communication that is to follow: it is an apocalypse. When the congregations hear that John is speaking about an apocalypse, they know what to expect. This opening section also establishes the authority of the book as coming from God, and this prologue-like material reveals key theological ideas that are developed further in the book.

Revelation 1:1–8: Prologue: John Reveals the Nature and Purpose of the Book

1:1. John signals listeners immediately that they are to hear a revelation. In John's setting, the word apocalypse (*apokalypsis*) had the specific meaning of a vision that revealed theological perspective on the present and the future that people would not otherwise know. John's apocalypse (revelation) casts a vision in dramatic images intended to help the listening community recognize the idolatry, injustice, exploitation, scarcity, and violence of the present broken age, and to point the congregation to the hope that God will transform the broken world into a new creation in which all circumstances mediate love, justice, peace, mutuality, and abundance. An apocalypse encouraged the congregations to be faithful through the struggles and destruction of the old age so they could become a part of the renewed world that biblical writers and contemporary preachers sometimes call the realm of God, sometimes called the new heaven and the new earth, or the new Jerusalem.[1]

John indicates that the book of Revelation is a letter (see Rev 1:4–5a). In antiquity, letters to communities were typically read aloud to the assembled group. The experience of the community was more of *hearing* with the

---

1. E.g., Mark 1:15; Matt 4:17; Luke 4:33; Acts 1:3; 1 Cor 15:24, 50; Rev 12:10.

ear than of *seeing* with the eye. As noted in the introduction, John assumes that someone reads the letter aloud with vocal emphasis to the assembled congregation. This practice suggests that the person who reads aloud from the book of Revelation in today's service of worship should read with expression and not with the flat speech often typical of lectors. Even better, readers could memorize the passage and present it with movement.

1:2. God gave the revelation to Jesus Christ, who gave it to an angel, who gave it to John. This statement establishes the authority of the apocalypse: it came from God. For the apocalyptic theologians, angels were intermediary figures between heaven and the world. Angels carried messages, and exercised power in God's behalf. Angels appear prominently in both roles in this book.[2]

The book of Revelation soon fills out the identity of Jesus Christ: He is the Ruler of rulers, a figure of awesome cosmic power, God's apocalyptic agent who conquered the powers of the old age and brought about the transition to the new (1:12–16). However, Jesus did not always appear to be the Ruler of rulers. John's readers know that the Romans crucified Jesus, an ignominious death from a Jewish point of view. How shall they understand the relationship between Jesus crucified and Jesus risen? What does it say about the power of God that Jesus was crucified? Later, John explains this relationship by turning to the image of the ruling Lion of Judah who was simultaneously the murdered Lamb (5:1–8).

According to John, events described in the vision "must soon take place."[3] Indeed, as the book unfolds, we discover that some things—particularly the judgment of the Roman Empire—are already underway. John did not attach a specific timeline to the end of the earth and the emergence of the new one. However, "soon" (*taxos*) means shortly, quickly, without much delay. While the time is not fully defined, John expected the final historical cataclysm to occur in the near future.

Believers have often been vexed by the fact that the new Jerusalem is yet to come. A preacher could help a congregation wrestle with this issue by reviewing alternatives, and helping the congregation identify a viewpoint that makes sense. A few Bible students, preterists, think that the events described in the Revelation actually took place in John's time and that the realm of God today is his rule in the heart. Premillenialists construct timelines (often very specific) with events and dates that indicate how close we are to the end-time events. Many Christians, perhaps a plurality, have a

2. As we note in the introduction, authority is an issue in the church today. See pp. xii–xv, xxxi–xxxiv for a discussion of the issue and possibilities for preaching.

3. This theme occurs throughout the book: Rev 2:16, 25; 3:11, 20; 6:11; 10:6; 12:12; 17:10; 22:6–7, 12, 20. Indeed, it comes as one of the final, climactic statements: 22:20.

general conviction that God will end this age and begin a new one, but they do not attach this transition to a specific time line. Some who partake of this general point of view take God's sense of time to be quite different from ours—e.g., "One day is like a thousand years, and a thousand years are like one day." Still others (including me) doubt that God will end this present age and replace it with another one. Indeed, some (including me) do not think God has the raw power to intervene in history in the dramatic way assumed by the book of Revelation, but see God attempting to lure the world towards greater love, peace, justice, mutuality, and abundance.[4] From this last perspective, possibilities for a renewed world are always at hand—they are always "soon"—in that God is ever present in offering them. We do not have to sit and wait for an indeterminate future. Our job is to respond appropriately to God's initiatives in the present.

Revelation 1:3: A Beatitude

1:3. In apocalyptic writings, to be blessed usually means to be included in the community that is moving from the present broken world to the new heaven and earth. Revelation 1:3 is an end-time beatitude declaring that the person who reads the book aloud in worship is blessed in this way, as are those who hear the book and then take the path of faithfulness that John commends. An implication is that those who do not follow the guidance of the Revelation are cursed. The ultimate curse is the lake of fire, where the cursed are tormented "day and night forever and ever" (20:10; cf. 14:11; 20:11–14).

According to recent scholarship, many members of the congregations to whom John wrote were becoming too acculturated to the Roman Empire. This beatitude says to them, "If you want to be blessed—if you want to be on the road to the realm of God—then you need to follow the prescriptions of this vision. Otherwise, you will be cursed, along with the rest of the empire."

Revelation 1:4–5a: A Letter to Circulate among the Congregations

1:4a. John now adapts the customary opening of a letter in the Hellenistic age. By casting the book as a letter, John indicates that the Revelation is to be read aloud in the congregations, probably during services of worship. This oral presentation functioned much like a sermon in today's congregation.

---

4. These theological matters are discussed further on pp. xxxi–xxxiv.

This insight suggests that the preacher might frame the sermon itself as a letter to today's listeners. Instead of talking *about* the book of Revelation, and explaining it in didactic fashion, the sermon could speak as if it is a direct word to the congregation. Such a letter-sermon might summarize the leading themes of the book of Revelation as a whole and address them to the context of the congregation, or it might focus on one passage from the book. This approach is especially amenable to the letters to the seven churches in Revelation 2:1—3:22.

The format at the beginning of the letter indicates (a) the sender (John, 1:4a), (b) the recipients (the seven churches, 1:4a), and (c) a greeting, "Grace and peace" (1:4b–5). The introduction to this book expands on the identity of John: an early Christian prophet (a figure in the early church who receiving messages from God), imprisoned on the island of Patmos because the Roman government perceived him as a threat to peace (1:9). The seven congregations may be a circuit that John traversed, prophesying in congregation after congregation, much like circuit-riding preachers in an earlier day in Methodism. The addressees (1:11) may also symbolically represent the larger community of congregations in Asia Minor (present-day Turkey).

The greeting in the typical Greek letter would begin with the word "greeting" (*cheirein*), rather like today's letter or email writer might begin, "Greetings" or "Hello." Instead, John begins with two of the most important words in the Bible: grace and peace. Grace refers not simply to unmerited favor; rather, "grace" (*charis*) sometimes translated the Hebrew *hesed*—that is, covenantal loyalty, faithfulness, trustworthiness, reliability, or loving kindness. Divine *hesed* is the foundation of God's relationship to Israel. Of special note to interpreting Revelation: when Israel was in trouble—threatened from without or from within—biblical writers often reminded the community that they could survive because of God's utter faithfulness. Peace, or *shalom*, refers not simply to absence of conflict, but to positive well-being in community. For John, the work of God through Jesus Christ is an expression of *hesed* that eventually brings about a transfigured community characterized by *shalom*: the new heaven and new earth of Revelation 21–22.

1:4b. John reinforces the reliability of the message by indicating that the promise of grace and peace come (a) from God, (b) from the seven spirits before God's throne, and (c) from Jesus Christ. The prophet describes God as "who is, who was, and who is to come." This expression points directly to God as an active agent in history ("who comes") in contrast to a more passive Greek formulation for a god as "who is, who was, and who shall be."

John mentions the seven spirits elsewhere (3:1; 4:5; 5:6). Many commentators, drawing on Isaiah 11:2–3, think the expression "the seven spirits" refers to the complete fullness of the Holy Spirit. However, because

Jewish literature of the period sometimes describes angels as "spirits," it seems more likely that the seven spirits are angels (on the order of "guardian angels"), that is, agents who carry out God's purposes.[5] By picturing angels headquartered at the throne of God, John reinforces the listeners' confidence in the roles the angels play in the last book of the Bible.

1:5a. The book of Revelation is ultimately theocentric, though as the book develops, John unfolds a high Christology. Revelation 1:5 explains how God's purposes come to expression through Jesus. John explains the significance of the ministry of Jesus in three related expressions. First, Jesus is the faithful witness (*martyr*) who interpreted the world from the perspective of God's purposes, and who endured in faithfully witnessing, even in the face of the most extreme opposition: being put to death.[6] Second, Jesus is the firstborn from the dead. God did not simply resuscitate Jesus' corpse. God brought him back to life in a resurrection body that will not decay. The end-time theologians of the Hellenistic age assumed that resurrection of the dead would occur after the end of the old world and as part of the birth of the new. The resurrected ones would live forever in resurrection bodies in the realm of God. Jesus is the first to be resurrected. His resurrection is the definitive evidence that the transition of the ages is underway.[7] Third, God has made the risen Jesus the ruler of the rulers (monarchs) of the earth. Jesus is God's agent. This bold statement means that God has given Jesus authority over all other authorities who rule in the world, including Caesar. This authority is for the purpose of remaking the world into the realm of God. All rulers (and all nations, communities, and cultures) will be judged by whether they have ruled according to the values and practices of the realm of God or have followed the attitudes and actions of the old age epitomized by the Roman Empire, systemic expression of Satan. The positive vision for the cosmic community, especially as set forth in the vision of the New Jerusalem, is the standard for all rulers (and all nations, peoples, and cultures).

The church today—like the church in many ages—struggles with how to interpret the meaning and significance of Jesus Christ. The preacher could

5. For examples of Jewish texts describing spirits as angels, see 1 En. 61:12; Jub. 1:25; 2:2; 15:31–32. As so often, the sphere of God and the sphere of Satan are mirror images. The spirits of God contrast with the demonic spirits—that is, the agents of Satan.

6. The same thing happens to the two witnesses in Rev 13:3–11. They make their testimony—interpreting the world from the perspective of God's purposes as set out in the book of Revelation—and the beast puts them to death. God confirms their faithfulness and the truthfulness of their testimony in the same way that God confirmed the faithfulness and testimony of Jesus—by raising them back to life.

7. One of the most explicit descriptions of the place of resurrection in end-time theology is 1 Cor 1:1–34. One of the most vivid descriptions of the resurrection body in Jewish literature is 1 Cor 15:35–57.

take Revelation 1:4b–5 as the basis for a sermon that does two things. First, it could explain the Christology of the book of Revelation using the three descriptions of Jesus in verse 5, taking into account how they are amplified in the rest of the book.

Revelation 1:5b–7: A Doxology that
Reveals the Work of Jesus

1:5b. In the typical Greek letter, a thanksgiving paragraph often follows the opening (sender/recipient/greeting). However, John moves directly to a doxology—an exclamation of glory, often accompanied by pithy descriptions of the reasons for giving glory and concluding with "Amen." Doxologies are often directed to God, though 1:5b–7 gives glory to Christ.

As we learn in 4:11, God should receive glory because God is worthy. To be worthy is to manifest integrity between divine purpose and behavior. God is worthy because the divine purposes and divine behavior (moving towards the new heaven and earth) are consistent. Christ is worthy to receive glory because Christ, who witnessed faithfully to God's purposes to the point of death, continues to witness to those purposes in Christ's post-resurrection life (which includes giving John the Revelation) and will complete those at the end of time.

Revelation 1:5b–6 identifies three activities of Christ—as God's agent—that indicate why he should receive glory. First, Christ loves us. In Jewish theology in antiquity, love is less an emotion and more an action for the common good. This love is the diametric opposite of the self-centered, exploitative, and repressive behavior of Caesar.

Second, Christ freed us from our sins by his blood. In apocalyptic theology, "sin" is more than a failure on the part of the human being. Sin is a power that seeks to enslave individuals and communities to the values and practices of the old world. Human beings become complicit in sin when they assume that the attitudes and behaviors of the old age (epitomized by the empire) are the limits of possibility, and when they live according to those limitations. The element of bondage is why John says that Christ *freed* us from sins.[8]

---

8. The English word "freed" translates a form of the Greek *luō*. Some ancient manuscripts of the Gospels and Letters have the word *louō*, which is often translated "wash." Virtually all scholars think that "freed" is the preferred reading. It is worth noting that the rendering "washed" contributed to the notion that believers are "washed in the blood," as in the hymn of that title (Hoffman, "Are You Washed," 229). A preacher could use this textual disagreement as a jumping-off point for a sermon or Bible study on issues related to Bible translation, and to the possibilities and limitations of translation

The expression "by his blood" does not likely refer to actual blood (as if the blood was itself a saving substance) but is a way of speaking of Jesus' death. That death is not salvific in and of itself, but is the occasion whereby the powers of the old age (manifest through the Empire) made their maximum effort to turn back the coming of the new world. However, that death gave God the opportunity to raise Jesus, which demonstrated the superiority of God's power over all other powers. Consequently, while Jesus' followers may still be pummeled by the powers of the empire, they can live in the confidence that the superior power of God will ultimately replace the Roman Empire with the divine reign.

1:6. Third, John draws on Exodus 19:6 to describe the church as a "realm, priests serving God." In Exodus, God appoints the *community* of Israel to the priestly vocation. The life of the community is itself to have a priestly function in relationship to its own members and to other communities in the world. The essential work of the priest is to represent the purposes of God in the world. By designating the church as a "realm of priests," the prophet indicates that the community, as community, is to represent life together as God wants it to be in the new Jerusalem. The life of the church is not for its own sake, but is for the purpose of representing the possibilities of the new world.

Just as the church today struggles with the meaning and significance of Jesus, so the contemporary church struggles with its own identity. Who are we? And what are we to do? The three parts of this doxology could suggest themes for beginning such a consideration. In a world in which Caesars continue to exploit, the church can offer love. In a world in which the values and practices of the old age continue to enslave, the church can point the route to freedom. In a world of radical individualism and pseudo-communities, in which people and groups lose themselves in their own self-absorption, the church can offer genuine solidarity as it seeks to move towards the community of the new age.

Revelation 1:7: Every Eye Will See the Final Revelation

1:7. The final events will be public so that "every eye will see," including those who "pierced him." This event will prompt "all the tribes of the earth to wail." The Romans, like many ancient peoples, put on public displays of imperial power intended to remind the general population of who was in charge. Yet even the most awesome/fearsome display of the *imperium* fades against the appearance of the ruler of rulers.

issues in formulating theology for today.

John draws on two passages from the Torah, Prophets, and Writings in Revelation 1:7. The statement that Jesus "is coming" derives from Daniel 7:13, where God appoints a figure in the heavenly court, "One Like a Human Being," who comes on the clouds as apocalyptic judge and redeemer. For John, Jesus is that figure, and he will return soon.

The references to piercing and mourning derive from Zechariah 12:10. Some scholars think that John adapts this passage from Zechariah to suggest that the reappearance of Jesus will result in universal salvation. They interpret the wailing in Revelation, like the wailing in Zechariah 12:10, as repentance for having pierced him. The difference is that Zechariah reports that only the inhabitants of Jerusalem wail, whereas John indicates that "all the tribes of the earth will wail." From this point of view, everyone repents. All are included in the new Jerusalem.

However, at the climax of this book—as in end-time theology generally—the wicked will be condemned to punishment and the faithful will be saved (19:11—20:15). All people will experience the trauma and pain of the final apocalyptic travail. Zechariah 12:1—14:21 contains a series of visions of apocalyptic cataclysm that depict deliverance for Jerusalem, but only after everyone suffers as part of the deconstruction (e.g., Isa 60:20; 61:3; Jer 31:13; Dan 10:2; Amos 5:16), and only the faithful are saved.[9]

This statement is an earpiece through which to hear the rest of the book of Revelation. To those in the Johannine congregations who are faithfully witnessing to the presence and coming of the Realm of God, the book is a word of pastoral comfort. This statement says, "You are about to hear a vision that can help make your way through the difficulties of the great period of transition." To those in the Johannine congregations who are colluding with the empire and other entities, values, and practices of the old age, the statement says, "You are about to hear a vision that reveals that you are unfaithful and on the path to perdition. You still have time to repent and to engage in faithful witness, but you need to act quickly or your wail will be that of persons consigned to the lake of fire." John wants people to recognize where they stand in this scenario, and to respond appropriately.

This passage is one of many in the last book of the Bible that could launch the preacher into a consideration of the degree to which the congregation truly believes that God will bring about a single season of apocalyptic re-creation, or the degree to which the congregation could believe God is active in the world for urging the world towards more realm-like qualities of life.

9. Boring (*Revelation*, 226–31) provides a thought-provoking discussion of universal salvation in the Revelation. Cf. his "Revelation" in Boring and Craddock, *People's New Testament Commentary*, 817–19.

Revelation 1:8: God Reveals the Trustworthiness of the Revelation

1:8. God speaks directly only twice in the book of Revelation: in 1:8 and 21:5–8. Each quotation has special force. This first quotation has two purposes. For one, it establishes God's credentials for the vision that follows. Revelation 1:8 is the ultimate statement of authority for the vision in the book. For the other, it implicitly invites the listener to compare the authority of God with that of Caesar (and the powers of the old age). The listener can count on history to unfold as it is presented in the book of Revelation because it is guided by One whose authority is inimitable.

Commentators almost universally point out that the opening words "I am" recall the name of God revealed in Exodus 3:14. This reminds the listener, who is daily under the heel of Caesar, that in an earlier time, God confronted Pharaoh and the gods of Egypt and proved superior.

God uses the first and last letters of the Greek alphabet, alpha and omega, to indicate that everything that takes place from the beginning of history to its ending occurs under divine aegis. From the viewpoint of the end-time theologians, God is omnipotent—that is, God either causes or permits everything that happens in history. God is the Almighty, the *Pantokratōr*, the ruler of all.

In connection with 1:4, we have already noted that the description of God as one "who was, who is, and who is to come" envisions God actively coming into history to reshape it. This expectation contrasts with a traditional formulation used of some other gods in the Hellenistic age: "who was, who is, and who shall be." The role of most deities in Mediterranean antiquity—including the gods of Rome—was to maintain the status quo, in particular to provide transcendent authority for the repressive social hierarchy that benefitted the wealthy and powerful while keeping the rest of the population in the service of those above them. By contrast, the living God comes to redeem and remake.

Today's preacher could contrast the God who comes to recreate the social world and the gods who maintain the exploitative status quo. Some Christian communities in North America—especially Eurocentric ones—interpret the God of the book of Revelation not as one who comes to remake, but as one who seeks to maintain the status quo, smiling at racial superiority, gender discrimination, economic exploitation, nationalism, and other violations of community. The preacher's vocation in this instance is twofold: (1) to critique such points of view and (2) to offer a positive vision of a God who seeks a new heaven and new earth, and compelling reasons for the congregation to embrace that God and vision.

Revelation 1:9–11: John Reveals the Setting
in which the Prophet Received the Vision

John provides some of the most direct evidence of any book in the Bible with regard to authorship, place of writing, and circumstance of writing. We have already considered these matters in detail in the introduction to this book (pp. xix–xxxi). Here we only briefly comment on such matters.

1.9. John identifies himself as "your brother." In antiquity, identity was communal, and kinship—relationship by blood or marriage—was basic to identity. By using a word that indicates close familial identity, John intimates that the congregations are a kinship network. For John—as for others in the Gospels and Letters who think this way—the church is a network of "fictive kin," that is, people who were not physically related by blood or marriage, but who were as committed to one another as kin. This way of thinking about corporate identity is so far removed from Eurocentric individualism; a preacher could explain and draw out its implications for a congregation. John shares the vision of the book of Revelation with the congregations with the intensity of a family member sharing urgent news.

In public communication in antiquity—as today—the speaker often began the communication with remarks intended to help listeners identify with the speaker. Toward this end, John identifies three things that he shares with the congregations: persecution, the hope for the realm, and patient endurance. While three-point sermons are out of favor in many circles today, the three notions in this verse would give the preacher a natural structure for a sermon that could overview several main themes in the interpretation of the last book of the Bible.

While the word *thlipsis* can mean "persecution," Jewish end-time writers sometimes used it to refer to the particular intensified suffering of the last days before the apocalypse, sometimes called "the tribulation." Since I think it less likely that John's congregations were persecuted, and more likely that they were in danger of accommodating to the culture during the period of intensified struggle shortly before the apocalypse, I think it is better to replace "persecution" with something like "I, John, your brother who shares with you the intense suffering of the last days."

John also shares the "realm" (*basileia*) with the listeners. The prophet here means that he shares the partial experience of the Realm in the present as well as the future hope of its final and full appearance. John also shares the "patient endurance" (*hypmonē*). The congregations need to remain faithful, and to persevere, even in the face of the struggles that occur as part of the transition of the ages. Endurance, here, is more than passively holding on. Those who endure actively continue to witness.

Patmos is a rocky island in the Aegean Sea, about ten miles long and about six miles broad, with a highest point of eight hundred feet. It is located about thirty miles from the mainland (present-day Turkey) and is sixty-five miles southwest of Ephesus. Patmos was a settled island with a military compound and shrines to the gods Apollo and Artemis.[10] Preachers often portray John as imprisoned on Patmos. However, recent scholarship concludes that the Romans did not use Patmos as a formal penal colony, though they did banish people there.

John claims that he was exiled to Patmos "because of the word of God and the testimony of Jesus."[11] John uses the double expression "the word of God and the testimony of Jesus" to summarize his message: God is about to replace the Roman Empire and the larger world with the Realm of God, and Jesus is the means whereby God will affect this metamorphosis. It is easy to imagine that representatives of the Roman Empire could have interpreted such preaching as a threat against Caesar.

1:10. John received the vision "in the spirit on the Lord's day." John does not purport to write the book of Revelation as an intentional author who seeks to persuade people to adopt the author's point of view. Instead, John reports receiving the book while he was "in the spirit," that is, in religious ecstasy. Apocalyptic writers in the Hellenistic age often received visions in this state. Many people in antiquity regarded such visions as authoritative.

This datum gives the preacher an opportunity to think with the congregation about the degree to which today's community regards ecstatic utterances (and private visions more generally) as authoritative. Moreover, the preacher may ask, "What does our community regard as truly authoritative, and why?"

The "Lord's day" is Sunday. The followers of Jesus began to worship on the first day of the week in commemoration of the resurrection of Jesus having taken place on Sunday.[12] The word "Lord's" calls to mind kyrios, "Lord,"

10. A preacher who uses a big screen could project a map of the Aegean and drawings and pictures of Patmos, including the Cave of the Apocalypse, to help the congregation get a feel for John's life there. Of course, the preacher should critically discuss elements of the island associated with "tourist Patmos" today.

11. Commentators point out that the expression "testimony of Jesus" could mean either the testimony that Jesus gave or the church's testimony about Jesus. Since John does not actually report the testimony that Jesus himself gave, I incline towards the church's testimony about Jesus. However, the two expressions are close enough in theological content that the choice does not significantly affect the interpretation of the book of Revelation.

12. Many communities of Jesus' followers remained closely tied to Judaism during the period John wrote. The prophet may have presupposed traditional Sabbath worship followed by Sunday worship. John never repudiates Judaism. Rather, the book of

an appellation which Caesar also used.[13] The designation "Lord's Day" thus critiques Caesarism.

Most commentators think John received the vision during worship. In worship, a community acknowledges the transcendent power responsible for its life and acts out its values and practices in liturgy. From this point of view, the worship of the church should (a) embody aspects of the Realm and (b) criticize the world as it is currently misshaped under Caesar. A preacher might reflect with the congregation on the degree to which the congregation's worship expresses the purposes John has in view, and the degree to which worship itself partakes in contemporary Caesarism.

John hears the great voice of an angel (who brings the revelation) like a trumpet. By this period of Jewish history, the sounding of a trumpet often signaled something momentous (e.g., Exod 19:16; Rev 8:6—11:19). The revelation that John receives is, indeed, momentous. Worship planners could take advantage of the reference to the trumpet in the text to include sounding a trumpet as part of the reading from Scripture.

1:11. John is to write the vision in a book. The book would be carried from congregation to congregation. Since the culture was much more oral-aural rather than print-based, the carrier or the worship leaders in the receiving congregations would speak the book, perhaps with dramatic emphasis. Indeed, since only a small percentage of the population was literate, oral presentation was essential.[14]

The voice instructs John to write to seven churches located in the western part of Asia Minor (modern Turkey).[15] John was likely a traveling prophet who prophesied in a circuit, including these congregations. Beyond that, many scholars think the seven churches John names (2:1—3:22) were not intended as the only congregations to receive the letter, but represented all the churches in Asia Minor. John, like other end-time writers, often used numbers symbolically, and, as is well-known, the number seven can represent completeness, especially in things pertaining to God.[16]

Revelation is so saturated with references to Jewish literature that one cannot understand the book without a working acquaintance with the Torah, Prophets, and Writings, as well as other Jewish literature. John does not think of the church as a separate religion, much less superseding Judaism, but as an end-time expression of the religion descended from Sarai and Abram.

13. The word *kyrios*, "lord," refers to someone who has authority over others, a ruler.

14. Estimates for literacy in antiquity range from 3 to 10 percent of the population.

15. A preacher who uses a big screen could project a map of Asia Minor showing the locations of the congregations, accompanied by an explanation of the symbolic function of the seven churches.

16. I have a lot of fun in Bible studies by asking people to name the seven churches without looking at their Bibles.

Revelation 1:12–20: John Reveals a
Vision of the Ruler of Rulers

The introduction of this book points out that John wrote much of the last book of the Bible in a kind of code—not a secret code, but in symbolic language in which word pictures point to wider associations. John does not try to hide the meaning, but the listener needs to know the codes to understand the elements in the vision. These associations typically come from the Torah, Prophets, Writings, and wider Jewish literature, supplemented by other ancient writings and associations. The preacher should approach Revelation 1:12-16 (and much of Revelation 4:1—22:5) with this question in mind: what does each element of the vision represent in its wider world of associations?

A preacher who uses a big screen could project images of the elements of the vision in Revelation 1:12–16. Or an artist could draw the elements into an image. The preacher could begin with a blank screen, name and discuss an element, add it to the screen, and continue adding to the figure until the image of the One Like a Human Being is complete.

1:12–13a. When John turned to see the voice that spoke to him, he saw seven gold lampstands. In Revelation 1:20, the prophet explains that the seven lampstands represent the seven churches. John sees the figure of the Son of Man, described in the next four verses, in the midst of the seven congregations—that is, in the context of the community at worship. The vision is thus an expression of continuity of God's work through Judaism. This multidimensional symbol of the lampstands also calls to mind the notion of Israel as the "light of the world" (e.g., Isa 42:6-7), and it evokes the prophetic nature of the light of Israel's witness.[17] The congregations have a vocation, even in their diminished state: to point prophetically to the coming of the Realm. John uses the seven golden lampstands to emphasize that the vision takes place within the congregation as community and is intended to shape the congregation's perception of itself and its mission.

John then describes one "like a Son of Man" at the center of the vision.[18] This figure is similar in form to a human being.[19] John refers to a

17. For John's perception of the prophetic vocation of the congregation, see the role of the two witnesses in Rev 11:1–14.

18. When I teach this passage in Bible study groups in local congregation, some people nearly always initially think the figure in Revelation 1:12–15 to be bizarre, even inexplicable. On the contrary, people in the world of John were accustomed to prophets and other writing in such colorful, symbolic ways. Here are just two examples: Ezek 1:4-28 and Dan 10:5-6.

19. While "Son of Man" is a typical and accurate translation for the technical expression *hohuios tou anthrōpou*, and while Jesus in his earthly manifestation was male,

figure from Daniel 7:13–14, "One Like a Human Being." In the latter passage—itself an apocalyptic vision—the One Like a Human Being is in God's
heavenly retinue. God appoints the figure as God's agent to judge the four
empires of Daniel 7:1–12, and to rule the ensuing new world. The followers
of Jesus used the One Like a Human Being to interpret the significance of
the ministry of Jesus (e.g., Mark 8:38—9:1; 10:35–45; 14:62; Matt 16:27–28;
26:64; 25:31–32; Luke 9:26–27). Jesus is the latter-day apocalyptic judge and
redeemer who began judgment and redemption during his earthly ministry
and who is now ruler of the rulers of the earth. He will return, per the book
of Revelation, to finish the destruction of Satan and the old world and to
complete the Realm of God.

John sees the risen and ruling Jesus present in the very midst of the
community. This vision signals John's congregations that the time of the
great transformation is underway, and it assures the listeners that, regardless of the conflicts at hand and ahead, the outcome is already in the hand
of this figure.

1:13b. The One Like a Human Being is dressed in a long robe and
wears a golden sash, both symbols of power. In Roman antiquity, most laborers wore short tunics made of rough cloth with a rope-like belt. People
with power wore long robes (e.g., Ezek 9:2, 3, 11). The One Like a Human
Being wears a golden sash rather than a simple rope belt, thus magnifying
the sense that this figure is powerful.

1:14a. The head and hair are luminescent white, a color that indicates
that the One Like a Human Being is from the heavenly world. This color
appears on the ancient one in the heavenly world in Daniel 7:9. It is the
color of the transfigured Jesus (Mark 9:2–8; Matt 17:1–8; Luke 9:28–36) and
is the color of the angels who announce the resurrection of Jesus and the
resurrected Jesus (Matt 28:1–10; 10:3; Mark 16:5; John 20:12; cf. Acts 1:10).
The presence of the color white thus reinforces the transcendent nature of
the one at the center of the visions.

1:14b. The eyes of the figure at the center of the vision are like flames
of fire. The eye is the organ through which a person sees the world. From
this physical use comes a transferred or symbolic use, namely the capacity

---

the use of "Son of Man" contributes to the repression of women. Moreover, according
to some voices in Jewish end-time thinking, individuals will not have gender or sexual-
ity in the coming realm (e.g., Mark 12:18–27; Matt 22:22–34; Luke 20:27–40). And
listeners not acquainted with the association of the end-time agent with the "Son of
Man" may think the latter phrase calls attention to the humanity of that figure rather
than to its heavenly origin (per Dan 7:13–14). Therefore, I will refer to this figure in
the language of Dan 7:13, "One Like a Human Being" (NRSV), and in various other
descriptive designations such as "apocalyptic judge and redeemer, cosmic ruler." I capi-
talize One Like a Human Being for emphasis.

to perceive situations accurately. While fire was a multifaceted symbol in biblical antiquity, its primary reference in the book of Revelation is with judgment. God uses fire (among many other things) to punish those who are disobedient (8:7; 9:17–18; 14:10; 16:1; 17:16; 18:8; 20:9–10, 14–15). Putting these associations together: the one with the eyes of fire accurately perceives the conditions of the world—including those who cooperate with God in the values and practices of the Realm, and those who collude with the attitudes and actions of the Roman Empire (the beast)—and God will rightly punish the disobedient.

Significantly, the first appearance of the One Like a Human Being in the book of Revelation is a vision that takes place in the congregation. The judgment represented by the eyes of fire begins within the church. As the focus of the book widens to life beyond the congregations in later chapters, God unleashes fire on the Roman Empire. But first, John warns members of the congregations to consider how the fiery eyes of God will fall upon their own attitudes and actions.

1:15a. The feet of the apocalyptic judge and redeemer are "burnished bronze, refined as in a furnace." Both Ezekiel 1:7 and Daniel 10:6 refer to burnished bronze in describing living entities that resemble human beings, but who are from the world beyond and through whom God shapes history. A similar force field operates through the figure in Revelation 1:12–16.

1:15b. The voice of the One Like a Human Being was "like the sound of many waters," that is, a sound that is very loud. Daniel 10:6 describes the sound of the words of the supra-historical being as "like the roar of a multitude." Ezekiel 1:24 says that when the creatures described above moved, "I heard the sound of their wings like the sound of mighty waters, like the thunder of the Almighty, a sound of tumult like the sound of an army." John's listeners would have understood this detail as identifying the origin, authority, and power of the figure at the center of the vision.

1:16a. The apocalyptic ruler holds seven stars in the right hand. According to Revelation 1:20, the seven stars are the angels of the seven churches (mentioned in 1:4, 10, and 12). According to John's world of thought, God assigned angels as go-betweens for the world of heaven and communities on the earth. Angels would act on behalf of God in pouring out blessing and in administering punishment.[20]

---

20. These angels are similar to the "guardian angels" that are popular in some Christian circles today. However, John's angels differ in two respects. For one, Christians often believe that God assigns a guardian angel to an individual whereas end-time thinkers conceived as angels having relationships with communities as well as individuals. Second, Christians typically think of "guardian angels" as doing only good things, whereas John's angels can condemn as well as bless.

In antiquity the right hand was the superior hand. A monarch's most powerful assistant often stood at the right hand of the throne. Indeed, people often avoided using the left hand in social interaction because it was commonly used for cleaning up after eliminating waste.

To say that the One Like a Human Being has seven stars (seven angels) in the right hand is to say that this figure controls what happens to the churches. Whether blessing or punishment, the congregations can be assured that their circumstances are not arbitrary, but come from the life-shaping hand of this cosmic figure.

1:16b. From the mouth of the One Like a Human Being "came a sharp two-edged sword." In antiquity, people believed that speech had the power to accomplish its content. Scholars like to refer to words as deeds, for words have the capacity to shape life. Isaiah famously voices this perspective by recording God saying, "My word shall not return to me empty, but it shall accomplish that which I purpose, and succeed in the thing for which I sent it" (Isa 55:11). Not surprisingly, then, Jewish literature sometimes refers to the speech of God and figures of heavenly origin as being similar to a sword or to having outcomes in community and in the wider world in ways similar to that of a sword (Isa 11:4; 49:2; Heb 4:12; Eph 6:17; cf. Rev 2:16).[21] One might think of the two edges of this sword as judgment and redemption. The power of this sword is manifest in Revelation 19:21 where the rider on the horse (the One Like a Human Being) kills the beast and the beast's cronies with the sword of the rider's mouth. As God created by the word in Genesis 1, so destruction takes place by the word.

1:16c. The face is "like the sun shining in full strength." The sun in full shining is powerful beyond the capacity of the eyes to absorb. Jewish writers of the ancient world sometimes refer to this quality of the sun (e.g., Judg 5:31; 2 Sam 23:4; Psa 19:5) This detail emphasizes the overpowering character of the presence of the One Like a Human Being.

John implicitly invites hearers to compare the One Like a Human Being with Caesar and his retinue, who dressed in ways that bespoke imperial power. Impressive as their garments—and places atop the social pyramid of the first century—may have been, the ruler of the empire was a pale imitation of the apocalyptic judge and redeemer. On the one hand, those who adhere to the word of God and the testimony of Jesus have nothing to fear from Caesar. Indeed, what they receive from the Realm is unimaginably

21. Although the Letter to the Hebrews is from a middle-Platonic world of thought, it testifies to the use of "sword" language to refer to divine speech in 4:12. "Indeed, the word of God is living and active, sharper than any two-edged sword, piercing until it divides soul from spirit, joints from marrow; it is able to judge the thoughts and intentions of the heart."

more generative now and forever. On the other hand, those who collude with the empire have far more to fear from the One Like a Human Being than they do from Caesar.

For faithful individuals and communities, the preacher can offer this vision as a source of strength. Modern-day Caesars can be things ranging from systemic racism and sexism to a disease such as cancer or an addiction to alcohol. For those who benefit from cooperating with the Caesars of the old world, the preacher can use this opening vision as a sober reminder of the consequences of continued collaboration.

While a preacher may locate a center of gravity in the historic Eurocentric congregation with regard to being more or less faithful and true, few congregations are purely one or the other. Since the faithful and the unfaithful may sit side by side on the same pew, the preacher may need to think pastorally about how to frame a single sermon speaking to these.

Revelation 1:17–20: Responses to the Vision of the One Like a Human Being

1.17. John responds to the vision of the One Like a Human Being by falling at the feet of that being "as though dead." This response contains multiple dimensions. Scholars rightly describe this reaction as one of profound awe mixed with a certain element of fear and fascination. In an earlier generation, scholars might have used Rudolf Otto's apt expression: John was overwhelmed by the experience of the numinous, the *mysterium tremendum et fascinans*.[22] Indeed, such responses occur elsewhere in the Bible and in Jewish end-time literature (e.g., Exod 33:20; Josh 5:14; Isa 6:5; Ezek 1:28; 43:3; Dan 7:17, 27; 10:7–9, 17). Beyond a response of bone-deep awe, I wonder if John fell down, as though dead, in light of the fact that the cosmic coming of the One Like a Human Being means the destruction of the present world and the eternal punishment of the disobedient. The prospect of such a cataclysm would be too horrible for me to contemplate: I would faint.

In the postmodern world, even as people are "getting over modernism" (as a friend of mine puts it), real awe seems to be in short supply today, except in response to something like a birth or a dramatic sunset. A sermon could help a congregation name and claim awe in response to God's presence and purposes. Indeed, a sermon on Revelation 1:12–16 could seek to induce the deep and complex feeling of the *mysterium tremendum* to help the congregation recover a sense of awe and wonder as constitutive of primary religious experience.

22. Otto, *Idea of the Holy*, 12–41.

1:17b–18. The One Like a Human Being placed his right hand on the immobilized John, saying, "Do not be afraid; I am the first and the last, and the living one. I was dead, and see, I am alive for ever and ever; and I have the keys of Death and of Hades."

As we noted earlier, the right hand is the hand of power. And as we have just noted, the picture of the One Like a Human Being that has just passed before John's eyes contains bone-chilling implications. Yet when the One Like a Human Being touches John with the right hand, we are reminded that the awesome power that can destroy the Roman Empire is even more fundamentally a power that touches life in behalf of life.

At one level, the expression "Do not be afraid" names at least one strain of John's response: John fears such a numinous one as well as the process destroying the present world and bringing down the new heaven at the new earth. At another level, this phrase typically begins an oracle of salvation (e.g., Isa 45:1–7; Jer 31:1–9; Hos 2:16–20; Amos 9:11–15). The prophets spoke these oracles when the community needed assurance, especially in the face of condemnation and other disasters. God often kept the promises of salvation through such means as returning the exiles from Babylon and sustaining the community when they lived as a colony of successive empires (for example, Persia, Egypt, Greece, and Syria). By using this opening phrase, the prophet John seeks to assure listeners that the community can trust the process of social and historical transformation God had already initiated to defuse the Roman Empire.

At one level, uncertainty and anxiety are often just below the surface of many Eurocentric communities today. Long-assumed personal, social, and economic structures are under pressure. The fear of the Other is sometimes palpable. It is not clear what the future holds, especially for those who seek a more Realm-like world. Such communities need reassurance of the kind offered by John. At another level, the preacher cannot assuage such anxiety simply by intoning, "Fear not." The preacher may need to help this congregation understand and experience the reasons they can move forward without fear.

John likely derives the expression "I am the first and the last" from passages such as Isaiah 44:6 and 48:12, where God asserts God's sovereignty over the gods (idols) of Babylon through similar utterances. John intends for these words to remind listeners of God's sovereignty over the first-century gods that the Romans used to justify their power. As God defeated the idols of Babylon, so God would put an end to the idols of Rome.

The One Like a Human Being is "the living one." God raised Jesus from the dead, the first resurrection of the present and coming Realm. Whereas the Caesars and their minions die, Jesus continues to live as the ruling

Christ. On the one hand, for the faithful, the confidence that Jesus is ever alive is reassuring. On the other hand, for the unfaithful—including the unfaithful in congregations—the confidence that Jesus is ever alive means that they are ever accountable for their disobedience. They should repent.

The phrase "the keys of Death and of Hades" refers to the fact that the apocalyptic judge and redeemer has the keys that lock and unlock the doors through which people pass when they die and when the dead come to the final judgment. As we note more fully in connection with 20:13–14, Death is not only a state of being, but a power opposed to the life-giving purposes of God. Hades, in this context, was not a place of punishment (such as the lake of fire), but was a somber, gray holding tank (so to speak) where the dead await the final judgment. While it was not a place of punishment, it was still a state of captivity to a reduced state of existence.

1:19. The voice instructs John, "Now write what you have seen, what is, and what is to take place after this." We earlier explained that the purpose of writing the vision in a book was to produce a copy of the vision in the following chapters that messengers could carry from one congregation to another. The book of Revelation reports what God revealed to John: a critical theological analysis of the present in the form of an end-time vision, and a projection in the same format of what will happen in the future, largely in the language of symbols.

Scholars and preachers give considerable attention to what John means by "what is to take place after this." The simplest explanation is that John believed God had already initiated the process of condemnation and renewal that would end the current age and result in the new heaven and the new earth. This process would come to completion in the relatively immediate future. In connection with Revelation 1:1, we discuss a possible theological approach to the fact that the apocalyptic event has yet to take place.

1:20. "As for the mystery of the seven stars that you saw in my right hand, and the seven golden lampstands: the seven stars are the angels of the seven churches, and the seven lampstands are the seven churches." John here provides explicit confirmation of the principle of interpreting the elements of the vision in the book of Revelation as a form of code or soft allegory in which one thing (e.g., the stars) stands for something else (e.g., the angels of the churches). We have considered the specific associations of lampstands, stars, angels, and churches in connection with Revelation 1:4, 10, 12, and 16.

Revealing Ambiguities in the Witness of the Church

I n Revelation 2:1—3:22, the One Like a Human Being dictates seven messages for the angels of the seven congregations. John may have been a circuit-riding prophet who went from congregation to congregation. In any event, many scholars think the prophet does not simply report the content of messages to specific congregations about particular issues, but uses the seven messages to speak to diverse conditions widely spread across the congregations in Asia Minor.

The messages are an interpretive grid through which to pass the circumstances of a congregation today. At which points in the messages are dynamics in congregation similar and different in comparison with the dynamics in the early churches? At which points are John's admonitions more and less applicable to communities today?

Prophetic Apocalyptic Messages[1]

Although Christians often refer to these communications as "letters," they do not follow the typical letter style of antiquity.[2] While scholars debate the precise literary or rhetorical categories for these letters, David Aune is on a good track by observing that they do not neatly fit any one ancient form. Aune thinks that John created the genre of these messages to resonate with prophetic oracles and with the tone of imperial edicts of rulers in antiquity.[3]

In traditional prophetic oracles, the prophet critically analyzes the situation of the community and suggests appropriate responses. For example, if the

1. A student of mine, Leah Yen, suggests the acronym PAM for prophetic apocalyptic messages.

2. See the discussion for Rev 1:1–2.

3. Aune, *Revelation 1–5*, 119. Cf. Blount, *Revelation*, 47–48.

community is unfaithful, the prophet might call for repentance. If the community is in danger, the prophet might assure the community that God would act for their salvation. In the book of Revelation, the critical analysis takes place through the lens of apocalypticism and identifies points at which the life of the church is consistent or inconsistent with the values and practices of the emerging Realm of God and suggests appropriate responses.

In an imperial edict, the ruler set out a policy that residents of the land should follow. The messages in Revelation 2:1—3:22 are not modeled in detail on imperial edicts, but their tone is reminiscent of such messages. Residents of the late first century were accustomed to receiving edicts from the Roman imperial administration. The seven proclamations in the book of Revelation remind the congregations of an administration in the cosmos that is higher than Caesar. Indeed, the congregations should now compare and contrast the edicts that come from Rome with those that come from God. In the same way that Rome judges residents of the empire on the degree to which they follow the directions of imperial proclamations, so God judges the empire on the degree to which it obeys the purposes of God.

The Pattern of the Messages

The seven prophetic apocalyptic analyses are arranged according to the following pattern, though John occasionally mixes these elements.[4]

a. Instructions to the angel.

b. The destination (the city).

c. Prophetic message formula: "These are the words of . . ." This expression is John's way of saying, "Thus says the Lord . . ." (a typical expression of the prophets).

d. Title for Jesus. These titles are often specific to the situation and congregation to whom the letter is addressed. The titles come mainly from Revelation 1:9–20.

e. Critical evaluation of the congregation. "I know . . ." The prophet describes, analyzes, and evaluates things that are taking place (or not) in the churches.

f. Counsel. The message counsels the churches in what to do. This guidance can contain exhortation, admonition, warning, and/or assurance, according to the circumstance of the congregation.

4. Aune, *Revelation 1–5*, 117–19.

g. Formula indicating the importance of the message: "Let anyone who
   has an ear. . ." This saying, which John cites in every prophetic message, echoes similar sayings on the part of Jesus in the gospels where it
   stresses the importance of responding decisively to the inbreaking of
   the Realm of God.[5] This formulaic statement underscores the importance of responding appropriately to the message.

h. Promise to the churches. If the churches respond appropriately—that
   is, if they conquer and are faithful—they will have a place in the new
   heaven and the new earth. Where necessary, the prophetic messages
   confront the failure of the community and call for repentance. But in
   each case, the message ends with a positive promise that functions as a
   lure towards faithful life and witness, even in difficulty.[6]

The discussion of each message in the following commentary is structured
according to this eight-part pattern.

Each prophetic apocalyptic interpretation is given to the angel of the
church to whom the interpretation is directed. The angels, as noted previously, are agents through whom the über-authorities of heaven—God and
Jesus—administer the divine purposes to the churches, including blessing
and curse, encouragement, and judgment.

Some Possibilities for Preaching

A time-honored approach to preaching on the declamations to the seven
churches is a series of seven sermons, one on each message. A preacher
following the lectionary could develop such a series by departing from the
assigned texts in Ordinary Time after Pentecost.

A few congregations today probably fall into clearly delineated categories of faithful and unfaithful. In the case of congregations that are similar to
unfaithful Ephesus and Laodicea, the sermon might urge repentance. When
the congregation is like faithful Smyrna and Philadelphia, the homily might
urge continued faithfulness.

---

5. Mark 4:9, 23; Matt 11:15; 13:9, 43; Luke 8:8; 14:35. Speakers in the Torah, Prophets, and Writings frequently underscore the importance of listening. Indeed, Deuteronomy 4:6, the Shema, a passage that defines Israel, begins, "*Hear*, O Israel." To listen in
the fullest sense, from the perspective of Deuteronomy, is not only to let the words fall
on the ear drums, but to act on the message.

6. The messages to Ephesus, Smyrna, and Pergamum follow this pattern. In the
other letters, the promise comes before the formula, indicating the importance of the
message.

My impression, however, is that most contemporary Christian communities are mixtures of faithfulness and unfaithfulness, as at Pergamum, Thyatira, and Sardis. For congregations in this category, the preacher needs to encourage critical reflection on aspects of community life that prompt repentance, and reinforce aspects that are faithful.

From week to week, a sermonic question might be, "What does our community learn from our consideration of a particular proclamation that helps us?"

Today's church sometimes struggles with Christology; that is, with how to make theological sense of the figure of Jesus Christ in relationship to other theological concepts and realities. Using item "d" from the previous list, the preacher could develop a series of seven sermons in which each sermon focuses on a different title for Jesus, perhaps with the help of visual images depicting the title on the big screen. What do the different titles imply about Jesus and the mission of the church? Of course, the series should go beyond discussing the individual titles in this book to helping the congregation consider how interaction with the titles helps today's community consider its own Christology. What do the titles in the book of Revelation offer? What are their limitations? What can the congregation *really* believe?

The genre of the messages suggests a possible movement for the sermon: a sermon in the form of a prophetic-apocalyptic message, albeit addressed to today's congregation. For example, the preacher might begin with "To the angel of the church in Tipton write, 'These are the words . . .'"

Revelation 2:1–7: Ephesus

The church in Ephesus was manifesting both appropriate and inappropriate attitudes and behaviors. As one of my students said, "They are doing okay in some ways, but they are not doing as well as they think they are." The message urges them to repent so they can become more faithful.

2:1a: Instructions to the angel. The One Like a Human Being instructs the angel to write.

The destination. Ephesus was a large, sophisticated urban city, a seat of Roman government, and famous for the temple of Artemis (a Greek goddess), one of the seven wonders of the ancient world.

2:1b: Prophetic message formula. Prophetic message formula: "These are the words . . ." As noted previously, this expression adds to the authority of the vision by the One Like a Human Being as the source of the message.

2:1c: Description of Christ. The description of Christ in 2:1c echoes the description of the One Like a Human Being in Revelation 1:12–16. This description highlights two details important to the church in Ephesus. For one, Christ holds the seven stars in the right hand—that is, the hand of power (cf. 1:16). The One Like a Human Being controls the angel of the church who will mediate judgment. For another, the statement that Christ walks among the seven golden lampstands reminds listeners that Christ is a living presence in the midst of the community. Consequently, Christ has firsthand knowledge of the attitudes and behaviors of the congregation. John soon declares that judgment is already at work in the empire (6:1–17). The church, too, will be judged. However, as we learn in 2:5, the churches in situations like that of Ephesus still can repent.

2:2–4: **Critical evaluation of the congregation.** The One Like a Human Being knows the works of the community. "Works" (*erga*) refer to the attitudes and the actions of the congregation in witness.[7] The community is laboring in patient endurance (2:2a), but it has not grown weary in its effort. The community wants to think of itself as faithful. Many congregations today want to see themselves in the same way, but, like the community in Ephesus, need to take steps like those proposed in 2:5–6 to align their self-perception with truly appropriate actions and attitudes.

In favor of the congregation in Ephesus: it does not tolerate evildoers who claim to be apostles, but who the community finds to be false. This falsehood was likely compromising the values and practices of the Realm with those of the empire. Many ancient churches engaged in community discipline—that is, assessing the faith and deeds of community members, and disfellowshiping those who violated community norms. To be sure, such processes have been misused, sometimes reprehensibly, over the course of Christian history. But this part of the text reminds us that the church has standards. Without recommending that today's church convene trials for heresy, the preacher could initiate a conversation regarding whether the church should place limits on what it will tolerate in the way of believing and doing. Should a congregation, for instance, tolerate the presence of members who are blatantly racist?

The congregation has "abandoned the love you had at first." While some interpreters think they have abandoned the love they had for Christ, that seems unlikely since the Ephesians see themselves as faithful. I agree

---

7. Some Christian circles typically use the term "works" in a negative way to refer to things that Christians do in order to earn God's favor. They often contrast "works" (trying to earn God's favor) with "grace" (the unmerited favor of God which cannot be earned). In the book of Revelation, John typically refers to "works" as what the community does *in response* to their perception of God's presence and work (and not to earn God's love). The question for the community is the degree to which the community responds with attitudes and actions that are appropriate (faith) or inappropriate (unfaithful or accommodating to the Roman culture).

with those who think that the love they abandoned is the love they once had for one another. Dynamics could have been similar to today, when people are often enthusiastic when they initially join a group but lose commitment over time. They let the community down. Moreover, loss of love-in-community was characteristic of life in the last days (e.g., Matt 24:12). On the one hand, this is a lively preaching theme for today. People sometimes disappear when the church loses its new car smell for them. A preacher could help the congregation think about what it can do to engender important and vital life and witness that can help people want to continue to engage.

2:5–6: Counsel regarding what the congregation should do. John introduces a theme here that recurs frequently in the book: repentance. John articulates a classic understanding of repentance as a positive and dynamic action: turning away from current disobedience and returning to obedience (2:5).

In the broad sense, repentance is a means of grace. The community deserves punishment because of its disobedience, but God graciously offers the possibility of returning to obedience. In the case of the churches in chapters 2 and 3, repentance is still possible. Many people outside the church have refused to repent and thus invite punishment upon themselves (e.g., 9:20–21; 16:9, 11).

The congregation should continue to "hate the works of the Nicolaitans." In English, the word "hate" (*miseō*) often carries a specific emotional dimension. In antiquity, the emphasis was less on the *feeling* of animosity, and more on the decision to keep one's distance. The congregation should continue to separate themselves from "the works of the Nicolaitans."

We have little data to identify the Nicolaitans. They were a group within the church. John says more about them as continuing the teachings of Balaam in 2:14–15. Many scholars think the group associated with Jezebel in 2:20–23 is Nicolaitan. John charges both Balaam and Jezebel with leading the people to eat food that had been offered to idols and with fornication—transgressions associated with idolatry and accommodation. See further on 2:14–15 and 2:20–23. The Nicolaitans, then, were likely participating in the imperial cult as a way of gaining access to the benefits of the larger Roman system.

2:7a: Formula indicating the importance of the message. "Let anyone who has an ear . . ." As we noted when discussing the elements of the prophetic messages, this statement underlines the importance of acting on the exhortation. It is time to repent.

2:7b: Promise to the congregation. The promise is for those who "conquer." This motif recurs often in the book of Revelation (2:11, 17, 26, 28; 3:5, 12, 21; 12:11; 15:2; 21:7; cf. 5:5). Conquering on the part of the faithful does not involve violence in beating down opponents. Rather, it is to remain faithful while patiently enduring the struggle of the transformation from the old age to the new. The community is to conquer the impulse towards cooperating inappropriately with empire.

The preacher might compare this kind of conquering with the person who is addicted to alcohol or drugs and who conquers by living into recovery. Indeed, participating in empire can be an addiction that requires detox and therapy. In this perspective, the church should be similar to Alcoholics Anonymous in helping its members maintain theological and ethical sobriety.

Those who conquer eat from the tree of life in the paradise of God. Apocalyptic writers sometimes used both the tree of life and paradise as figures to represent the eschatological world.[8] A popular phrase among interpreters of apocalypticism is "The end time will be like the beginning time," that is, the new heaven and the new earth will be a world in which all elements are in mutually supportive community as in Genesis 1:1—2:25. The tree of life was an ancient symbol of the continuing power of generativity. In Genesis 3:3, 22–24, the original couple ate from the tree of the knowledge of good and evil and invited judgment upon themselves and subsequent generations. In the Revelation, God promises not only to reverse the damage caused by inappropriately eating from the tree, but to multiply generativity in the new world (22:2). By contrast, the fruit of the empire (and those who eat it) will be destroyed (18:14).

The word "paradise" was originally a Persian word borrowed by Jewish writers. It means "garden" or "park"—that is, the new heaven and the new earth will be similar to a garden. In contrast, the old world of Rome is disintegrating—a haunt of foul spirits, a place of pestilence and mourning and famine, the smoke of the burning city in the air, and in torment (18:2, 8, 9, 15).

Three preaching themes come to mind. For one, the Jewish community borrowed a familiar word from Persian culture, "paradise," to speak of the garden of Eden, and later of the new heaven and the new earth. The preacher might borrow imagery from culture today to help the congregation get a feel for the new world. Second, the preacher might invite the congregation to compare and contrast paradise with the world of Rome. In which do they want to live? What can the congregation do to help the world become more like the paradise of God? Third, many Christians think of eating of the tree of life and of being in paradise only in terms of what happens to the

8. E.g., 2 Esd 7:52; 8:36.

individual at death. The sermon could stress that the notions of the tree of life and of paradise presume community.

Revelation 2:8–11: Smyrna

This congregation is faithful and suffers as a consequence. The prophet sends a message of encouragement.

2:8a: Instructions to the angel. See the comments on 2:1a.

2:8b: The destination (Smyrna). Smyrna, a seaport, immediately evoked the awareness of empire as the city was a major center for Roman imperial worship, including temples to the goddess Roma and a temple to Caesar.

2:8c: Prophetic message formula. See the comments on 2:1b.

2:8d: Title for Jesus. Both titles for Jesus are important in themselves while implying contrast with Caesar and Rome. Echoing Revelation 1:17, Jesus is the first and the last—that is, he controls the great parentheses at the beginning and end of history. John may use this designation because Smyrna competed with other cities to be "first in Asia."[9] The city—and the empire—may see itself as "first now," but its end is already in view.

Jesus was dead, but God brought him back to life. The resurrection reveals the fundamental nature of God's life-giving purposes and the extent of God's power; it can bring life out of death. By contrast, Caesar controls the current state of existence (pseudo-life) with the threat of death.

2:9: Critical evaluation of the congregation, "I know . . ." The critical evaluation identifies points at which the congregation acts faithfully but suffers as a result. The community is afflicted, that is, the congregation suffers because its witness to the new world brings them into conflict with the powers that rule the old one.

The community is also impoverished. The congregation may simply have been comprised of people from the lower classes; the Roman system exploited them by benefiting from their cheap labor. Per the introduction of this book, an alternative explanation is possible. In order to dissociate with the empire, they may have withdrawn from participating in its economic life. Trying to function in an alternative economic system, they became impoverished.

John does not tell the community they have "spiritual wealth" to encourage them to accept passively their material poverty. The community may not be rich in the sense of material resources that are immediately

9. Travis, "Cultural and Intellectual Property Interests," 637, citing the geographer Strabo.

available, but in the sense that the faithful already have a place in the new heaven and the new earth whose resources are unimaginable.

The prophet further believes that the congregation "is slandered on the part of those who say they are Jews and are now, but are a synagogue of Satan."[10] The word "slander" renders the Greek *blasphēmeō*, which elsewhere in the book of Revelation typically refers to words and actions that give Caesar and the empire the recognition that belongs only to God (13:1, 5, 6; 16:9, 11, 21; 17:3). Evidently the slander took the form of some "Jews" calling the attention of Roman authorities to violations of Roman expectation on the part of the Smyrnean congregation, causing some members to be imprisoned or threatened with imprisonment (3:10). Likely the faithful refused to engage in emperor worship. The Romans may have perceived their talk about a new heaven and a new earth as anticipating revolution.

Who are "those who say they are Jews and are not, but are a synagogue of Satan?" John does not devalue Judaism. Indeed, John was Jewish, wrote out of the deep well of Jewish literature, commends Jewish values, and sees the book of Revelation as setting out a Jewish vision. The Johannine church was a Jewish sect. The best explanation for those "who say they are Jews and are not" is that they are gentiles who recently converted to Judaism, who had only a partial understanding of Judaism, who encouraged accommodation to the empire as a natural continuation of their prior life.[11] Perceiving themselves as Jews, they may have thought the church's talk about a new Realm could cause Rome to think of the whole Jewish community as a threat to the *Pax Romana*.

In a general sense, John viewed Satan as a personal being who sought to wrest control of the world away from God. More especially, John viewed the Roman Empire as a social expression of the rule of Satan in a similar way to Paul's view of the church as the "body of Christ" (12:18). The "synagogue of Satan" in Smyrna, then, is the group described in the previous paragraph. By slandering John's community, they serve not God but Satan.

A preacher might explore the degree to which the present-day church fails to live up to the best of its vocation by abandoning or otherwise betraying Christians and others with whom it should be in solidarity. To what degree might a Christian community today be characterized as a "church of Satan"?

Contemporary commentators almost universally make this point: Christians today should not use this passage to justify anti-Semitism.

---

10. Similar motifs occur in Rev 3:9.

11. They were likely similar, in many respects, to a comparable group in Rome to whom Paul wrote Romans. See Stowers, *Rereading of Romans*, 36–41.

Indeed, apropos of the prominent theme of repentance in the book of Revelation, today's preacher should encourage the congregation to repent of such mistakes. With respect to Judaism today, the preacher should find ways to emphasize continuity between Judaism and Christianity, and to explore possibilities of shared witness of love, peace, justice, mutuality, freedom, dignity, and abundance to the world.[12]

2:10: Counsel. The admonition seeks to prepare the listeners for the possibility that the devil will throw some of the members of the church into prison to test them.[13] Taking account of John's view that the Roman Empire is an agent of the devil, the prophet means that the threat of Roman imprisonment might be just ahead. Rome seldom used prison as a direct means of punishment. Rather, the empire imprisoned people either to motivate the prisoner to obey an edict of the state or to hold people before execution. Since there is little evidence that Rome executed large numbers of followers of Jesus in John's time, John likely foresaw Rome using prison to compel members of the church to accommodate. The book of Revelation is a counter-motivation to the followers of Jesus to remain faithful.

The members of the community will have affliction for ten days. The reference to ten days is likely not literal, but a figurative expression for a limited but intense period, recollecting Daniel 1:12–13, where the young Israelites remained faithful when challenged by the monarch to disavow their Jewish traditions. John wants the addressees to do the same.

The English translation "affliction" does not catch the sense implied in the Greek *thlypsis* that the struggle to remain faithful while suffering incarceration is part of the eschatological struggle. The prophet essentially says, "You have been faithful so far. You can be faithful in the intensified period of imprisonment." Today, in some contexts, the preacher can direct this admonition to congregations who have been faithful in difficult situations in the past, but whose current missions portend increased struggle ahead.

"Be faithful to death" in order to receive "the crown of life," John admonishes. To today's listener, the word "crown" probably calls a metal headpiece to mind, but the ancient author has in mind a wreath made of leaves that was awarded to people who did significant things—e.g., victorious athletes. Speaking of "the crown of life" is simply a way of saying that those who remain faithful will be included in the new heaven and the new earth.

2:11a: Formula indicating the importance of the message. See the comments on Revelation 2:7.

---

12. One of the best guides is Williamson, *Mutual Witness.*

13. Roman prisons tended to be underground, and were often dark, damp, and dank. Imprisonment was especially uncomfortable.

2:11b: Promise to the church. As so often in book of the Revelation, the reference to "conquering" refers to beating the impulse to accommodate, and hence to remain faithful.

John thinks of two deaths. The first one occurs at the end of one's present life, at which time the self enters an interim state while awaiting the final judgment. At that time, the unfaithful are consigned to a "second death"—that is, to eternal punishment (21:8)—while the faithful begin life in the New Jerusalem.

Revelation 2:12–17: Pergamum

Pergamum is another congregation whose life is a mixture of faithful testimony and dangerous accommodation.

2:8a: Instructions to the angel. The One Like a Human Being instructs the angel to write.

2:8b: The destination (Pergamum). Pergamum was a large city with a population of one hundred thousand, serving as a seat of Roman government and containing a large political-religious complex which John calls "Satan's throne" in 2:13. The complex included the emperor cult and temples to Zeus and Athena. Pergamum was the site of the first temple dedicated to a Caesar, erected in 29 BCE.

2:8c: Prophetic message formula. See the comments on Revelation 2:1b.

2:8e: Title for Jesus. Jesus is the one who has the sharp two-edged sword. This image, which we discussed at Revelation 1:16, reminds the listening community that the ruling Christ has the power both to condemn and to save by means of the word. This theme resurfaces in 2:16: Christ threatens to destroy some of the members of the church because they are unfaithful.

2:13–15: Critical evaluation of the congregation. The congregation lives "where Satan's throne is." As noted, John sees the Roman Empire as a system embodying the values and practices of Satan. The phrase "Satan's throne" probably refers to the complex of ideas mentioned above (2:12b).

A preacher might muse on places in today's culture where religious buildings and other symbols are intertwined with empire buildings and symbols. To what degree do expressions of contemporary religion serve empire, as in Pergamum?

Even with Satan incarnate in empire in the building across the street, so to speak, the congregation has held fast to the name of Jesus and has not denied its faith in Jesus. By "faith in me," the prophet means the confidence that God is bringing about a new world through Jesus. They have not accommodated.

One of their number, Antipas, was killed. John does not indicate whether Rome executed him or a vigilante action, associated with empire values, put him to death. Unfortunately, we know nothing else about Antipas, the only martyr whom the prophet names in the book of Revelation. While there is no evidence that Rome put believers in the new world to death on a large scale, John's mention of Antipas is a pastoral signal to the congregation to be prepared to hold fast to the limits of testing.

A preacher might point to persons and situations today in which Christians maintain faith and witness in the face of opposition, and even death. Few congregations in North America risk death for witnessing to the new world. But a preacher can raise the question of the limits of risk the congregation is willing to take in the name of social reconstruction.

At the same time, the One Like a Human Being has "a few things against" the Pergamumites. Some hold to the teachings of Balaam. These teachings are probably the same as those of the Nicolaitans and of Jezebel (see 2:4 and 2:20). While it is possible that "Balaam" was literally a teacher in the prophet's congregation, it is more likely that John uses the name Balaam symbolically to interpret the teaching and behavior of a group in the community: they did in John's day what Balaam and followers did in an earlier time. According to Numbers 31:6, the ancient Balaam led a group of Israelite men to have sex with non-Israelite women, who then led them into worship of the god Baal of Peor.[14] According to John, the idolatry involved both eating food which had been offered to idols and fornication, practices of accommodation in John's immediate world. People who offered food to idols would take a pinch of the food and place it on a fire in front of the idol, believing that all who ate from that food would be under the power of the idol. Fornication may refer to the practice of engaging in sex with temple prostitutes as part of idol worship. John thinks that the Balaamites/Nicolaitans engaged in these customs. By doing so, they implied that idolatry and its consequence—the unjust and violent Roman society—was acceptable to God.

2:16: Counsel. As in the case of Ephesus, John admonishes the community to repent. In this instance, repentance means to stop eating food offered to idols and participating in cultic prostitution. To fail to repent is to invite the One Like a Human Being "to come and make war against them with the sword of my mouth," an image recalling the double-edged sword of

---

14. Num 25:1–17 describes the incident.

2:12. To "make war" is to condemn; Christ will condemn those who practice idolatry.[15] As we observed earlier, judgment begins with the church.

While we do not eat food offered to idols today, many people in North America relate to food in ways that undermine self and community. Many are overweight, filling up on foods that have minimal or negative health values. Regarding an otherwise positive movement, many are mesmerized by things like the slow food movement without considering the significant numbers of the world population living in food insecurity. And while we do not visit temple prostitutes, many North Americans commodify sex and objectifying and abusing women.

2:17a: Formula indicating the importance of the message. See the comments on Revelation 2:7.

2:17b: Promise. To all who conquer, the One Like a Human Being promises two things. First, Christ will give them hidden manna in a way similar to God providing manna to the people in the wilderness (e.g., Exod 16:31–35; Num 11:6–9). Brian Blount calls to mind a Jewish tradition slightly earlier than John in which Jeremiah, prior to the Babylonian conquest of Jerusalem, hid the ark, which contained some morsels of the manna from the wilderness. According to 2 Maccabees 2:4–8, God would reveal the ark and its hidden manna only in the last days. By invoking this memory, John indicates that the last days are present. God will sustain the Pergamum community in the eschatological transformation just as God sustained Israel in the wilderness. This motif invites the preacher to explore sources of hidden manna—resources for spiritual sustenance today that may not be obvious to the congregation.

The meaning of the white stones is uncertain. The best explanation is to see them as amulets. In the ancient world, many people wore amulets representing the gods they worshiped. An amulet was like the brand on a steer indicating the owner. God issues amulets—white stones—to the faithful. In Revelation 19:12, John reveals that the one known as Faithful and True (Jesus) is the identity of the one with the "new name" on the white stones. Of course, this reference to amulets is symbolic. The amulets are not physical. But for those who bear the name of Christ, the name itself has the function of an amulet. The preacher might help the congregation imagine the amulets that God provides—things that remind us of our identity and destiny as we aim for social transformation.

---

15. The conquering Christ makes war against the enemies of the Realm in Rev 12:7; 13:14; 17:14; 19:11.

Revelation 2:18–29: Thyatira

The congregation at Thyatira is another one in which streams of faithfulness and unfaithfulness run side by side.

2:18a: Instructions to the angel. See the comments on Revelation 2:1a.

21:8b: The destination. While Thyatira was smaller and less prominent than most of the other cities to whom John spoke, one of the city's distinguishing characteristics was important to understanding the communication. Thyatira was known for its trade guilds, such as carpenters and workers of leather, linen, bronze, garments, pottery, and baking. These groups—which were similar to unions today—often included rites with meals where they ate food that had been offered to idols (see 2:15–16).

2:18c: Prophetic message formula. See the comments on Revelation 2:1b.

2:18d: Title for Jesus. This use of "Son of God" derives from Psalm 2:7, a hymn in Israel on the day the prince was elevated to ruling monarch. On coronation day, God adopts the young person as "my son." This reference has three functions here. First, it interprets the relationship between God and Jesus: God appointed Jesus as ruler of the coming Realm. Second, it contrasts the lineage and authority of Jesus and Caesar. Roman documents sometimes refer to the emperor as son of a god. The contrast is between God and the gods. Third, the reference foreshadows the quote from Psalm 2:8 in Revelation 2:29.

The "eyes like a flame of fire" recollect 1:14: Through accurate perception (symbolized by the eye), Jesus can perceive faithful and unfaithful actions and can render judgment accordingly (fire is often a symbol of judgment). Here, as in 1:15a, the burnished feet reveal the cosmic Christ as a history shaper in the same way that God shaped history in the days of Ezekiel and Daniel.

2:19–21: Critical evaluation of the congregation. At one level, the congregation puts forward good works—that is, the people live and witness with love, faithfulness, service, and patient endurance characteristic of the Realm. Indeed, the church's most recent works are greater than its first works.

Yet the community tolerates Jezebel, "who calls herself a prophet."[16] John probably borrows the name "Jezebel" from the Canaanite who married Ahab, ruler of Israel (1 Kgs 16:31), and whose behavior (such as idolatry, persecution, and unethical dealings) made her name a symbol for covenantal viola-

16. John is also a prophet. The issue is this: which prophet is closer to the purposes of God? Then, as now, congregations had to discern true prophets from false.

tion (1 Kgs 18–19; 2 Kgs 9). According to John, the Jezebel in the church leads her followers to fornicate and to eat food sacrificed to idols.

Fornication and eating food sacrificed to idols are described at 2:14–15. Those who eat food sacrificed to idols bring the eater into the domain of authority, practices, and values of the idol. Eating food offered to idols sometimes included cultic prostitution, through which worshipers hoped to please the gods. Many people in the Roman world took part in such activity as part of their everyday lives. Moreover, the rites of many of the trade unions in Thyatira included eating food that had been offered to idols. For the unions, such meals were not simply social occasions, but were experiences through which the trade union would receive the blessing of the god whose food they ate. From John's theological point of view, eating food offered to idols was a compromise too far because those who ate dramatized their trust in the idols (representing the unjust empire) for community well-being.

Christ had given Jezebel (the false prophet in the congregation) an opportunity to repent, but she refused. Most interpreters agree that John means that her opportunity is exhausted. She can no longer repent and, according to 2:22, is sentenced to death.

2:22–25: Counsel. John first admonishes the congregation to understand the seriousness of Jezebel's situation. Christ will throw Jezebel on a bed (2:22a). Here John invokes Isaiah 57:1–13, which condemns those who stayed in Jerusalem during the exile for making their beds with idols (Isa 57:7–8) and who will die as a consequence (Isa 57:13b). Jezebel is sentenced to death, most likely the second death of 20:11–15 that leads to the lake of fire.

John then admonishes those who committed idolatry with Jezebel to repent (i.e., those who believe the false prophet; 2:22b–23a). Otherwise, they will be part of the great tribulation—the intensified suffering that accompanies the transition of the ages—and Jesus will strike them dead at the final eschatological judgment with a second death.

The One Like a Human Being can, like God, search the minds and hearts of the community (Jer 17:10; cf. Pss 7:10; 64:6–7). Given this searching, the One Like a Human Being can judge rightly. There can be no secret, hidden devotion to idols.

At the final judgment, Jesus "will give to each of you as your works deserve" (cf. 20:11–15). In the book of Revelation, God has graciously taken the initiative to do what people cannot do for themselves: to begin the cosmic transformation that will result in the end of the empire and the coming of the heaven and the new earth. From John's perspective, people must respond to this gracious initiative by living and witnessing to the

Realm. If they respond inappropriately by continuing to manifest attitudes and actions of the old age, they will lose the grace they have been given, and will be punished.

Many preachers today struggle with this perspective, as many believe that God's love is unconditional, whereas from John's point of view, the initial invitation is unconditional, but repentance and obedience are conditions for continuing to the new Jerusalem.

John further admonishes the Thyatirans to "hold fast" to the good works they are doing until the One Like a Human Being returns. They rejected the teaching of Jezebel which "some call 'the deep things (*bathys*) of Satan.'" Since the Roman Empire is a social embodiment of Satan, "the deep things of Satan" bespeak participating in the empire. Moreover, in Paul's apocalyptically oriented writings, the apostle refers to the "deep things (*bathos*) of God" (1 Cor 2:10) and to the "depths" (*bathos*) of the knowledge of God (Rom 11:33). The "deep things" include inexhaustible resources for transformation that are beyond human comprehension. By contrast, the "deep things of Satan" contain possibilities for destruction that are hard for the human mind to grasp.

2:27–28: Promise. Revelation 2:27–28a pledges that those who are faithful until the end will share in the rule of Jesus in the new world (5:10; 20:4, 6; 22:5; cf. 4:4, 10). John draws on Psalm 2:9 to help interpret this claim: "I will give authority over the nations." Psalm 2:9 presumes that God will defeat Israel's enemies, which John takes as assurance that God will defeat Rome. Moreover, the monarch of Israel was to see that God's values and practices of God shaped the life of the community. For John, those who honor the word of God and the testimony of Jesus will rule with Christ in the new world. However, according to 22:3–5, this "rule" is not the arbitrary exercise of power, but is serving the purposes of God in the new heaven and the new earth. John implies contrast with the arbitrary, self-serving rule of Caesar and his devotees.

The One Like a Human Being promises further to give "the morning star" to the community. Revelation 22:16 indicates that Jesus is "the bright morning star." John again invites comparison with Caesar. The Romans thought of the morning star as the heavenly form of the goddess Venus. Isaiah 14:12 uses the language of "Day Star, Son of the Dawn" to speak of the ruler of Babylon, whom God dethroned in a way similar to God dethroning the emperor and the emperor's deities. Jesus (not Venus) is the real morning star.

2:29: Formula indicating the importance of the message. Ordinarily, this formula occurs prior to the promise. For the meaning of this formula, see the comments on Revelation 2:7.

This prophetic apocalyptic message raises the question for today's preacher of how to discern which prophets and teachers to trust and which to repudiate. From John's perspective, the ones to trust are those whose visions of life are consistent with that of the book of Revelation. The untrustworthy are those who, like contemporary Jezebels, bless accommodation.

Another possible issue for the pulpit is the degree to which Christians might participate in job-related affairs and social occasions in which empire attitudes and actions prevail, analogous to eating food offered to idols and fornication in Thyatira. Nearly everyone in North America participates in empire to one degree or another. On the one hand, it would be easy to generalize: Christians should be a part of such affairs as little as possible in order to make a moral statement. On the other hand, being present in such affairs could afford an opportunity for witness. For me, this issue is contextual, and is resolved by considering the degree to which presence implies complicity or provides opportunity witness.

Revelation 3:1–6: Sardis

When John looks at the congregation in Sardis, John essentially sees a burial ground, a repose of the dead.

3:1a: Instructions to the angel. See the comments on Revelation 2:1a.

3:1b: The destination. Sardis had been known as an impregnable fortress. But twice in earlier centuries, the city's defenders did not pay attention to approaching enemies, who slipped into the city and conquered it. This association may be in the background of John's description of the congregation: "You have a name of being alive, but you are dead" (3:1e). In other words, "You think you are safe, but you are the same as dead if you do not repent."

3:1c: Prophetic message formula. See the comments on Revelation 2:1b.

3:1d: Title for Jesus. Jesus is the "one who has the seven spirits of God and the seven stars." The phrase "seven spirits" refers to the seven angels of the churches (1:16, 20).[17] Angels can mediate both encouragement and judgment and both are in view here. Angels can be instruments of condemnation if the church continues on its present path, but they can be instruments of encouragement if the congregation conquers (that is, turns away from the route to death and turns to walk with Jesus, per 3:4b).

---

17. For the seven spirits as a way of speaking about the seven angels of the churches, see our comments on Rev 4:5 and 5:6.

3:1e: Critical evaluation of the congregation. The problem in the churches represented by Sardis is that, evidently, they saw themselves as "alive" and enjoyed that reputation among others, but thought that others but were moving towards death.[18] Their situation is the opposite of that of Christ and similar to that Rome. Christ had been dead (put to death by the empire), but is now alive. The empire appeared to be alive but was, according to John, already dying. Indeed, this congregation is an ecclesial version of the empire.

Some congregations today fall into this category. From the standpoint of institutional success—e.g., attendance, income, public recognition—they appear to be alive. But their values and practices learn towards those of contemporary empire.

3:2–4: Counsel. It is not too late for Sardis. John exhorts the congregation to "Wake up and strengthen what remains." The community may be "on the point of death," but there are "remains" of faithfulness that can wake up and come back to life.[19]

The way forward is to "remember" what the community "received and heard," and to "obey" and "repent." This statement is a classic prophetic summary of the practice of the heart of Jewish identity in the service of John's apocalyptic critique of the community: remember the promises of God and the responsibilities of the community, live according to the responsibilities (commandments), and repent when violations occur.

The One Like a Human Being will return at an unknown hour, "like a thief"—that is, he will return for the final events at a time the community does not know. John intends for this image, borrowed from the larger Jesus tradition (e.g., Matt. 24:43; Luke 12:39), to compel the listeners to take the action necessary to be a part of the final manifestation of the Realm.[20] On the one hand, I appreciate John's intention: to activate the listeners' sense of urgency. On the other hand, I am troubled by the image of returning like a thief because theft is part-and-parcel of the old age. Theft violates victims and community. To be sure, John does not sanction theft, but the image unintentionally suggests that Jesus violates the communities to which he returns. A pastor might use this incongruity as a jumping-off point to explore the kinds of language that are appropriate for inviting people to participate

18. Although John seems to pronounce the congregation "dead" in Rev 3:1e, the succeeding verses indicate that the congregation is only nearing death. Recovery is still possible.

19. On waking up as a figure for preparing for the apocalypse, see Mark 13:34–37; Matt 24:42–43.

20. Similar imagery occurs in 1 Thess 5:2–4; 2 Pet 3:10, and Rev 16:1.

in the movement towards the Realm, and patterns of speech that, even when well-meant, undermine aspects of that invitation.

When John says that "some in the community have not soiled their clothes," the prophet draws on an established Jewish tradition of speaking of the covenantal life in the language of dress (e.g., Zech 3:1–5; Matt 22:11–14). The "soiled clothes" represent unfaithful behavior. By contrast, the few who have been obedient to the values and practices of the Realm will be dressed in white—that is, they will be part of the eschatological world.[21] They wear white robes because they are worthy, meaning that they manifest the integrity of the Realm.[22]

3:5: Promise. After reaffirming those in the congregation who will also be dressed in white in the eschaton, John introduces an idea that troubles many Christians: the names written in the book of life. Many apocalyptic writers believed that God wrote the names of the people who would be welcomed into the Realm in such a book. In connection with Revelation 20:12, we discuss the complicated thinking relating this book to the book of deeds opened at the final judgment, along with the notion that God wrote these names "from the foundation of the world" (13:8). For now, it is enough to note that, whereas listeners today sometimes think of the book of life as limiting the names of the saved, the ancients took the book as indicating that no name that deserved to be saved would be lost.[23]

In addition to naming the hesitation of some contemporary people about such a book, the preacher could help the congregation understand that the function of the motif of the book of life in antiquity was to assure people that they would be part of a better world. However, the presence of one's name in the book was not a once-and-for-all guarantee. As Revelation 2:5 implies, God blots names out of the book when people soil their clothes. A name is written in the book by grace, but it stays in the book by faithful witness.

One of my students once suggested that "the book of life for today" is the roster of those who have stood up for justice, especially in situations that are uncomfortable. Preachers might formulate contemporary books of life along lines that are appropriate to the preaching context.

21. White robes are characteristic of the dress of people in the heavenly world (4:4; 7:9, 13, 14). The church is in clean linen in 19:8.

22. On the notion of worthiness, cf. 4:11.

23. This seems to be the case in Exod 32:32–33; Ps 69:28; Isa 4:3; Dan 12:1; and Mal 3:16. Commentators sometimes point out that many ancient cities kept track of citizens (a more specialized category than today), recording their names in a city register. For a person to have the full rights of a citizen, a person's name had to be in the register.

John, like most apocalyptic writers, assumed a final judgment at which the members of the human family would give an account of how they lived. John claims that the risen Jesus will confess the names of the faithful before God and the angels on that occasion (3:5b). Jesus vindicates those who have conquered (as in Matt 10:32 and Luke 12:8).[24]

While some present-day believers do not believe in such a final judgment, this theme does remind us that all actions have consequences, some of them long-term. A preacher might describe a scene other than a court room in which circumstances come together to cause a person to feel judgment (because of complicity with Rome) or vindication (as a result of standing for the Realm). The sermon could encourage people towards vindicating attitudes and actions.

3:6: Formula indicating the importance of the message. See the comments on Revelation 2:7.

Revelation 3:7–13: Philadelphia

The congregation at Philadelphia has kept Jesus' admonition to patient endurance.

3:7a: Instructions to the angel. See the comments on Revelation 2:1a.

3:7b: The destination. The history of Philadelphia is a backstory to this letter. The city was devastated by an earthquake in 17 CE. The emperor Tiberius favored Philadelphia with reduced taxes and imperial aid in rebuilding which prompted the city to add "Neocaesarea" to its name. Wanting to solidify its relationship with Emperor Vespasian, the city added his family name, Flavia, to that of the city. In so doing, the civic authorities aligned themselves with the vision and morals of Rome. By contrast, the One Like a Human Being will write on the prophetic community "the name of the city of my God" (3:12).

A preacher might meditate on how names signal—and help create—worldview. What do the names of the congregation and its denomination signal? Could the congregation or denomination call itself something that points more directly to "the name of the city of my God"?

3:7c: Prophetic message formula. See the comments on Revelation 2:1b.

3:7d: Title for Jesus. The description of Jesus is "holy" and "true." To be holy is to have sovereign identity and power set apart from all other identities

---

24. Dan 7:9–14 recounts a similar scene in which the Ancient of Days pronounces judgment in the presence of thousands of angels. One of the clearest pictures of a final judgment in the Gospels and Letters is Matt 25:31–46.

and powers. Jesus, like God, is not dependent on the power of the Roman
Empire or any other entity, but exercises power only according to the divine
aims. In Isaiah 65:16, the Septuagint, the translation of the Hebrew Scriptures
into Greek, the word "true" (*alēthinos*) refers to God in contrast to the idols.
God and Jesus are true and trustworthy, whereas Caesar and the Roman Empire are based on false values and are untrustworthy.

 John reinforces these themes by citing Isaiah 22:22: "who has the key
of David . . . and no one opens." In Isaiah 22:15–25, God effects a transition
in leadership among the servants in the house of David. Shebna, who man-
aged the household, was self-serving. God decided to replace Shebna with
Eliakim. God would give the key to the household, a symbol of responsibility and authority, to the latter. Eliakim would have authority to open and
shut the door—that is, to oversee the operations of the household.

In John's time, Caesar was a functional equivalent of Shebna—using
the resources of the world in self-serving ways. God would replace Caesar
with Christ, who would oversee the reinvention of the new heaven and the
new earth.

The excerpt from Isaiah in Revelation 3:7 is the text for the fourth of
the seven contemporary "Great O's," a series of antiphons—short liturgical
texts—often chanted or sung in Advent.[25] A preacher might use the appearance of this Great O for an Advent sermon on the message to Philadelphia
to reflect on the relationship of Advent, the first coming (Christmas), and
the second coming (the final transition).[26]

3:8: Critical evaluation of the congregation. The One Like a Human
Being has offered the church represented by Philadelphia the opportunity
to pass through the open door—i.e., to be part of the movement towards the
Realm. No one can close that door. Compared to the power brokers of the
old age (especially the empire), the witnesses in Philadelphia "have but little
power," yet they have remained faithful. They have "kept my word and have
not denied my name." Members of this community have refused to accommodate to the empire. They have exercised their power wisely.

3:9–12: Counsel and promise. Admonition and the promise in-
termingle in this message. The speaker intends to make the members of
the synagogue of Satan bow down before the feet of the Philadelphia

25. Historically, the church used one of the seven Great O's each day from December 17 to 23. The "key of David" is the fourth (December 20). However, churches now
use the Great O's in other ways and at other times. For example, some congregations
recite the Great O's on Sundays during Advent or on Christmas Eve or Christmas Day.

26. A preacher might develop a series of sermons on the Great O's: one sermon
each on the four Sundays of Advent, Christmas Eve, and the two Sundays of Christmas.

congregation so the former "will know that I love you."[27] As at 2:9, the synagogue of Satan is likely comprised of gentiles who converted to Judaism without giving up their affinity with the empire. In the hierarchical social structure of antiquity, people did acknowledge those who were above them in the social pyramid, often by bowing.

The function of this affirmation is to reinforce the Philadelphians in keeping Jesus' word. At the same time, I am troubled by the notion. It simply reverses the occupants of the social pyramid, assuming a hierarchical social structure like that of the old age. While those who have been degraded might find it satisfying to rule over those who degraded them, such a reversal does not really reconstitute the people involved as human *community*. The nature of the social structure itself needs to change in the direction of offering love, peace, mutuality, justice, and abundance.

As we have noted, many apocalyptic theologians believed that an intensified period of suffering, sometimes called the time of trial (*peirasmos*), would occur as the end approached and the powers of the old age entrenched to resist the coming of the Realm.[28] The One Like a Human Being promises to keep the church in this coming period (3:10). This expression cannot mean that the Philadelphians will not be present during the great *peirasmos*, since John is clear that this ordeal will affect all peoples and the creation itself (7:14).[29] Rather, the prophet means that God will support them as they make their way through it.[30]

In many congregations, a preacher could profitably compare and contrast the exegesis above with that of the popular premillennialists who anticipate the rapture—an event in which God physically removes believers from the world, so they will not experience tribulation, leaving the rest of the human family to suffer in the chaos and pain until Jesus returns.[31] In the view of most progressive scholars, God does not remove the church from suffering, but strengthens the church for witness in it.

27. John takes the notion of enemies bowing down before the faithful from Isa 60:14, where gentiles kneel before Israel, thus reinforcing the idea that the synagogue of Satan is made up of gentile converts who have not fully embraced Judaism.

28. Here, as throughout the book of Revelation, "the earth" has a negative connotation. It is associated with the broken old age, the domain of empire.

29. Aune, *Revelation 6–16*, 240 points to the following: 6:2–17; 8:6—9:21; 12:13–17; 13:7; 16:2–21; 17:6.

30. Gundry, *Church and the Tribulation*, shows that John 17:15, which contains the same wording, "keep from," does not refer to God removing faithful people physically from the trouble, but precisely preserving (keeping) them within it.

31. Pretribulation premillennialists and post-tribulation premillennialists debate how Rev 3:10 relates to their end-of-the-world timelines.

John refers to Jesus "coming soon" to encourage the congregation: they would not have to struggle through the great trial for too long (3:11). Moreover, if they "hold fast," they will receive a crown. While the image of the crown (*stephanos*) evokes the wreath awarded an athlete who won a contest, it also echoes Isaiah 17–22, when God removes Shebna's crown and gives to Eliakim. The crown is a symbol of being part of the final eschatological world. The promise of the crown is one of John's ways of motivating the community to hold fast for that day.

John ramps up the motivation in Revelation 3:12 by using images that work together to promise one thing: those who conquer in the present will be part of the everlasting New Jerusalem. The images also imply contrast with aspects of the Roman Empire, whose promises are pale and passing away.

The One Like a Human Being will make those who conquer a pillar in the temple. A temple represents the presence and purposes of a deity and makes those things accessible. The Revelation frequently uses the architectural symbol of the temple that John sees in heaven as a way of representing the divine presence and purposes (7:15; 11:1–2, 19; 14:15–17; 15:5–8; 16:1, 17). The reference to "pillars" partakes of this architectural symbolism to say that the community that holds fast is in the divine arms and manifests the divine purposes. By contrast, the Roman temples—representations of gods—are on the way to destruction.

In antiquity, to receive the name of another was to be in included in the community of the other. Revelation 3:12b employs three images associated with the notion of "name." (1) Recollecting Isaiah 43:7 with its promise that God would reunite and restore all who are called by the divine name, Jesus will write the name of God on the faithful. (2) Anticipating Revelation 21:1–5, Jesus will write the name of the city of God, the new Jerusalem, on the faithful, foreshadowing the Philadelphians' citizenship there. (3) Perhaps appropriating Isaiah 62:2 with its assumption that giving a new name befits a new level of community life, Jesus will write his own new name on the faithful as they move towards the new Jerusalem. John never reveals the content of the "new name," but it signals a new world.[32] While each image has its own nuances, the three reiterate the point made through the symbol of the pillars: the names of the Philadelphians who conquer will forever belong to God in the new Jerusalem.

This passage implies a backstory for those who act in the name of Caesar (including those who accommodate); John soon reveals that Caesar and

---

32. On the new name, see further on 19:12.

Rome come from Satan and the depths of chaos (12:18—13:1). Those who accommodate will share the fate of that city, which is destruction (18:1–24).

3:12: Formula indicating the importance of the message. See the comments on Revelation 2:7.

John's tone in this message suggests an approach for a sermon. The prophet positively reinforces the congregation's witness and urges them to continue what they are doing; he seeks to *attract* hearers to the movement to the new Jerusalem. Preachers might search for contemporary images that are as compelling as pillars. Moreover, the preacher might ponder how today's community experiences the security represented by receiving the name of God, the name of the new Jerusalem, and Christ's own name.

Revelation 3:14–22: Laodicea

The letter to Laodicea is likely the most well-known of the seven letters because of the famous painting by Warner Sallman, "Christ at the Heart's Door," and because the image of Christ spitting out lukewarm Christians has a sizable place in the popular Christian imagination.

3:14a: Instructions to the angel. See the comments on Revelation 2:1a.

3:14b: The destination. Located at the hub of several trade routes, Laodicea was known for wool and eye salve, both themes in 3:17. Laodicea was a Roman administrative center and was so wealthy (a theme in 3:17) that when an earthquake destroyed the city in 60 CE, the city did not accept government help. The city's water supply was drinkable but foul; much of Laodicea's water came through an aqueduct from hot springs six miles away so it was lukewarm by the time it reached the city.

3:14c: Prophetic message formula. See the comments on Revelation 2:1b.

3:14d: Title for Jesus. The first title for Jesus, "the Amen," draws inspiration from the root meaning of "amen:" to be trustworthy, to be faithful, to affirm. Scholars rightly point to Isaiah 65:16 and the title "God of faithfulness" (which could be transliterated "God of *amen*") as a theological resonance chamber for Jesus as "the Amen." God can be trusted to create a new heaven and a new earth (Isa 65:17–25). The Realm-initiating ministry of Jesus is an expression of God's faithfulness in moving towards the new world.[33]

33. While John may not have been influenced by 2 Cor 1:19–20, he evidences a similar spirit in calling Jesus "the Amen": for the prophet, Jesus is God's confirmation that the Realm is on the way. In Rev 1:7d, John writes *nai, amen*, which the NRSV renders

Jesus is "the faithful and true witness," which John partly invoked in 1:5 when speaking of "the faithful witness." We commented on John's use of "true" (*alēthinos*) at 3:7d. The combination "faithful and true" anticipates Revelation 19:7.

The prophet does not speculate about the specific role of Jesus in the process of creation when speaking of Jesus as "the origin [beginning] of creation."[34] The prophet implies authority and trustworthiness on the part of Jesus. Since God acted through Jesus as part of the creation of the world, God can act in a powerful way in recreation. Moreover, this theme reverberates with the notion that the end-time will be like the beginning time.

3:15–17: Critical evaluation of the congregation. Both hot and cold water have distinctive functions: hot for such things as cooking and cleansing, and cold for such things as refreshing and preserving. Lukewarm water is good for neither. Similarly, the works (the witness to the Realm) of the Laodiceans are neither hot nor cold (3:15). The works are not sufficiently faithful. Consequently, the One Like a Human Being will spit them out— i.e., will condemn them at the last judgment (3:16).[35]

The expressions "I am rich, I have prospered, and I need nothing" indicate that the Laodicean congregation was relatively well off socially and economically. Commentators often hear two echoes here. First, in Hosea 12:8, Ephraim (the northern nation, Israel) thought itself secure when it became rich through exploitation and injustice but consequently faced judgment. Second, the affluence of the congregation comes from the idolatrous practices that make possible the affluence of the city of Laodicea. The congregation was accommodating to prevailing Roman attitudes and actions to maintain the congregation's comfortable material life. They wanted to see themselves on the way to the Realm while continuing to benefit from Rome.

The church had a false impression of itself that would result in Jesus spitting them out. John reveals their real situation: "wretched, pitiable, poor, blind, and naked" (3:17b). Apocalyptic writers sometimes use such designations for the conditions of the old age that will be condemned at the final judgment. Moreover, commentators sometimes see the poor, blind, and naked as exposing the false security of leading Laodicean industries—finance,

---

"So it is to be. Amen." The Greek *nai* is often translated "Yes," as in 2 Cor 1:19–20.

34. Scholars often call attention to thematic similarities between this phrase and Col 1:15–20, especially v. 15. John may use the notion of wisdom as a model for interpreting the role of Christ in creation (e.g., Prov 8:22; Sir 24; Wis 7:22–25).

35. The verb "spit out" (*emeō*) could be translated "vomit" as in the Septuagint of Lev 18:25, 28; 20:22, where the land vomits the Canaanites (archetypal idolaters) out of the land.

eye salve, and clothing. The circumstances of the congregation are like that of the Roman Empire: both appear to be in peak condition, but both suffer from interior rot that is itself the means of punishment. Consequently, John prescribes salve for their eyes, so they will be able to see themselves as John sees them (3:18c).

Many congregations today are like the Laodiceans, enjoying relative prosperity, thinking themselves Christian while largely following principles and behaviors of the various empires in which they are embedded. While the Prosperity Gospel may be the most egregious example of this phenomenon, many of the state churches in Europe fall into this category. While the United States cannot have an official state church, many churches are effectively state churches, that is, chaplains to the empire cultures that infuse the United States.

3:18–20: Counsel. The visionary uses three vivid images to counsel the congregation to repent. First, they can buy gold refined by fire (3:18a). People converted ore into pure gold by thrusting the ore into fire, which then burned away the slag. The gold in view, however, is not the gold of the old age, but gold as a figure for life in the new heaven and the new earth. If the Laodiceans repent, they can survive the final judgment and walk the streets represented by transformed gold (21:21).[36]

Second, the church can get white robes to clothe them and to cover their shame and nakedness (3:18b). The white robes are the dress of those who dwell in the new Jerusalem (1:13; 3:5; 4:4; 6:11; 7:14; 22:24). Per Ezekiel 16:36, nakedness is a way of speaking about judgment on those who have cooperated with idolatry and injustice. The church thinks the fine garments for which Laodicea was known are adequate clothing. However, in their present condition, the Laodiceans will be subjected to shame and nakedness at the final judgment. If the church repents, they may experience difficulty, but after the final judgment they will wear white robes forever in the new world.

Third, John prescribes salve for their eyes so that they will be able to see themselves as John sees them (3:18c). In Jewish physiological symbolism, the eye often represents the capacity for theological perception. While Laodicea was known for its eye ointment, that medicine would only allow its users to continue to misperceive their relationship to old Rome and the new Jerusalem. Repentance, however, makes it possible for them to discern their situation and to take the necessary steps to see the new Jerusalem.

36. The prophets sometimes speak of communities undergoing a theological and ethical smelting (e.g., Jer 9:7; Zach 13:9; Mal 3:3).

In 3:19, John articulates a classic Jewish notion in the tradition of Proverbs 3:11–12: God disciplines those whom God loves. Through prophets, God tells the beloved community what they are doing wrong and disciplines them, not as an end but to motivate repentance, so the community will make the adjustments necessary to join the movement towards the Realm.

Revelation 3:20 with Jesus standing at the door and knocking is an iconic image in Christian community, but is often understood in a reduced way when Christians think of Christ knocking at the door of the individual, pleading for that person to accept him as personal savior. John, instead, uses the architectural image of Jesus standing at the door of the house in which the church at Laodicea meets. In response to the message of the letter in Revelation 3:14–22, the church opens the door—that is, repents.

Many scholars think that 3:20b—Jesus eating with the church—refers to the One Like a Human Being present with the church through the loaf and the cup. Many apocalyptic theologians in antiquity anticipated that after the apocalypse, God would invite the residents of the new world to a festive victory meal (sometimes called the eschatological banquet or the messianic banquet). In Revelation 19:9, John refers to this celebratory meal as "the marriage supper of Lamb." From these points of view, partaking of the bread and cup in the church is a prolepsis—a meal when the church in the present anticipates the final eschatological meal.

Theological illiteracy in today's church often includes a vacuum of understanding the breaking of the bread and the pouring of the cup. This text provides the preacher with a golden opportunity to think with the congregation about John's conviction that, when gathering at the table, the church can experience the presence of the risen Jesus as part of a larger anticipation of the Realm. Yet this perspective comes with a question. Does the congregation gathering at the table really anticipate the transformed community of the new Jerusalem? If not, what might the preacher suggest as steps in that direction?

3:22: Formula indicating the importance of the message. See the comments on Revelation 2:7.

3:21: Promise. Although the formula indicating the importance of the message comes before the promise, the final promise is a lovely benediction on the seven prophetic apocalyptic messages. To those who conquer, the One Like a Human Being will "give a place with me on my throne." As we noted earlier, John imagines that the faithful will share in Jesus' reign in the post-apocalypse world (1:6; 5:10; 20:4, 6; 22:5). However, as we see in 4:10 and 22:3b–5, the faithful carry out this rule by serving the purposes of God in the new heaven and new earth.

Many Christians today think of "heaven" as an extension of the best qualities of their own lives in the present. Although I have had few conversations with lay people in the historic churches specifically about "ruling" in the next life, when that issue has come up, the lay perspective has universally been simply to extend their own hope to the future. They envision God reversing the hierarchy of rule from the old world to new, as if the followers of Jesus now lord it over those who lorded it over them. As someone said, "We get a turn." John sees these things quite differently. John revalues "rule": those who rule in the new heaven and the new earth do so by serving the qualities of life God ordains for the new Jerusalem.

Revelation 4–5

Revealing the Power of God

R evelation 4:1—5:14 takes place in the throne room of heaven. A preacher might imagine Revelation 4 as a wide-angle view of the throne room within which to place the more selective focus of Revelation 5.

The Throne Room: A Wide-Angle View

When preaching or leading studies on the book of Revelation in congregations, I often engage interest with trick questions. "How does John describe heaven?" Nearly everyone answers in terms like "a city with golden streets." While such answers get partial credit—Revelation 21 and 22 do picture a heaven as well as a new earth—the trick is that Revelation 4 is actually the passage that gives John's fullest discussion of heaven per se. Of course, Revelation 4 is not a blueprint, but represents abiding realities through vivid pictorial symbols.

Beginning a sermon or Bible study on Revelation 4 with the group's preconceptions of "heaven" is often a bridge to help them think about a difference of emphasis between their questions and that of the prophet. Today, many people want to know, "What will heaven be like when I go there?" John reframes that question in the vision of the new Jerusalem, but in Revelation 4, he implies the effect of the vision of the heavenly throne room for the church living in the midst of the empire.

An important perspective of apocalypticism is in the background. Things in heaven determine things on earth. The realities that John sees in the world above shape possibilities in the world below. This vision clarifies who is on the throne of the universe: God is the absolute ruler of heaven and earth. Pointedly, Caesar is not on that throne. Consequently, the congregation can believe the interpretation of the present and the anticipation of the future that John unfolds in the next chapters.

Perhaps today's preacher can join John in hoping that the vision in Revelation 4, picturing realities that endure amidst the uncertainties and struggles of life in the Mediterranean Empire, will inspire worship of God amidst the uncertainties and struggles of life in an increasingly empire-like world. To those who accommodate to the Empire and the old age, this vision is a multimedia memorandum: you will be called to account for your life and witness before the one on the throne. To those who struggle to witness faithfully, this vision is multimedia declaration of assurance.

While the sermon should keep in mind the overarching purpose of the passage, the preacher may notice that particular images speak with particular power to the preaching context. For instance, the preacher might correlate the image of the sea like glass (4:7a) with the situation of a congregation in chaos.

Revelation 4:1: John's Journey to Heaven

4:1. Much of the rest of the book of Revelation is a seer's journey to heaven, a common motif in apocalyptic literature. The purpose of the journey is to reveal to the seer (and to those who hear about the journey) the things in heaven that determine things on earth. In that tradition, John, in a state of ecstasy ("I was in the spirit"), is transported through a door that opens in the dome between the earth and heaven. John's journey differs from many others in that other such travels often unveil a specific timeline of events that will soon occur. John's heavenly sojourn articulates a lens through which to interpret significant things in the present (exposing the empire and teaching how to respond) and points generally to future developments (the ultimate destruction of the empire and the coming of the new Jerusalem), but does not dwell on minute speculation.

The affirmation that "these things must take place" is in the mood of promise. John's congregation can have confidence in the great transformation, and hence can risk being faithful to the word of God and the testimony of Jesus.

John grounded his interpretation of life in a form of authority that people accepted in his culture (the heavenly journey). A preacher might reflect with the congregation on forms of authority that the congregation recognizes, and may have a spirited conversation on how they relate to the heavenly journey.

Revelation 4:2–6: The Throne Room:
Experience of Transcendence

John's description of the throne room is similar to typical royal courts of Mediterranean antiquity.[1] The prophet implicitly invites the listener to compare the throne of God with the throne room of Caesar.

4:2. The throne is a symbol of power; the one who sits on the throne rules. John's description has a polemical edge. The description of the throne room is similar to the Roman imperial court. Caesar sits on a throne, but as a pretender.

4:3. In the tradition of Judaism, John does not describe the being of the one seated on the throne, but compares the appearance of God to the effect of precious stones radiating color—carnelian and jasper. Carnelian is typically red, and jasper is usually a shade of red, yellow, brown, or green, but is clear (without color) in 21:12. While the analogy is imprecise, the effect evokes a sense of wonder like that of a brilliant spotlight reflecting off of the hundreds of mirrors on a rotating disco ball.

The throne is surrounded by a rainbow that, strikingly, is emerald green. Several apocalyptic writers compare the transition of the ages to the time of the great flood of Genesis 6:1—8:22. The Roman Empire is disobedient as the world was before the great flood. God will destroy the present age, but afterward God will open a new, revitalized world. The rainbow is a reminder of the promise of a new beginning awaiting those who are faithful during the period of intense struggle.

The rainbow around the throne is the first of several symbols in the book that is transformed. It is no longer a rainbow that would be found in the sky of the old world. It is emerald in color, and one presumes that it does not vanish from the heavenly world. This sign of promise endures.

4:4. Twenty-four elders surround the throne. Commentators debate the identity of these figures. Given John's conviction that the work of God is continuous from Israel through Jesus to the apocalypse, and that the twelve major figures in Israel and the twelve apostles are both mentioned as foundational to the new Jerusalem (21:12–14), they seem to be heavenly representatives of the twelve tribes and the twelve apostles. Their white garments are the dress of heaven. Their crowns indicate that they have real power and that they rule. They are in the very presence of God, thus assuring their earthly counterparts (the Jewish community and one of its sectarian expressions, the church) that God has ultimate control over those who are faithful

---

1. For the description of the heavenly court, John draws extensively on passages in the Torah, Prophets, and Writings, and in other apocalyptic traditions, especially Isa 6:1–13; Ezek 1:1–28; and Dan 7:1–14.

in the teeth of empire, and that God will bring them into the new heaven and new earth. Later, the elders instruct John on how to interpret things that he sees (e.g., 5:5; 7:13–14).

Similar courtiers surrounded Caesar in the imperial court. But in 4:10, John implies a dramatic contrast between the elders and devotees of Caesar.

4:5. The "flashes of lightning, rumblings, and peals of thunder" are characteristic of theophanies—dramatic phenomena that demonstrate the awesome power of God (e.g., Exod 19:18–21; Psalm 29: Ezek 1:4; Dan 7:9–10). A theophany is often the equivalent of bold print in today's book: it highlights the meaning of the event or the teaching with which it is associated.

Seven flaming torches, which John identifies as the seven spirits of God, burn before the throne. The discussion at 1:4 concludes that the seven spirits of God are the angels of the seven churches. The presence of the torches/spirits/angels before the throne is another statement that God has definitive control over what happens to the churches in the ongoing and final struggle between God and the forces of Satan. God's promises to the faithful and true—as well as the condemnation of the disobedi-ent—are guaranteed.

4:6a. "Something like a sea of glass, like crystal," is also before the throne. In the Ancient Near East, water was sometimes associated with cha-os. In the ancient worldview, chaos was the presence of incredible energy that was not focused towards community-building. Indeed, people viewed chaos as community- and order-destroying. Yet, here God has not only calmed the sea but has materially altered it so that it is no longer composed of water that can continually reform itself in new expressions of chaos. In-deed, the transformed sea is a thing of beauty.

The seven torches and the sea are both before the throne. While John does not likely picture the torches in the sea, that image is theologically apt. The churches in the Roman Empire are in a period of chaos. Yet, through the spirits (the angels of the churches), the chaos does not destroy the pos-sibility of witness.

4:7b–8a. Interpreters sometimes struggle with the significance of the four creatures. Since some of the other elements in the throne room rep-resent things on earth, it follows that the four creatures are emblematic of human and animal life, and, by extension, the broader natural world.[2] The creatures in the throne room do what is appropriate to creatures: they praise

---

2. Irenaeus, in the middle of the second century, was the first to leave a record coor-dinating the four creatures with the four gospel writers: the human being for Matthew, the lion for Mark, the ox for Luke, and the eagle for John. However, the Bible itself does not suggest this symbolism.

God day and night. The activity of the creatures in the throne room is a pattern for activity that is appropriate to creatures who live in the world: to live in community that manifests the covenantal purposes of God, so that all can be blessed.

Interpreters offer multiple suggestions for why John mentions the four specific creatures—lion, ox, human, and eagle.[3] They may represent leading species from different categories—wild animals (lion), domestic animals (ox), the human, and flying things (eagle). These four, then, evoke the awareness of other elements of creation whom God intends to dwell in the community as described in Revelation 21:9—22:5.

The eyes add an important dimension to the meaning of the creatures. As we have already noted, in Jewish theological symbolism, the eye is often a representation of the capacity to perceive from the perspective of the community's deepest convictions. In the heavenly throne room, these creatures are covered with eyes, front and back. I admit that this picture gives me the creeps when trying to visualize it. But John's message is that, when informed by God, living things understand what is needed to be fully receiving and giving members of community. They see what they need to see.

Moreover, the creatures can fly. John borrows descriptions of the wings on the seraphs from Isaiah 6:1–3. In the realm of earth, three of the four creatures can only walk, but in heaven, God transforms them so that not only can they use their eyes 360 degrees, but they are not limited by the horizon. By flying, they can see things that they could not ordinarily see. This is a way of saying that their theological acuity is unlimited.

In this passage, John points the preacher to a striking theme by stressing that the immediate presence of God is transforming. The entities in the heavenly throne room retain continuity with their earthly nature and function, but God remodels them to serve God's intentions in a fuller way. The heavenly court of God is thus dramatically different from the imperial court where Caesar commands people and animals to serve the *Pax Romana*.

The churches to whom John wrote were still in the old age where the empire continued its brutal rule. Against this, the four living creatures are both an assurance and an aspiration. They assure the church that true community already exists in heaven, and the church is moving towards its expression in the new heaven and new earth. And the passage offers the church a vision towards which it can aspire. People, animals, and nature can live towards the new heaven and new earth, even in the present.

---

3. Ezek 1:5–22 and 10:12 mention the same four creatures, but in Ezekiel, each creature has all four faces, and they carry God's throne-chariot.

Revelation 4:8b–11: The Throne Room:
Giving Glory to God

In the opening paragraphs of this chapter, we referred to a lay tendency to think of heaven in terms of the best qualities of their present lives. In Bible study groups, I sometimes challenge this predisposition by pointing out that Revelation 4:8b–11 mentions the inhabitants of heaven doing nothing day and night except singing praise to God. This heaven is not a great family reunion where all the children eat their spinach and people can pull in twelve-pound basses every time they cast their lines. Just as God remakes things in heaven, so also God remakes the very way of thinking about the nature and meaning of existence.

A different way of thinking and valuing takes over John's presentation of what happens in heaven, which is paradigmatic for what should take place everywhere. In the throne room of heaven, praising God day and night is the *raison d'etre*. A preacher's question is this: what can the congregation do in order to praise God in its earthly setting?

4:8b. John has already alluded to the themes of this initial song coming from the creatures.[4] John takes up the heart of Isaiah 6:3 to shape this hymn. As we observed at 3:7 and 4:8, God is holy because God is not dependent on other powers. God manifests integrity of being, purpose, and action. God always does what is right because God can do no other. God ever acts consistently with God's purposes. The threefold repetition of the quality of holiness underscores the importance of this essential quality of God.

At 1:8 we explain that to call God "almighty" (*pantokratōr*) is to indicate that God has more power than any other entity, including Caesar. Formula used of several Greek and Roman deities state that they "were, are, and shall be," which emphasizes their continuity of being. By contrast, at 1:4 and 1:8 we stress the emphasis of the final line of the prophetic hymn: God is coming to the world with judgment and salvation. From the perspective of a world in the grip of Rome, God needs to go beyond continuity of being to assertive redemptive engagement to be truly holy. Indeed, in the book of Revelation when people and creatures and nature praise God, they tend to do so in response to God's intention to recreate the world.

4:9–10. The "living creatures give glory and honor and thanks to God." John frequently writes multimedia scenes such as 4:9–10 into the book (e.g., 5:11–14; 7:10–17; 11:15–19). In these settings, multiple descriptors of the qualities of response attributed directly to God intensify the hearer's

---

4. Liturgical scholars refer to this hymn as the triasgion, from its Greek roots meaning "three times holy" in reference to repeating "holy" three times.

awareness of these characteristics and turn the listener's imagination into a chamber resonating with a fully sensory, even visceral awareness of God, fueled by the content of the particular concepts. Intellect, intuition, and feeling intertwine in a *gestalt* of perception. The effect of such texts is to create in the listener multiple and reinforcing perceptions of God, along-side which fade the ceremony of the imperial court, Roman civil religion, and other public rites.

Many African-American congregations embody an analogous situation when the music, visual, and congregational participation in the first part of the services—perhaps lasting an hour or more—reaches a fever pitch and the congregation is in ecstasy. Such worship goes beyond both emotion and intellect and becomes a transcendent dimension of understanding. In the face of racism and other systems that repress African-American life, moments of high worship help reinforce personal identity, build community, develop critical perspective, bestow mission, and empower courage.

The twenty-four elders represent the communities that witness to God from the Torah, Prophets, Writings, and followers of Jesus. When they fall before the throne and place their crowns before one on the throne, they explicitly symbolize the mission of these communities: to take their power and place it in the service of the purposes of God. As previously noted, the crown indicates that they have real agency. They can make things happen. Their choices make differences. They do not use the power represented by their crowns for their own glory (as Caesar does), but they use their power to point to the new heaven and the new earth with its love, peace, joy, freedom, dignity, egalitarianism, and abundance for all.

4:11. God is worthy to receive glory and honor and power because God created all things. At 1:5b–7, we indicated that to be worthy in the prophetic world was to manifest integrity between divine purpose (bringing about the new heaven and the new earth) and activity (the way in which God brings it about). God is worthy because the divine purposes and divine activity are ever consistent.

When I first studied the book of Revelation, I wondered why John included this emphasis on creation in Revelation 4:11. After all, is not this apocalyptic discourse about the *new* creation? Commentators have since helped me see that Revelation 4:11 connects God's worthiness to God's work at creation. As Creator, God endowed all things to live in mutually reinforcing community (Gen 1:1—2:4). Although people violated that plan and invited the divine curse on humankind and nature, leaving the world broken and suffering the wound of empire, the God who created the world did not give up on the original plan. Revelation 4:11 implies that since God had the power to create, God now has the power to recreate. God is sovereign over all things—including things claimed by the Roman Empire.

Although John did not focus on ecology and concern for the earth in a contemporary way, a preacher could get to those matters from conversation with Revelation 4:11. John foresaw the present world disappearing and God replacing it with a new heaven and a new earth (21:1). Consequently, John had little reason to advocate traditional Jewish respect for ecology.[5] I disagree with John's overarching perspective in that I do not believe God will destroy and remake the world in this singular fashion. I believe the world will exist until the sun burns out, and that human beings need to do all that we can to restore nature to its supportive relationship with humankind. If we do not take such action, the empire thinking that fuels human abuse of nature could very well cause the structures that support life to collapse prematurely.

While I disagree with this key aspect of John's unconcern with preserving the present natural world, John does presume that the new heaven and the new earth will be a material (physical) realm in which all elements cooperate for mutual blessing. A preacher could extend John's vision for the new earth into a vision for which people could work today. While we cannot create a whole new earth, we still have time to recreate a healthy ecology that will bless every living thing.

The book of Revelation contains nine hymns: 4:8-11; 5:9-14; 7:9-12; 11:15-18; 16:5-7; 19:1-4, 5-8. A preacher could construct a series of nine sermons in which each sermon focuses on one hymn. The worship team could plan hymns and other pieces of music that coordinate with the preaching texts. For example, in connection with 4:8-11, the congregation could sing "Holy, Holy, Holy."[6] When 19:6 appears, the choir (and perhaps the congregation) could sing the "Hallelujah" chorus from Handel's *Messiah*.[7]

---

5. Some Christians, especially influenced by premillennialism, claim that the human family does not need to engage in ecological stewardship because the world will not be here very long. Why preserve something that God will soon destroy? For them, nature is the stage on which human beings act, and not an integral covenant partner with humankind and animals. Unfortunately, this attitude only hastens ecocide while lowering the quality of life for those awaiting the end.

6. Heber, "Holy, Holy, Holy," 4.

7. Blount, *Revelation*, 95-98 provides an excellent discussion of the hymns that could guide the foci of the sermons in the series.

Revelation 5:1–11: At the Center of the Throne Room

John's focus now shifts from a wide-angle view of the throne room (4:1–11) to a more selective focus on characters and things. In 5:1–5, the prophet focuses on an unopened scroll with seven seals. In 5:6–10, John reveals Christ in the image of a slaughtered Lamb who can open the scroll. In 5:11–14, the visionary sees growing choirs praising the work of God through the Lamb.

Revelation 5 has several main purposes. One is to reinforce the authority of Christ as God's agent in cosmic transformation, and hence to reinforce the trustworthiness of the theological interpretation of present history and the future that becomes more specific when Christ opens the seals in Revelation 6:1–16. Revelation 5 explains why the church can believe that the crucified Jesus—the Lamb who was slaughtered—is now the instrument of recreation.

This chapter clarifies the nature, extent, and purpose of God's power as manifest through the Lamb. In this respect, John implies a comparison with the character, reach, and aim of the power of the empire. While not explicitly named in this chapter, John here lays a foundation for later admonishing the church to follow the Lamb—that is, to stand up to the principalities and powers in the pattern of Christ.

One approach to a sermon might take its starting point from the christological uncertainty of many congregations today. The preacher could explain the Christology of John as revealed in this passage and bring that Christology into conversation with Christologies at work in the church today, with an eye towards helping the congregation move towards a mature understanding of Jesus.

Revelation 5:1–7: The Power of God
Revealed through the Lamb

5:1. In the midst of the sensory vision of the throne room, the prophet sees a document in God's right hand, with writing on the inside and outside of the document. Although there is some debate on whether the document is in the form of a scroll or of an ancient book, the fact that John models this part of the scene from Ezekiel 2:9–10 suggests that it is a scroll. In apocalyptic writings, a scroll often contained interpretations of the meaning of the present and future. That the scroll contains writing on the inside and out indicates that it contains everything the congregation needs to know.[8] This scroll contains God's plan for history.

8. Brownlee, *Ezekiel 1–19*, 30.

Writers of documents in antiquity put a seal on a document to guarantee its authenticity. The presence of seven seals indicates that the message is of divine origin. The opening of the seals will reveal the content regarding how listeners should understand the present and what they can anticipate in the future. Ezekiel, for instance, says, "Written on it [the scroll] were words of lamentation and mourning and woe" (Ezek 2:9) in reference to the coming siege of Jerusalem—an act of divine judgment.

5:2. John sees a mighty angel who speaks in a loud voice. The designation "mighty" here and in reference to other angels in the book of Revelation emphasizes the angels' power. Here the angel is powerful, but strength alone does not make the angel worthy to open the scroll. Elsewhere, the mighty angels serve purposes given to them by the one who does open the scroll (10:1; 18:21). The angel speaks in a voice loud enough so that many in heaven can hear.

The angel wants to know, "Who is worthy to open the scroll and break its seals?" To open the scroll and beak the seals is not only to make known the contents of the scroll—per our comments on 5:1—but is also to set in motion the process of cosmic metamorphosis. Only one who is worthy in the same way that God is worthy—that is, by manifesting integrity between intention and action in regard to the Realm of God—can open the scroll.

5:3. John draws on a traditional three-story view of the universe—heaven above, earth in the middle, and a domain under the earth—when pointing out that no one is "able to open the scroll or look into it." By mentioning the three stories, John calls attention to the utter paucity of those who are worthy.

5:4. John weeps bitterly. Listeners immediately feel the disappointment evoked by the weeping. In the apocalyptic mindset, John is sorrowful because the world is in the grip of Satan embodied in empire and, hence, permeated by idolatry, injustice, exploitation, scarcity, and violence. John mourns because John can see no end to this quality of existence.

5:5. One of the elders points out that "the Lion of the tribe of Judah, the Root of David, has conquered," and consequently can open the scrolls and the seals. As we noted in connection with the prophetic apocalyptic messages to the seven congregations in Revelation 2:1—3:22, "to conquer" in this vision is to continue to live according to God's covenantal prescriptions and to witness faithfully even in the teeth of Roman opposition. The conqueror is one who endures patiently in behalf of the values and practices of the Realm of God, even when accommodating to the empire would immediately lessen one's struggle. Jesus endured patiently, and thereby made it possible for the church to do so.

Preachers need to carefully handle the designation of "Lion of the Tribe of Judah, the root of David." Christians, influenced by a long history of anti-Judaism and anti-Semitism, often contrast their belief in a crass Jewish militaristic messianism with the superior love of Jesus exemplified in the upcoming image of the Lamb. However, John's theology does not fall prey to the supersession that sees good Christianity replacing bad Judaism. Indeed, as we shall see in connection with 5:6–10, the seer interprets God's power in relationship to Jesus' death in a provocative Jewish way.

John's listeners would recognize that the image of the lion of the tribe of Judah (Gen 49:9) and the "Root of David" (e.g., Isa 11:10) are associated with power. Among the tribes, Judah was powerful (e.g., Isa 49:8–12). The monarchy of David was the zenith of Israel's power as an independent state. These images suggest that the power of God moves through the Lamb in ways that are similar to its movement through a lion, through the tribe of Judah, and through David, who defeated numerous enemies. John thus suggests that the one worthy to open the scroll has power greater than that of the exploitative and brutal empire.

The picture of the elder in 5:5 raises a possibility for preaching that focuses on the vocation of preaching itself (and stretches to the broader vocation of ministry and of the church). The elder performs a classic function of that office in both Judaism and the church: the elder teaches the prophet by drawing on sacred tradition to offer a theological interpretation of the present. In this regard, the elder touches on the oldest and one of the most important functions of religion: to help people make sense of life, to help a community create meaning. A sermon on these purposes could be timely in congregations besieged by other understandings of preaching; for example, preaching as popularized psychotherapy, as baptizing a particular political party, or as the way to prosperity.

5:6. When the prophet turns to see the Lion of the Tribe of Judah, the Root of David, the prophet does not see a warrior wearing a tunic and armor and carrying weapons. Instead, the prophet sees a Lamb who had been slaughtered. At this point in book of Revelation, the Lamb does not seem to be on the throne, but is near it, and is in the midst of the four creatures and the elders. The figure of the slaughtered Lamb, of course, refers to Jesus, who had been murdered by the Romans. Since the four creatures and the elders represent earthly counterparts, we can see this picture asserting that the effect of the Lamb's work continues in the world.

The incredible power represented by the lion works through the Lamb. While the Lamb appears to be weak, its slaughter is the occasion for God to reveal the irrepressibility of divine power. God raised the slain Lamb from the dead and placed it in the throne room, the control center of the universe.

When the Lamb receives the scroll, God invests it with authority to carry out God's intentions, which are revealed in the scroll.

An important issue is how the death of Jesus (the slaughter) functions in the last book of the Bible. Many believers immediately interpret the figure of the slaughtered Lamb in light of traditional Christian doctrine that sees the death of Jesus repairing a broken relationship between humankind and God—e.g., as Jesus' dying for us so that we do not have to suffer punishment for sin. Some Christian theologies attribute saving power to the shedding of Jesus' actual blood. However, I join those who do not think John sees the death of Jesus (the slaughter of the Lamb) as appeasing an unhappy God and bringing about a change of relationship between God and humankind. Indeed, nothing in the immediate context directly suggests this line of thinking, and the book of Revelation seldom uses language associated with such interpretations.[9]

Rather, I follow those who see the death of Jesus in Revelation as a demonstration of Jesus' faithful witness in the face of the empire (see 1:5; 3:14; cf. 1:2, 9).[10] The prophet does not suggest that God sent Jesus to die. Rather, the death of Jesus resulted from the heinous behavior of Rome. The empire believed that Jesus was a threat to the *Pax Romana* and the domination of the empire, and so put Jesus to death to end that threat. Jesus could have prevented his death by accommodating to Rome. The death of Jesus revealed the depth of evil at the heart of the empire.

Jesus gave up concern for his own safety and well-being with three effects. First, his death exposed the idolatry, injustice, and brutality of the empire. Rather than organize itself under the ways of God, the empire behaved as if it were god. Rather than act out of generosity for the well-being of community, the empire acted out of fear to protect its own power.

Second, the death of Jesus testified to Jesus' confidence that God would replace the present empire with a new Jerusalem. In a crude manner of speaking, "Jesus bet his life on God." God "saw this bet" by raising Jesus from the dead and preparing for Jesus to return to complete the transformation (22:20). Believers can have similar confidence. The death of the Lamb is not directly salvific. Jesus' death did not change God's mind from condemnation to forgiveness or unacceptance to acceptance, but rather confirmed that the season of transformation was underway and that death itself could not prevent the great change.

9. Many commentators take the appearance of the Lamb to connect to the sacrifice of Lambs as part of Israel's liturgical practice. Shortly, I posit a positive association with the blood of Passover.

10. Blount, *Revelation*, 108–12.

Third, the faithful witness of Jesus is a model of witness for his followers (2:13; 11:3; 17:6; cf. 6:9; 11:7; 12:17; 20:4). They are to witness as tenaciously as Jesus, even when confronted by similar threats. The witness of the church is not salvific per se, but it makes possible salvation for others by alerting them to the possibility that they can repent—that is, step away from Rome, and join the movement to the new Jerusalem.

John emphasizes that the Lamb is standing. This posture shows that the power of transformation continues to be at work in the world and hence can support the churches in their faithful witness. Those who stand with Jesus for the values and practices of God amid the temptations and pressures of empire can also stand with him in the eschatological world.

The Lamb has seven horns and seven eyes, which are the seven spirits of God that God sends throughout the earth. Following Daniel 7:8, 20, and 24, the horns are symbols of power. The number seven indicates that they represent the power of God. We mentioned earlier that the eye is a symbol of perception (1:18; 2:18; 3:18; 4:6) and that the seven spirits of God are the angels of the seven churches (cf. 1:4, 16, 20; 2:1; 3:1; 4:5). Through the angels, the Lamb fully understands what is happening in the world—both the situation of the saints and the exploitative behavior of the empire. Also, in keeping with the motif that Satan seeks to deceive the world through the beast (Rome), the beast partially imitates the Lamb by having seven heads.

The church today theologically struggles with what to say about the death of Jesus. The preacher could use this text (and John's wider perspective on the death of Jesus) as a way to enter this struggle. John offers an alternative to traditional Christian interpretations that center on ritual violence intended to satisfy a disconsolate deity. Indeed, many Christians today could be inspired by John's approach. I know a lot of people today who want to point the world to the possibility of the Realm. A preacher who is inclined towards sermons that make points could use the three effects of the death of Jesus discussed here as an outline for a message.

This passage (and this theme in book of Revelation) is a sober pastoral reminder that such witness can invoke hostile response. John wants readers to be prepared for such an eventuality. At the same time, a preacher does not want to encourage a narcissistic approach to suffering and Christian life.

5:7. The Lamb takes the scroll from the one seated on the throne. This visual detail establishes that God, in fact, gave the scroll to the Lamb, thus showing the divine authorization of the Lamb's role in the final cosmic drama.

Revelation 5:8–14: Responding to the Lamb

The scene that John sees in the throne room, Revelation 4:1—5:14, establishes the trustworthiness and authority for the more specific aspects of the symbolic vision that continues in Revelation 6:1—22:7. The overwhelming assurance of this scene prepares the listener for the bracing events that follow, especially the violent condemnation befalling not only the Roman Empire, and the old age more broadly, but also members of the church who have accommodated to Romanism. John wants the congregations to turn away from collusion with Caesar and to be faithful to the God and to the Lamb. The vivid theological imagery of 5:8–14 is intended to fill the intuitive and intellectual sensorium of hearers so as to solidify that commitment.

This final scene centered in the throne room begins with the somber 5:8–10, and then moves to sensory fever pitch with three developments whose effects on the listener are cumulative. First, the crowd of heavenly beings—myriads of myriads—come to voice (5:11–12). Second, every creature in heaven, on the earth, under the earth, and in the sea swells the chorus (5:13). Third, the four living creatures and the elders pronounce a benediction on the scene (5:14). The exegetical and theological motifs in 5:11–14 have almost all appeared previously, and require little explanation.

5:8-10. The living creatures and the elders fall before the Lamb, each holding a harp and a golden bowl filled with incense. To fall before the Lamb—as they fell before the one seated on the throne in 4:10—is to acknowledge both his divine authorization and their willingness to serve his purposes. Since the creatures and the elders betoken the communities of nature and humankind, and especially Israel and the church, their behavior demonstrates what residents of the world should do: witness in the way of the Lamb.

In the Mediterranean world, the harp was often used to accompany singing in the temple and elsewhere (e.g., 1 Chr 25:6–31; Pss 33:2–3; 43:4; 57:7–19). Singing infuses the remainder of this scene. Since many congregations are likely to imagine the harp as a large, curved golden instrument, the preacher might describe an ancient stringed instrument and even find a musician who could play one. Congregations with a big screen could project a line drawing or picture of an ancient harp.

Incense was also characteristic of worship in many religious settings in antiquity. Incense brings an olfactory dimension to worship. Here John sees the incense, representing the prayers of the saints, rising from bowls to God.[11] John does not specify the content of the prayers of the saints here.

11. When this text is used in a service of worship, planners might accompany it with incense. In congregations which do not regularly use incense, this liturgical feature

Preachers sometimes speak rhapsodically of the beauty of incense as an image for prayer. However, two subsequent passages suggest the content of these prayers. In 6:8–11, John pictures martyrs sheltered under the altar crying for vengeance. And in 8:3–4, an angel casts the fire—from a bowl holding incense—down to the earth as punishment on the wicked. These latter passages raise a significant theological problem that we address at 6:8–11: whether seeking vengeance is an appropriate way to pray.

The elders sing "a new song." On the one hand, commentators often rightly say that the new heaven and the new earth call for a new song. The Psalms and Isaiah both speak of singing new songs in response to God's fresh acts of deliverance (e.g., Pss 33:3; 40:3; 96:1; 98:1; 144:9; 149:1; Isa 42:10–14; 65:17–18). John's song is new in this sense. On the other hand, this new song does not signal a break with the past, but comes in response to the awareness that God's promises and actions are ever creating fresh possibilities pertinent for the present and future. A new heaven and a new earth calls for such a new song.

New songs do not have to be brand-new to be new. I grew up in the 1950s and 1960s when our congregation sang many of "the old songs," by which we meant the gospel songs of the late 1800s and early 1900s, typified by the works of Fanny Crosby. I went through a phase in which I consigned this music to the theological trash bin. But through deeper life experience, greater appreciation for the multiple levels of language, and theological circumspection, I have come to sing many of these old songs as "new songs" in John's sense. At the same time, I served on the committee that prepared *The Chalice Hymnal* and learned many songs that were recently composed, "new songs" according to the timeline of history, but evoked the best of the past for the new day.

Recollecting earlier themes, the elders affirm that Jesus is worthy to open the scroll. For Jesus was slaughtered and his blood ransomed people for God. As we noted in connection with 1:5, the reference to blood does not attribute magical power to the blood itself, but uses the language of blood as a figure for death in reference to the consequences of Jesus' faithful witness.[12] Scholars point out that the word "ransomed" is borrowed from

could occasion a sermon on the history and symbolism of incense, which could lead to broader consideration of symbolic dimensions of worship, including the relationship of liturgy and life in which the actions of liturgy are a symbolic model for the actions of life.

12. The function of the blood of the Lamb at the Passover is instructive here. The blood did not have salvific properties in and of itself. When a Hebrew family painted the blood on the doorpost, the blood signaled the angel of death to pass over the house. Similarly, the faithful witness of Jesus confirms that God is moving history to its end-time.

the marketplace, where it was a way of speaking of liberation. A slave was freed (ransomed) when someone paid the price for the slave.

Tying these themes together: the faithful witness of Jesus is both a demonstration of, and means through which, God is releasing the old age from the grip of empire. We might paraphrase John: "For you were slaughtered, and by your faithful witness, God signaled that the process of liberation is underway."

Genesis 12:3 is in the background of John's description of the community of the ransomed: saints from "every tribe and language and people and nation." For God promised Sarai and Abram that through them God would bless all the peoples of the earth. In the life of Israel, God modeled the way of blessing. According to the early church, God grafted gentiles into that way through Jesus Christ. John's multicultural vision reveals the boundaries of the community of the new heaven and new: it embraces repentant people from every ethnicity, language, and nation seeking new world community while maintaining key elements of their identities. Diverse groups dwell together in mutual support according to the values and practices of the Realm. The community that John sees in heaven is a prototype for the makeup of the community of the church in the world.

However, such diversity is not in-and-of-itself proof that a community shares the characteristics of the Realm. The Roman Empire imitates the diversity of the Realm, but in a deceptive way. Indeed, John uses almost the same language to describe the populace of the empire (11:9; 17:15; cf. 13:11). However, the Roman Empire did not encourage mutual support among the groups that exist under its aegis. Instead, it repressed them under the aegis of its idolatry and lavish self-centeredness.

We have already explored what it means for John to say that Christ made this community a "realm, priests serving . . . God" (1:6). The community is itself priestly in that God intends for it to perform the essential work of the priest, which is to represent God's purposes in the world. John uses the same word, *basileia* (realm), to designate the new heaven and the new earth (1:9; 11:15; 12:10), and thereby to imply the quality of the community's life: the church is to manifest the qualities of the new heaven and new earth in its own life and as part of its priestly work in the world.

The theme of communities maintaining identity while living together in mutual support steps almost directly from the ancient setting into the pulpit today. Indeed, this theme is quintessential for the postmodern world with its emphases on relativity and diversity. The diverse community around the throne is a pattern for diverse community in the church, which is supposed to model that community for the rest of the earth in a priestly way.

Unfortunately, many congregations—especially in churches of Eurocentric origin—mirror the separations of tribe, language, people, and nation.

5:11–12. The vision in 5:8–10 focused on the four living creatures and the elders. The 5:11–12 vision adds the many angels around the throne, so that they number "myriads of myriads and thousands of thousands," that is, almost more than a person can imagine. As in Daniel 7:10, this scene overflows the senses of the listener in the manner just described.

The chorus repeats the earlier affirmation that the Lamb who was slaughtered is worthy (5:12a). Whereas the elders offered three ascriptions to God in 4:11a, the intergalactic choir puts forward seven qualities of which the Lamb is worthy: power, wealth (material resources necessary for a good life), wisdom, might, honor, glory, and blessing.

The Lamb is worthy because the Lamb uses these things in the service of the movement towards the new heaven and new earth. Some interpreters note that the Roman imperial court sought or made use of these qualities, not for the common good, but to enforce its own oppressive interests. Hearing these qualities associated with the prompt moves listeners to compare how they function under Roman rule. For example, whereas God and the Lamb use power and wealth (material resources) for blessing in community, the empire uses power to maintain its unilateral control of the social world, and it uses material resources to provide for its own pleasure.

A preacher might develop a sermon series in which each sermon focuses on a different characteristic in light of how that characteristic functions in the larger book of Revelation. A sermon in this series should not be just a word study, but should explore the background of the word, its use in book of Revelation, the network of theological realities with which it connects in that vision. A preacher can often contrast the Lamb's embodiment of the quality with that of the Roman Empire, which typically appropriated the word and its resonating notions for Rome's coercive aims.

Christians who believe in universal salvation—the idea that no one will be forever condemned but that God will ultimately save every single person—sometimes cite Revelation 5:13 in support.[13] For John does speak of *every* creature in the various modes of existence acknowledging God and the Lamb. However, John is later quite clear that God punishes some living things forever (14:11; 20:10).

Interpreters deal with this discrepancy in different ways. Some argue that the rules of logic cannot be applied rigorously in the case of poetic works. Others see the prophet as simply inconsistent. However, because of

---

13. The Gospels, for instance, sometimes speak of "all" the people of certain regions in this hyperbolic way—e.g., Matt 3:5; Mark 1:5.

the clarity with which John articulates the punishment of the unfaithful, I do not think John envisions universal salvation. I think John speaks hyperbolically here (and in other similar places) in a way similar to other biblical writers speaking in the hyperbolic "all." John's immediate concern is not to satisfy a professor of systematic or constructive theology, but to evoke a positive response in the listener: "I want to be part of *this* chorus, and not those who sing in praise of Caesar." Nevertheless, preachers and congregations need to clarify what they mean by salvation, and also to consider the degree to which they believe a God of love would consign creatures to eternal punishment.

5:13. The choir swells again to include every living thing in heaven, on earth, under the earth, and those in the sea. While much of the song in v. 13b occurs in 4:11 and 5:12, John adds two distinctive elements. The first is that the choir sings to both God and the Lamb, which says that God and the Lamb are not completely conjoined. God is still apparently seated on the throne, with the Lamb standing nearby. The last book of the Bible is theocentric, but God's power works so completely through the Lamb that the cosmic choir can hymn them together. The second addition is related. John affirms that the Lamb, like God, will reign forever and ever. This motif is in stark contrast to the reign of the Roman Empire which, from John's perspective, is on a short timeline for destruction.

5:14. The four living creatures respond with "Amen," thus affirming all that has been said and sung in the throne room. Their behavior and that of the elders suggests a response: John's hearers can join the living creatures and the elders in saying "Amen" and falling down in worship. To prostrate oneself is not only a significant expression in the liturgical moment, but is a symbolic act of committing one's total life.

Revealing How Judgment Is
Already Beginning Now

In Revelation 6:1—22:7, the prophet uses word pictures to indicate that God's judgment on the Roman Empire is already beginning, as is the transformation of the world. John's pictorial commentary begins as the Lamb opens the seals on the scroll. The opening of the first six seals offers theological commentary on particular elements of John's world through symbols. The opening of the seventh seal sets in motion a fresh set of comments.

A broad Jewish framework related to covenant is in the background of the opening of the seals and of much of the book of Revelation. From this perspective, God made a general covenant with humankind through Noah (Gen 8:20–22; esp. 9:1–17; cf. Gen 12:3)[1] and a more specific covenant with Israel (Gen 12:1–3; 15:1–21; Exod 20:1–21; Deut 5:6–21; 2 Sam 7:1–17). In covenant, God promises the things necessary for security and blessing, and provides principles by which to live. Obedience to those principles brings about blessing. Disobedience invokes curse (punishment). When a community becomes aware that its disobedience has resulted in curse, then, as an act of grace, God provides the possibility of repentance as a way to turn away from the attitudes and actions that led to the curse

---

1. Some Jewish theologians in antiquity began moving toward an articulation of the Noahide covenant in a more systematic way by identifying the laws that God provided for gentiles. While the impulse for this articulation seems to have been to account for the righteous among the gentiles (gentiles who were obedient to the Noahide laws), the inverse is also true. Disobedience among gentiles accounted for curse. The seven laws are prohibitions against idolatry, blasphemy, murder, theft, sexual immorality, eating live flesh, and the positive admonition to establish courts of justice. The Roman Empire violated these laws (e.g., Jub. 7:20–28; t. 'Abod. Zar. 9:8:4–8; 9:4; b. Sanh. 56a/b. Jubilees was written about 150 BCE. While scribes gave the Tosefta its present form about 300 CE and the Babylonian Talmud its present form about 600 CE, these documents contain traditions that are much older.

and to become obedient and to turn towards God's values and practices designed for blessing. God can bless and curse through both social process and activity in nature.[2]

Apocalyptic theologians adapted this framework. The disobedience of people, institutions, and communities in the old age would invite curse. God would replace the old world with a new one of blessing. A time of intense struggle and suffering (the tribulation) would occur just before the great transformation. These themes all come into play in the book of Revelation.

Most of the seals reveal disobedience taking place in the Roman Empire that call down curse.[3] The curses coming from the seals are lenses through which to interpret things happening in John's world. The social and natural conditions unleashed by the seals (and by the trumpets and bowls) are the part of the tribulation when God unleashes eschatological curses, as part of the deconstruction of the present as a prelude to the new heaven and new earth.[4] When the congregations understand the meaning of events around it, they can respond appropriately.

The number of seals—seven—indicates completion and is associated with God: God is in control of the processes that the seals reveal. The opening of the seals does not depict a timeline of events, as if the first seal occurs, and then the second, and then third. Instead, the seals reveal conditions—curses—that are already taking place simultaneously in the Roman Empire.

Revelation 6:1–8: The First Four Seals

The four riders of Revelation 6:1–8 have become iconic in some circles. A preacher might begin the sermon by referring to such a use. For example, sports writer Grantland Rice wrote in 1924: "Outlined against a blue-gray October sky, the Four Horsemen rode again. In dramatic lore they are known as Famine, Pestilence, Destruction and Death. These are only aliases. Their real names are Stuhldreher, Miller, Crowley and Layden."[5] A preacher

2. The Deuteronomic theologians give this point of view its fullest expression in Deuteronomy, Joshua, Judges, 1–2 Samuel, and 1–2 Kings, esp. Deut 11:1–31. For a passage detailing obedience and disobedience, blessing and curse, see Deut 28. The Deuteronomic theologians wrote when Israel and Judah had manifest behavior like that of an empire, and thereby invoked the curse of national destruction and exile. A similar framework is present in the Priestly writings, e.g., Lev 26:21–39.

3. The sixth seal does contain a moment that anticipates blessing (7:1–17). The seventh seal (8:1–2) opens into the next series of visions—the seven trumpets.

4. Note broad similarities with Mark 13:3–23; Matt 24:3–31; Luke 21:7–24.

5. Rice, "Four Horsemen," para. 1. If the reference to the "four riders of Notre Dame" is too limited for today's congregation, an online search of the four riders of the

who uses a big screen could project images of the four riders, as well as of the other things to come out of the seals.

The use of different colored horses to represent different conditions is from Zechariah 1:7–15 and 6:1–8. Zechariah emphasizes that God's rule extends over the Persian empire, a theme directly pertinent to John, who envisions God's rule over Rome. Moreover, the circumstances invoked by the opening of the seals are characteristic of curses that God inflicts on Israel as a result of disobedience.[6]

6:1–2. The first figure to come from a seal is a conqueror on a white horse. The white color has confused some interpreters into thinking that the figure is Christ. However, contemporary scholars almost unanimously agree that this horse and rider represent the Parthians, whose army was known for its cavalry archers. Parthia was poised on the eastern edge of the Roman Empire, where northeast Iran is today. John envisions eventual Parthian military invasion as part of the punishment of Rome.[7] The Parthian victory did not take place as John imagined, but the anxiety created by external threat caused the empire to direct resources to the military, rather than to strengthening the quality of life of the larger community.

6:3–4. The second figure to come from a seal is a red horse carrying a rider who was "permitted to take peace from the earth so that people would slaughter one another." This rider was given "a great sword," another reference to divine oversight of this process. A significant number of commentators see John referring here to tension in the social order and outbreaks of violence, even during the *Pax Romana*. Indeed, the imperial peace breeds brutality.

The red of the horse is reminiscent of the red of the blood of the slaughtered. The Greek word for "slaughter" (*sphadzō*) is the same here and in the description of the slaughtered lamb (5:6). These mutual references derive from an important principle of Jewish theology in this period: God punishes people by the means by which they sin. In this case, those who slaughtered the Lamb will themselves be slaughtered.

6:5–6. The third figure to come from a seal, on a black horse, held a pair of scales. A voice identified only as "in the midst of the four living

---

apocalypse will reveal more historical and contemporary images, movies, poems, and books than a preacher can use.

6. For backgrounds in earlier Jewish literature interpreting conditions like those resulting from the seals as punishment for disobedience, see the following examples: Lev 26:26; Deut 28:21, 25, 38–39, 48, 63; Jer 5:6; 8:17; 15:2; 21:17; 56:56; Ezek 5:12, 17; esp. 14:21; Hos 18:7–8.

7. God uses the bow to discipline Israel in Lam 3:12–13 and Hab 3:9, thus suggesting that God uses the Parthian bow to discipline Rome.

creatures" cried out something similar to grocery prices regarding wheat, barley, olive oil, and wine—e.g., "A quart of wheat for a day's pay." The voice seems to come from heaven, suggesting that God is responsible for these conditions. The black horse is not directly associated with death—as contemporary congregations might expect—but with threat of famine.

Scales consisted of two pans suspended at the opposite ends of a balancing rod. A transaction required balancing the pans. For the third seal, the scale is figurative: a quart of wheat on one side and a day's pay (a denarius) on the other, and three quarts of barley on one side with (again) a day's pay on the other. These prices were outrageous, perhaps as much as eight times the usual rate. The ratios suggest significant shortages of the basic foods for most of the population.

A plausible explanation for "not harming oil and wine" comes from an edict by Domitian, combined with the aristocrats' response.[8] During John's time, Asia Minor did not grow enough grain and barley for the population, but imported significant amounts, especially from Egypt. Asia Minor did produce sufficient oil and wine. The profit margins on oil and wine were significantly higher than on grains. Production shortages of grain in Asia Minor or Egypt caused prices to escalate and could threaten famine.

In 92 CE—about the time John spoke—Domitian ordered vineyards to be cut back, and the land turned to growing grain. However, the landowners—wealthy Romans—complained so loudly about the possible loss of income that the emperor withdrew the order. From John's perspective, Roman selfishness is so systemic that even when the emperor makes an unusual decision for the common good, the system reacts to preserve the lifestyles of the rich and famous.

6:7–8. The fourth figure to come from the seal, on a pale green horse, is Death, followed by Hades, and "they were given authority over a fourth of the earth to kill with sword, famine, pestilence." Pale green was associated with the faces of the sick.

John personifies Death and Hades. As we noted in connection with 1:18, death is a power that opposes the life-giving purposes of God. Many apocalyptic theologians believed that at death, a person went to Hades, the abode of the dead, roughly equivalent to Sheol. In Hades, the diminished self—sometimes called a "shade"—awaited the final judgment.

John assumes that Death takes people from life and sends them to Hades via means of death typical of the Roman Empire: sword (violence), famine, pestilence, and being eaten by wild animals. The 97 percent of the

8. Krodel, *Revelation*, 174–75. For a review of interpretive options, see Blount, *Revelation*, 128–30.

population in the lower part of the social pyramid were especially suscep-
tible to these means of death as they furnished soldiers for the army, did
not have the resources to buy their way through famine, lived in crowded
conditions that hastened pestilence, and were more likely to be exposed to
wild animals.[9]

Death was one of the consequences of the fall. The opening of this
seal is John's way of saying that the processes of death under Roman rule
indicate that the final transfiguration of the world is underway.

Christians are sometimes puzzled by Death having authority over "a
fourth of the earth." This reference means that while the final transfiguration has begun, that movement still has a long way to go. John will soon
indicate that the world is moving closer to the final transformation by saying that the destruction embraces a third of the world (8:9–12).

From my theological window, John's description of the seals raises
disturbing questions. When speaking about each of the first four seals, the
visionary uses verbs in the divine passive to indicate that God is ultimately
in control of what happens, as when John says the rider of the first horse
"was given" a crown. As indicated in the introduction, I do not believe that
a God of unconditional love would deliberately cause the kind of suffering
spelled out in the opening of the seals, even to punish the things. That would
contradict the divine nature. Moreover, I do not believe God has the singular power to cause or control military action, widespread social conditions,
famine, and death.

I do think that human violation of the divine purposes for humankind
and nature can lead to the consequences that John names. The prophet intended for the congregations to use the opening of the seals as lenses through
which to interpret events taking place in the empire. Today's preacher may
not be able to see militarism, social tensions, famine, and death as signs
of the end or as direct punishments from God. However, a preacher could
interpret such conditions as revealing continuing disobedience. God does
not directly punish the human family, but we create our own punishment
(so to speak) by allowing such things to undermine community.

In the bigger picture of the Revelation, social conditions like the ones
embodied in the opening of the seals can be the occasion for repentance.
We can turn away from trust in militarism, from cooperating with various
forms of social oppression, from assuming that social polarization and chaos are just the way things are, from allowing food deserts in North America

9. In the Garden of Eden, human beings and animals initially lived together in
peace. After the fall, tension developed between humankind and animals. The threat of
wild animals is itself an indicator of the brokenness of the old age. In the new age, God
will restore the mutuality of human and animal communities.

while sitting on food reserves, and from permitting conditions that pave the way for death. We can turn toward peace, mutuality, community, and sharing abundance.

Revelation 6:9–11: The Fifth Seal

When I finished the first draft of this commentary and read through it, I realized that the central image of the fifth seal—the cry of the martyrs under the altar—plays a more key role in the theology of the book of Revelation than I had realized. By replacing the present world with the new one, God vindicates God's own faithfulness in the face of the murder of these witnesses. This theme—and related themes—recurs repeatedly in the Revelation.

6:9. When the Lamb opens the fifth seal, we see an altar in heaven under which are the souls of the faithful witnesses who had been slaughtered. They have not accommodated with the empire, but have witnessed to the word of God and given their testimony.[10]

Many thinkers in the ancient world believed that a temple in heaven was the model for an earthly temple. That interest was less in architecture and more in symbolism, since the temple above was the model for the temple on earth as a visual representation and reminder of divine presence and providence, as well as of the human responsibility to live in response to such grace. The Romans destroyed the Jerusalem temple in 70 CE, a generation prior to John. But the Romans could not destroy the temple in heaven.

From John's point of view, the Romans aimed to destroy faithful witness. Although John specifically mentions the martyrdom of Antipas (2:13), there is no evidence of widespread executions of church members in John's time. The prophet probably recollects persecution under Nero in the 60s, and anticipates intensifying conflict with the empire in the future. The souls under the altar represent the fate of past voices while preparing listeners for things to come.

Not only are the souls alive, but the altar symbolically indicates that God has gathered them into a place of safety. God is faithful. Their suffering is over while they await the new heaven and the new earth in which God and the Lamb will be the temple (21:22). John's listeners can expect similar providence when they, too, interpret the word of God, give testimony, and suffer.

By using the picture of the witnesses under the altar, John does not intend to give a news report on the state of the afterlife, but uses this picture—like so many others—to make a point in figurative language: even after death, God is faithful. God will gather those who die in keeping the

10. On the word of God and testimony, see 1:2, 9; 20:4.

words of this book to the great transformation, into a place of protection
and safety that is beyond the reach of Rome.

6:10. The souls under the altar cry out with a loud voice. As in the
reference to the loud voice of the angel in 5:2, this one is loud enough so
that everyone in heaven can hear. Moreover, John mentions the loud quality
of the voice to catch the listeners' attention. "Sovereign Lord, holy and true,
how long will it be before you judge and avenge our blood on the inhabitants of the earth?" The phrase "inhabitants" of the earth in John's vision does
not refer generally to "the folk," but more specifically has in view idolaters
and people who exploit and engage in injustice (9:20–21).

Nearly every time I have taught this passage in a congregation or in
seminary, students have become theologically disturbed by the cry, "How
long will it be before you judge and avenge our blood on the inhabitants of
the earth?" The students imagine a discontinuity between a God of love and
a plea for God to act the most unloving way possible. A student once burst
out, "So the souls under the altar want God to be as violent as the Romans."
Another: "Retaliation: that's the name of what they want." Another: "Sounds
like retribution. I will ask God to do to you what you did to me." Still another asked, "What happened to love your enemies?"

Commentators often push against such criticism and seek to portray
the cry of the souls in theologically acceptable ways. These commenators
claim that the plea is a cry for justice. The souls under the altar do not aim
to be vindictive, but to be vindicated. Plenty of other passages in the Bible
pronounce severe judgment on evildoers. The souls under the altar do not
seek to carry out revenge themselves; they trust God for that. Many people—especially in the Eurocentric middle and upper classes—who object to
the cry of the souls have never suffered prejudice, degradation, exploitation,
and violence in the same way as the faithful witnesses, and, consequently, do
not understand the deep longing for justice and vindication.

As a friend of the Bible, I am sympathetic to such attempts to put a
positive theological face on the cry of the souls. Each line in defense of
the passage has something to commend it. The verb translated "avenge"
(*ekdikeō*) is indeed related to the word-family for justice (*dikē*). Here it does
have aggressive punishment in view. To avenge, here, refers to God inflicting harm on those who have wronged the faithful witnesses. The notion
of justice in antiquity did sometimes call for the scale of justice to balance
violence inflicted and punishment received. At its best, however, justice in
some biblical traditions involves much more than wrongdoers receiving the
punishment they deserve. It calls for restoring relationship in community so
that all have access to means of blessing, and so that the community is one
of mutual support.

In my view, the cry of the souls does call for God to engage in behavior that is antithetical to the character and purposes of God. If the fundamental character of God is love, and if God is worthy (i.e., has integrity), then inflicting pain on others would violate that character.[11] It may be satisfying to see one's adversaries punished, especially if the punishment takes place in the same manner as one's own suffering, but such suffering does not necessarily "teach a lesson" to the punished nor does it necessarily enhance community. It may just add to the suffering of the world. Indeed, it can add to the spiral of violence that is circling ever larger in the contemporary world.

A preacher could offer the contemporary movement in restorative justice as a promising way forward. Consistent with deep biblical perspectives on justice, restorative justice seeks to bring together victim and offender to restore relationship and community through a process of calling for victims to express pain to offenders. It presents offenders with the opportunity to acknowledge that they understand the pain of the others, and to take responsibility for their behavior. In theological language, restorative justice makes it possible for offenders to repent in a way that makes a difference to victims. Such efforts cannot undo what has been done, but it can help both parties enter into the next phase of life less weighed down by the consequences of crime. One of the best-known examples of such efforts is the Truth and Reconciliation Commission of South Africa.

As indicated earlier, I do think disobedience sets in motion attitudes and actions that eventually lead to collapse of community. While God may not slaughter those who slaughter faithful witnesses, those who slaughter set in motion a spiral of violence that will eventually disrupt all communities.

In my mind, a preacher needs to do several things. The first is to explain the passage and to criticize it theologically. The second is to posit a positive alternative (such as restorative justice). The third is to take the wider pastoral step of helping the congregation recognize that we can fully express our immediate feelings to God, even when they are similar in tone to the cry of the martyrs. A preacher can help the congregation take the next steps of reflecting on those feelings to determine whether they are appropriate for empowering behavior. I may feel the desire for retribution, but that does not mean that retributive behavior serves God's purposes.

The souls receive white robes, typical dress for those in heaven and further indicating that they are in the protective arena of God. Since Jewish sources sometimes use clothing to represent the ethical life, the robes may

---

11. Moreover, if God's power is indeed limited, as I believe, then God cannot singularly slaughter those who slaughtered the witnesses. As indicated earlier, I do think disobedience sets in motion attitudes and actions that lead to the collapse of community.

also indicate that they are dressed in their faithful witness (see comments on 1:13; 3:5, 18; 7:9, 13–14).

6:11. They are told to rest "a little longer, until the number would be complete both of their fellow-servants and of their brothers and sisters," who would also be martyred. John draws on the concept found in some apocalyptic writings that God predetermined certain things, including the number of those who would be martyred before God would bring about the end.

On the one hand, the idea that God would have a quota to be killed appalls many Christians today. This sounds like quantified violence. A preacher who believes in a God of unlimited love rightly objects to this notion. On the other hand, from the perspective of John's worldview, this quota is a way of saying that God will limit the amount of suffering prior to the end; listeners may be better able to continue the struggle if they know their suffering is not unlimited. A preacher might take this part as a lure to consider ways the congregation might try to reduce the conflict and pain that often comes with personal and social transformation.

While the visionary does not posit a particular time frame for resting "a little longer" until the great transformation, John did not imagine a delay of two millennia. This text is one of many in the book of Revelation which the preacher could use as a springboard to acknowledge that while John was wrong about the timeline, the text is still a reminder that God is dissatisfied with the world in its present state and seeks renewal. Communities today can enhance the timeline of renewal by cooperating more energetically with God's purposes.

Revelation 6:12–17: The Sixth Seal

When the Lamb opens the sixth seal, we initially see the natural world coming apart (6:12–14). Someone I know describes this process as "un-creating" the world. It occurs because disobedience has interrupted the state of covenantal community in which God intended for people to live. After un-creating, God can recreate the new heaven and the new earth. This is a standard dimension of apocalyptic thinking.[12]

6:12–14. When referring to earthquakes, the darkening of the sun and moon, the stars falling from heaven, the sky rolling up, and the islands disappearing from the sea, John does not have natural disasters in mind as we typically think of them—that is, as catastrophic events in nature that

12. E.g., Mark 13:3–24; Matt 24:3–31; Luke 21:5–28; cf.; Isa 13:7, 9–10, 13; Joel 2:30–31.

result from weather phenomena acting without moral purpose. "These [latter] things just happen," someone once said in class, "because electrons and protons bump up against each other in accidental collisions, and boom, hurricanes, mudslides, and droughts." Instead, John imagines God using the forces of nature to curse humankind and nature itself.

The earth is one of the foundations of existence. Earthquakes can signify judgment that shakes the very thing on which of so much of creation rests (Amos 8:8; Ezek 38:19; Joel 2:10; 4 Ezra 5:8; 2 Bar. 70:8). Moreover, the ancients took the heavenly elements—such as sun, moon, and stars—as symbols of the reliability of creation. The sun in the dome arching over the earth is a source of light. When the sun darkens, life cannot continue as usual because people cannot see. The sun, moon, and stars are elements that help hold the dome in place over the earth. When they fall from heaven, they no longer hold up their parts of the heavenly dome.

Going beyond these considerations, ancient peoples viewed the sun, the moon, and the stars as astral deities. Yet, from the Jewish view, they are nothing more than elements of creation. The sky—the dome over the earth—will be rolled up like a scroll (Isa 34:4). The mountains and islands are removed. Mountains are awesome symbols of power and reliability on land, and islands represent the firmament even when surrounded by water.

The effect of these events is to dismantle the structures of life that God put in place in Genesis 1. While God intended those structures for blessing, the dragon (Satan) co-opted them for Satan's own empire, expressed through Rome. God cursed the earth, and, representatively, all of nature (Gen 3:17). By destroying part of the natural world in Revelation 6:12–17, God destroys the instruments through which the dragon and the beast (Satan and Rome) created their empire. The very materials of empire will disappear.

Revelation 6:12–14 opens a natural hermeneutical pathway for a sermon that deals with the relationship of humankind and nature. While nature does not have moral agency in the same way as human beings, the natural world is more than a stage on which human action takes place. According to Genesis 1:1-2:4, God designed humankind and nature to exist in mutually responsive relationship. When that relationship is disturbed, the power to support life diminishes. While John does not have the human-nature relationship in mind, we can go beyond John to notice that many parts of the human family are disobedient in regard to that relationship today. The plain fact is that we are moving towards ecocide. While today's congregation may or may not believe that God will destroy the created world as punishment, we are certainly in danger of "un-creating" the structures that support life. While clarifying the differences between John's use of nature motifs in the book of Revelation and today's ecological concerns, the preacher could use this text (and others like it) as a jumping-off point for a sermon seeking to restore mutuality between humankind and nature.

6:15–17. The visionary now describes the response of people who are part and parcel of the Roman system. John lists seven groups: five from the top of pyramid of power, including monarchs, magnates, generals, rich, and powerful. These groups are all accustomed to ruling the world so that it serves their pleasure and power. John lists two additional groups from the lower strata of the social pyramid—slave and free. While these latter are not rulers, they are trapped in the system of power, and they suffer the effects of the disobedience of the upper classes. To adapt a proverb that was used in Israel, "The powerful classes have eaten sour grapes, and the teeth of the whole social order are set on edge."

When the empire and its leaders see the consequences of their disobedience—the collapse of the systems that made empire possible—they hide in caves and among the rocks and mountains, and they cry out, "Fall on us and hide us from the face of the one seated on the throne, and Lamb, for the great day of their wrath has come, and who is able to stand?" (6:15). They attempt to run from judgment.

This scene is pathetic: the most powerful people in the world try to hide in the very places that will be destroyed—caves and mountains. These leaders who are accustomed to giving orders now plead to be crushed by rocks rather than face the judgment of God. Indeed, by asking for the rocks to fall on them, they invite a form of judgment on themselves.

This scene reveals the theological ignorance and the theological arrogance of the empire. God had earlier provided repentance as a way to avoid this consequence. Yet these monarchs and magnates refused to seek that path or to take it. These leaders practice a form of denial as they deny the ways that can lead not only to life, but to a new heaven and a new earth.

Even more sobering, the scene foreshadows the fate of the members of John's congregations who accommodate to the empire. By participating in the values and behaviors of both the empire and the church, they attempt to get something from both worlds, but they too will be caught in the cosmic rock slide.

The preacher might meditate on how some leaders and communities today are ignorant of—or arrogantly deny—pathways that would point towards blessing for all. They would rather live with destructive consequences than take steps that could lead to reconstitution of community.

John closes this section with a question similar to one posed by the prophets (e.g., Joel 2:11; Nah 1:6; Mal 3:2). "Who is able to stand?" John has provided listeners with the answer: those who witness to the word of God and the testimony of Jesus can withstand the final day of judgment and join God in the new Jerusalem.

A preacher might develop a series of six or seven sermons in which each sermon focuses on one seal. The pastor would then have an opportunity to explain more fully the meaning of the seal in its immediate context and in the wider book of Revelation, as well as focus hermeneutically in more detail on issues posed by the text. For instance, it is easy to imagine a sermon series with the following theological reflections:

Revelation 7:1–8: The Intriguing Case of the 144,000

The opening of the first six seals takes place in rapid fire. John describes each seal briefly. The combination of speed and brevity creates a sense of urgency: the forces of destruction are already at work. However, in Revelation 7:1–17, the prophet slows down this intensity by interjecting two scenes that interrupt the opening of the seals—the sealing of the 144,000 (7:1–8) and the vision of the multitude no one could count (7:9–17). These visions remind listeners that they can endure the pain of the great season of transformation (represented in the seals) because God is sealing them in the present (7:1–8) and gathering them into the eschatological multitude (7:9–17).

These two scenes are not events on a timeline marching towards the final judgment. God gives John these visions as prolepses—images of the future that come to expression in the present to give the congregations a positive vision of the future so they can live more faithfully and determinedly in the present.

7:1. God has commanded four angels at the four corners of the earth to hold back the four winds. This is the prophet's way of saying God has decided to delay the decisive apocalyptic moment. Forces dismantling the social order will continue their work, but the cosmic denouement awaits. John is signaling the congregations that they need to prepare for a long wait, but not to mistake the wait for a cancelation.

7:2–3. One provision for the wait that God makes is to seal the 144,000 servants of God on their foreheads. Scholars debate the identity of the 144,000. The number is symbolic. The number twelve represents community embodying God's purposes. Squaring a number and multiplying by thousands were ancient ways of intensifying. The 144,000, then, represent not a head count of 144,000 individuals, but a large community of servants dedicated to God's purposes.[13]

13. This conclusion is reinforced by the facts that the names of the twelve tribes

Having been influenced by post-Holocaust theology, I seek to find as much common ground as possible between Judaism and Christianity. I would like to see the 144,000 as a symbol for those in Israel who turned away from idolatry (as in Ezekiel 9:1–10). But when John more fully describes the 144,000 in 14:1–5, they are clearly followers of Jesus, albeit likely Jewish followers whose mission is in continuity with that of Israel.

Some see the 144,000 as martyrs—those who have been and would be killed—but such a limitation is unlikely, since John does not typically limit the "servants" to those put to death. Rather, John uses the notion of "servant" more generally for prophets and others who are obedient to God's covenantal aims (e.g., 1:1–2; 10:6; 11:18; 15:3; 19:5, 9).

The best explanation, then, is that expression "144,000 servants" is a way of speaking of all the faithful and true witnesses, including the martyrs. John's use of number symbolism (144,000) derived from the life of Israel unmistakably indicates that the work of God through Jesus to restore the world continues the work of God through Israel. The church does not replace Israel. The church is not a "new Israel" (an expression never used in the Gospels and Letters), but a chapter in the ongoing story of God keeping God's promises through Israel.

The long list of tribes in 7:4–8 mentions each tribe in parallel format. This repetition compounds the sense of the size of the community. It is also reminiscent of a military roll call of those preparing for combat, as in 1 Chronicles 4:1–7:40.

The angels mark the servants on their foreheads. In the ancient world, insignia on the forehead sometimes signaled the identity or function of the person. Judaism prescribed frontlets for the forehead (e.g., Exod 13:16; 6:8; 11:18). Aaron wore a holy rosette on his forehead (Exod 28:38). The figure in Revelation 17:15 had a mark on the forehead (cf. Jer 3:3).[14] As we indicated in connection with 6:1–17, the seals in antiquity indicated that something belonged to an owner or had a particular status. In Ezekiel 9:1–10, God is about to punish idolaters in Israel when God commands the prophet to put a mark on the foreheads of those who opposed idolatry so they would be spared. To offer a crude analogy, the seals are like brands that cattle ranchers place on free-range cattle.

---

contain anomalies. This is the only list in the Bible in which Judah comes first, explained by the claim that Jesus comes from that tribe (5:5). Moreover, John replaces Dan with Manasseh, perhaps because tradition remembered Dan as unusually idolatrous (e.g., Judg 18; 1 Kgs 12:28–30; Jer 8:16–17).

14. The presence of the mark on the forehead of the harlot in Revelation 17:5 is a way whereby the beast seeks to imitate God.

While the seals indicate that the servants belong to God, the seals do not prevent the servants from conflict with the empire or with other believers regarding how much accommodation to the empire is acceptable. The seals assure the servants that God will see them through the long season of suffering and bring them into the new heaven and new earth. John uses this scenario to communicate to his listeners that they are sealed, they are secure, when they turn away from accommodation. God gives them a sign that God will carry them through the time of transformation.

A preacher might think with the congregation about things that can function as seals, or signs of the assurance of God's presence in the midst of the contemporary struggle to witness to Realm, but which leave no physical mark. The first ones that come to mind, of course, are immersion (baptism) and partaking of the loaf and the cup. Others include anointing with oil, the laying on of hands, and the kiss of peace. Moreover, people gathered in communities of mutual support witness sometimes act as seals to one another.

The preacher might use popular curiosity about the 144,000 as a starting point for a sermon on the large and spacious nature of the grace of God. In congregational studies on the Revelation, I am sometimes asked about this number in such a way as to indicate that the questioners fear that they might not be among the 144,000 who will be saved.[15] Indeed, some Christians mistakenly take the 144,000 as the total number of the saved. As we indicated above, John uses the number with the opposite emphasis. A little historically plausible information often acts as a huge theological antacid.

Revelation 7:9–18: A Great Multitude that No One Could Count

In a way similar to one picture dissolving into another on the big screen in worship, Revelation 7:4–8 dissolves into 7:9–17. The first slide in John's PowerPoint (so to speak) recalls the continuity of the promises of God to and through Israel. The second slide, 7:9–17, anticipates the completion of those promises, especially God's promise to Sarai and Abram: "in you all the families of the earth [i.e., gentiles] shall be blessed" (Gen 12:3).

7:9. In the spirit of Genesis 12:3, with its emphasis on God blessing all peoples, Revelation 7:9 pictures a "great multitude that no one could

---

15. People often ask about the teaching of Jehovah's Witnesses regarding the 144,000. According to that church, only 144,000 faithful will fully go to heaven, where they will reign with Christ as monarchs and priests, but many others will spend eternity in a resurrection body on a renewed earth, while the unfaithful will spend eternity in Gehenna.

count, from every nation, from all tribes and peoples and languages." Many progressive preachers in the early twenty-first century are drawn to the inclusive nature of this community. But, as we noted earlier, preachers need to be circumspect in considering this motif. For in addition to emphasizing the positive diversity of the community of the new Jerusalem, this description has a polemical edge. The Roman Empire was also made up of people from many different tribes, peoples, and languages. The presence of diversity does not in and of itself guarantee that diversity serves the purposes of God. Mutual support characterizes pluralism in the community of God, whereas exploitation characterizes relationship in the empire of Rome. Whereas the multitude of God is so great that no one can count, the Roman Empire sought to count people for taxation so people would pay for their own oppression.

The members of the crowd are robed in white, a garment whose color is explained in connection with 7:14, as those who came through the great tribulation are now gathered around the throne. The multicultural crowd waves palm branches, calling to mind an event from the year 165 BCE. The Jewish population in Judea had been under the domination of the Seleucid Empire and its representative Antiochus IV Epiphanes. (The designation "Epiphanes" evokes the notion of "god manifest.") Antiochus forbade the practice of Jewish rites and customs, ordered the worship of Zeus, and erected an "abomination of desolation" (probably a statue of Zeus) in the temple (Dan 9:27; 11:33; 12:11; 1 Macc 1:54; 2 Macc 6:1–5). However Jewish forces under the leadership of the Maccabees family threw off the Seleucid Empire, reclaiming the temple in the year 165 BC. According to 1 Maccabees 13:51 and 2 Maccabees 10:7, the Jewish people waved palm branches on this occasion. Palms then became a symbol of Jewish independence. The crowd in Revelation 7:9 waves palm branches in celebration of God similarly liberating the faithful community from the Roman Empire.

With respect to preaching, my impression is that few congregations know the stories of the Maccabees behind the seemingly casual reference "with palm branches in their hands." The preacher who tells the fuller story from the books of the Maccabees will likely find the congregation engaged in the sermon and exegetically enlarged.

7:10. Some people are initially confused by the expression "Salvation *belongs* to our God." What does it mean to say that salvation "belongs" to God? A clearer working understanding is, "Salvation comes from our God."[16]

---

16. The Greek text does not contain a distinct word for "belongs." The Greek uses "God" in the dative case, probably as a dative of possession, meaning that God is the one who possesses the things that make for salvation.

The cry of the multitude in v. 10 is one of many polemical affirmations in the book. The crowd rightly acknowledges that God and the Lamb are responsible for "salvation" (*sōtēria*). While "salvation" could be associated generally with "victory" or "deliverance" in the ancient world, in apocalypticism, "salvation" is a one-word expression for the result of dismantling the old age and bringing the new Jerusalem into full and final expression. The point is that the new world comes from *God* and not from Caesar or Satan. In the broader perspective of book of Revelation, Satan attempts to deceive people into thinking that Caesar's rule is salvation when, in fact, that rule leads to exploitation, fractiousness, and violence.

7:11–12. The long-time residents of heaven (angels, elders, living creatures) now affirm the insight of those who have come through the great tribulation by saying "Amen" and offering an ascription of praise similar to those at 4:11 and 5:2.

Acclamations in the vein of 7:10 and 7:12 are sometimes part of Christian worship today. However, my sense is that congregations typically voice these statements generically, without recognizing their life-defining character. A preacher could help the congregation deepen and broaden its understanding that making such an acclamation is simultaneously saying "yes" to God (and to the values and practices of the new Jerusalem) and "no" to Caesar (and the attitudes and actions of empire).

7:13. Preachers are sometimes perplexed by the question of the elder: "Who are those robed in white, and where have they come from?" How can the elder have been present in the scene described in 7:9–12 and not know the answer? In my early encounters with the book of Revelation, I thought this elder was similar to some church members—and some students—who can be at the table for a discussion and ask a question or make a remark indicating that their bodies may have been present, but their minds were not. The elder also reminded me of people who just do not get it, not because they are inattentive, but because their worldviews do not have appropriate frameworks for processing particular materials. From a literary point of view, however, the question is simply a narrative device to call attention to the explanation of the identity of those robed in white in vv. 14–17. Indeed, the elder knows the answer to the question.[17]

7:14. The people in white robes "have come out of the great ordeal" (*thlypsis*). As noted previously, many apocalyptic theologians (John among them) believed that the suffering of the world—and the struggle of the

---

17. Rev 7:14a deals in a subtle way with the issue of authority that so permeates this book. John does not himself purport to interpret 7:9–12. Rather, John shifts the authority for interpretation to the elder, who is a member of the heavenly court: "Sir, you are the one that knows."

faithful in particular—would increase as the time of the apocalypse became closer (e.g., Dan 12:1; 1 Esd 13:16–19; 15:19; 16:19; 2 Bar. 25:1–2; cf. Matt 24:21, 29; Mark 13:19, 24). Satan and the rulers of the old age, fearing their eminent defeat and loss of power, would dig in their heels in opposition to God and to the faithful. Apocalyptic writers sometimes used the Greek *thlypsis* to speak of this great ordeal.

In a sermon, the preacher might call attention to the facts (1) that the King James Version famously translated the phrase "great ordeal" as "great tribulation," and (2) that this expression is popular today in dispensational theologies. Family similarities do exist between John's "great ordeal" and the "great tribulation" in dispensationalism, but a key difference is that John thinks generally of his own time as leaning into the great ordeal without tying the relationship of the great ordeal to a specific timeline, whereas most forms of dispensationalism attach the great ordeal to a particular chronology and include events (such as the rapture) that are not part of John's immediate theology. Indeed, some voices in dispensationalism promise that believers can avoid the great tribulation by being raptured, whereas John seeks to prepare all members of the community to remain faithful within it.

As noted several times, I do not embrace apocalypticism as a theological worldview, which means I do not anticipate a specific "great ordeal" shortly before an apocalypse. However, I do think that the notion of the "great ordeal" reminds us that the forces of evil and empire often seek to reinforce their power. The preacher can help the congregation see that John's admonition to believers opens the door to an empowering word: believers need to be prepared for the struggle of witness in their ordeals, but the promise of the eschatological world can sustain them.

Some commentators struggle to relate various theories of atonement to the multitude who "washed their robes and made them white in the blood of the Lamb." Atonement-like associations are reinforced in the Christian mind by the church's widespread use of the expression "washed in the blood" in association with salvation. For example, a popular hymn asks, "Are You Washed in the Blood?"[18]

However, when discussing 1:5 and 5:6–9, I sided with interpreters who see Jesus' death and the language of blood in the book of Revelation not in reference to closing a gap between God and humankind, but as a demonstration of Jesus' confidence in God's power to bring the new Jerusalem, and as an expression of his true and faithful witness, even when confronted by death. Indeed, the empire's ultimate threat is the power to put people to death. John's description "they washed their robes and made them white in

18. Hoffman, "Are You Washed?"

the blood of the Lamb" extends the same thinking to faithful witnesses in the congregation. As already mentioned, Jewish tradition used the language of robes (and other clothing) to speak figuratively of life and behavior. This tradition also used the language of "washing" to speak of taking actions that result in faithful living (e.g., Isa 1:16; 64:7; Zech 3:3–5). As we noted in conversation with 1:5 and 5:6–9, the language of "blood" often functions in the book of Revelation as a way to speak figuratively of death. Likewise, "white" is a color associated with God and the new world. Thus, to say that the multitude "washed their robes and made them white in the blood of the lamb" is to say that they were faithful to God by doing what Jesus did: when threatened by the empire, they kept faithful to the word of God and the testimony of Jesus.

Since there is no evidence of widespread persecution or martyrdom in Asia Minor at the time John wrote, the prophet was not commenting on a contemporaneous condition of many people being faithful unto death, but was anticipating a growing conflict between the empire and the faithful as the great ordeal intensified. This vision implicitly encourages the congregations to exhibit patient endurance in witness and thus to become a part of the great multitude.

In addition to clarifying the meaning of washing their robes in the blood of the Lamb, the preacher can call attention to the ironic but powerful logic at work. In the world of empire, a person washes a robe and makes it presentable for public use by conventional means—that is, a person goes along with the values and practices of empire. In traditional Jewish language, of course, such behavior would lead to a soiled robe and condemnation. Accomodation dirties one's robe, so to speak. By contrast, those in the force field of the Realm of God wash their robes not in conventional water, but in the blood of the Lamb that is, in devotion to the Realm that may end in suffering. In the old world, this action would leave the robes stained and unwearable. But in the transformed world of the Realm, God uses standing up for God in defiance of the empire as a way of washing robes. From this perspective, those who wish to clean their robes for eschatological wear must bloody them in witness.

7:15–17. The prophet concludes this scene by drawing on images from books in the Torah, Prophets, and Writings that were written when Israel was under the control of the Babylonian Empire. The implied message is that just as God sustained and liberated the community during that period, so John's congregations could count on that activity again.

7:15. Continuing the use of figurative associations of 7:13, the prophet enhances the positive picture of the ultimate state of the faithful multitude by describing them worshiping night and day in the temple of God where

God shelters them. To be honest, I know a fair number of Christians for whom 24/7 worship in the style of Sunday morning or Saturday night would be less than a delight. Indeed, some people cannot stay awake for a fifteen-minute sermon. For Judaism and for John, however, the temple and its liturgy had more symbolic power than the typical church building and service of worship today.

The temple functioned in Judaism as both a means and symbol of covenantal relationship between God and the community. When fulfilling its purpose, the temple and its rites assured the community that the providence of God was present and at work in behalf of the people. Psalm 84 is one of many passages bespeaking this perspective. In the best Jewish theology, God was omnipresent. God was not present only at the temple, but the temple symbolized God's presence everywhere.

The Babylonians destroyed Solomon's temple in 586 BCE and sent the leaders of Jerusalem into exile. The priestly theologians imagined this period as a wilderness. When they retold the story of Israel wandering in the wilderness, they spoke of God tenting with Israel in the same way that God dwelled in the tabernacle, thus suggesting God's living presence in the wilderness of the exile while the exiles awaited liberation (e.g., Lev 26:11–12). Indeed, in 7:15b, John uses the word *skēnoō* to describe sheltering the multitude. *Skēnoō* is from the same word family that priestly theologians use to speak of God "tenting" with Israel.

Ezekiel, who also anticipated God liberating the exiles from the Babylonian Empire, heard God declare, "My dwelling place shall be with them" (Ezek 37:2). Ezekiel looked forward to a renewed temple (Ezek 40:1—48:35; cf. Zech 2:10). In both cases, the emphasis is not simply on God being there, but on the divine presence sustaining the community and recreating a circumstance free of empire where the community can live in full blessing.

The Romans, of course, destroyed the Jerusalem temple (the third temple, or "Herod's temple") in 70 CE. John uses the symbol of the faithful multitude serving in the heavenly temple to assure John's community that the presence of God is operative for them apart from the temple. It will sustain them in the wilderness of the Roman Empire and it will liberate them at the transformative moment. Revelation 21:22 brings this theme to its eschatological climax when John does not see a temple in the new Jerusalem because "its temple is the Lord God the Almighty and the Lamb." At that time, the community will no longer need a symbol of assurance (such as the temple) since God's purposes for blessing will be fully and finally manifest in the new heaven and the new earth.

7:16–17. The second Isaiah, author of Isaiah 40–55, was a priestly theologian. Isaiah 49:10 is the background of the function of Revelation

7:16–17. Isaiah 49:1–6, the second servant song written when the leaders of Israel were in exile in Babylon, sees the vocation of Israel as being "a light to the nations," that is, a model for living according to the values and practices of God as the way to blessing. This vocation includes remaining faithful to the living God and turning away from the Babylonian idols, even when despised and rejected (Isa 52:13—53:12).

Isaiah 49:10 is part of God's promise to the exiles in 49:7–13. If they continue their vocation—even in exile—God will release them from domination by empire and return them home in a second exodus (from Babylon to Jerusalem). While the priestly retelling of the first exodus—especially the wandering in the wilderness—depicted the community beset by such things as hunger, thirst, heat, and weeping, the second Isaiah depicts the second exodus as free of those (49:10).

The conditions in Isaiah 49:10 and Revelation 7:17 are not just elements in the texts. They symbolize qualities of life under the heel of empire. As in Babylonian life for the exiles, life in the Roman Empire sometimes left people hungry, especially during food shortages. Clean water was hard to get in Rome. Jewish literature sometimes spoke of people weeping and mourning over the brokenness of the old age and their inability to repair it (e.g., Matt 5:4). Moreover, Jewish people sometimes used the language of hungering and thirsting to describe the longing for the Realm of God (e.g., Joel 2:12–14; 2 Macc 13:12; Matt 5:6).

In this setting, the prophet uses 7:16 in a twofold way. First, it implicitly reminds the congregations, like Israel, to make a faithful witness in the face of empire. Secondly, it assures the congregations that faithful witness will lead them to a time of abundance and security characterized by the qualities in the verse.

7:17. John concludes with the kind of inverted logic found in 5:6–7 where the power of the Lion of Judah is revealed in the Lamb "standing as if it had been slaughtered." In 7:17, we see the Lamb, now with God at the center of throne, as shepherd of the faithful multitude. Indeed, the Lamb guides the crowd to the springs of the water of life. The one who usually requires care (the lamb) becomes the one who expresses care (the shepherd). This is a surprise, and might prompt the preacher to wonder, "Where in today's world do I see people, ideas, and movements that I initially judge to be lamb-like (weak and needy) but that turn out to be shepherding vehicles of the Realm?"

Many contemporary Christians think of the shepherd giving tender care to the sheep. But people in the ancient world recognized that shepherds needed to do whatever was necessary to help the flock develop in a healthy way. This work included not only finding adequate and safe pasture and water, but also providing health care and even disciplining the sheep as needed. Figuratively, then, the ancients sometimes referred to rulers as "shepherds" (e.g., 2 Sam 7:7; Isa 44:28; Jer 3:15). One of the purposes of a ruler was to adequately provide for the care of the flock. Ezekiel famously contrasts true shepherds, who adequately provide, from false shepherds who not only do not provide adequately but themselves eat the sheep (Ezek 34:1–31)

The Roman Empire was a false shepherd as it kept the flock to serve its own interests, and provided few resources to sustain the flock. As God said of the false shepherds of Ezekiel's era, "With force and harshness you ruled" (Ezek 34:4). The Lamb became the true shepherd by pointing faithfully to the qualities and behaviors of the Realm, even when the empire put him to death. The Lamb cares for the flock by helping facilitate the coming of the new social and cosmic worlds. The true shepherd is the one who *gives* in the service of the purposes of God while the false shepherd *takes* from the sheep in self-service.

The image of the "springs of the water of life" derives from Isaiah 49:10 and calls to mind primal associations of water with creation and life force. From God, for instance, comes the "fountain of life," the power to generate and sustain (Ps 36:9). Such associations are especially resonant because the availability of water was not something that people could take for granted in John's world. While these waters erupt fully and forever in the new heaven and the new earth (21:6; 22:1), they refresh those seeking to be faithful in the present. The "springs of the water of life" contrast with the stale water stored in a cistern or the waters of empire on which Babylon sits, waters polluted by the spillage from fornication (17:1–7).

As we have noted, John does not have ecological theology in mind, but a preacher could turn a sermon that direction. When it comes to water (and other things in nature necessary for supporting life), empire-minded nations, corporations, and individuals often pollute it for the purpose of making profit without regard for consequences for the web of life. The preacher can invite the congregation to consider ways to help maintain and recover sources of water that can truly function as springs to be water for *life*.

As noted just above, the reference to tears resonates not only with the general sorrows that come with life, but with the mourning that accompanies the awareness of the depth of brokenness of the present age, especially the grip of empire. God will wipe away those tears by replacing the present order with the new one.

Preachers often instinctively turn to this passage and others like it for comfort at the time of death. While this use is appropriate, the passage reaches beyond the immediate occasion of death to offer hope to people in all forms of wilderness and exile, under domination by empire. Indeed, Isaiah, Ezekiel, and John all use the promise of transformed circumstances not only as comfort in discouraging times, but also to empower witness in the midst of the struggle.

Revelation 8–11

Revealing the Consequences
of Not Repenting

Hearing the book of Revelation for the first time, listeners reach the end of the first six seals and are ready for the seventh seal to be the climactic transition from the old world to the new. Instead, the seventh seal opens into seven trumpets whose pattern is similar to that of the seals: four short notes followed by three longer ones, with an interlude between the sixth and seventh trumpets.

John uses the repeating pattern from seals to trumpets to bowls to indicate that during the season of transformation, the qualities of life described in the seals, trumpets, and bowls continue to move like a spiral through history.[1] While John shifts the imagery from seals and riders to trumpets and plagues, John continues to help the congregations understand the significance of events around them and to respond appropriately. The end will not come immediately. Congregations need to be prepared for a prolonged struggle to the end. From the seals to the trumpets to the bowls the degree of suffering increases. John uses this device to indicate that the suffering of the world is increasing as the time of the apocalyptic conclusion grows near. However, the prophet refrains from setting out a detailed time line.

Revelation 8:1–6: Silence in Heaven
and the Prayers of the Saints

8:1. When the Lamb opens the seventh seal, heaven is silent "for about half an hour." This quiet is a surprise given the increasing intensity of the actions issuing from the opening of the seals. The silence recalls similar silences in

1. As noted in the introduction, the figure of a spiral suggests movement from one point to another (similar to a straight line) but with repeating patterns of action (the circles in the line).

other apocalyptic literature prior to God creating the world out of the original chaos (2 Esd 6:39) and again recreating the world out of the chaos it had become (2 Bar. 3:7). Moreover, Beale points out that silence is sometimes associated with divine judgment.[2] The silence prepares the reader for the chaos ahead as God destroys the empire (8:5—20:15). As God created out of chaos once, so God can do it again.

When reading the Bible in worship, the lector might become silent for several seconds after 8:1. This pause would dramatize the significance of the text.

While John used the motif of silence as a literary device to signal the coming apocalypse, the preacher might use the silence in the text as an opportunity to encourage the congregation towards its own silence—a pause in the hurly-burly of everyday activity to think critically about ways in which reconstruction might come out of the contemporary chaos.

8:2. The seventh seal opens into seven angels, each with a trumpet. As we saw in connection with 1:10, a trumpet often announces important activity, especially God's eschatological actions (Isa 27:13; Zeph 1:1–14; Zech 9:14; 2 Esd 6:23; Matt 24:31; 1 Cor 15:52; 1 Thess 4:16).

8:3–5. John now describes an angel using a golden censor to offer smoke with the prayers of the saints before the altar in the temple in heaven. The angel places fire from the altar in the censor and throws it on the earth, whereupon dramatic geophysical events take place.

The seals interpreted John's era of history as the great tribulation through which the church was passing. In Revelation 6:9-10, the souls who had been slaughtered cried out for God to avenge the faithful by judging "the inhabitants of the earth." John now describes those prayers ascending to heaven with the incense.

By depicting the angel filling the censor with fire and throwing the fire on the earth, John confirms that God has heard those prayers and is acting in judgment. While fire is a multivalent symbol in Jewish tradition, it here implies divine condemnation (e.g., Gen 19:24; 2 Kgs 1:10–14; Pss 79:5; 86:46; Jer 4:4; 15:14; Ezek 22:31). Moreover, commentators point out that several texts in Jewish literature bring together references to fire, thunder, lighting, and earthquakes in the service of announcing divine judgment (Exod 19:16–18; Ps 77:18–19; Isa 29:6). This casting of the fire and geophysical phenomena prefigures the final judgment.[3]

---

2. Beale, *Book of Revelation*, 451–54, offers a penetrating discussion of silence.

3. Similar themes recur in Rev 11:19 and 16:18–21, both of which have the final catastrophe in view.

Revelation 8:3-5 raises the same troubling theological issues for preaching identified in connection with 6:9-11. A sermon might follow a theological route similar to the one sketched there.

Revelation 8:6-21: The Trumpet Blasts

John derives inspiration for the seven trumpets from the plagues that God sent to Egypt leading to the liberation of the Hebrew slaves (Exod 7:14—12:32; 14:4-9). The prophet does not simply reproduce the plagues as they occur in Exodus, but mixes elements from the Egyptian plagues with similar material. John does not envision actual events (e.g., a star falling from heaven), but uses the language of the plagues figuratively to interpret the meaning of John's moment in history.

By using the plagues, John implies that the Roman Empire is in a similar situation to that of the Egyptian empire. According to Exodus, the plagues were simultaneously part of the liberation of the Hebrew slaves and "mighty acts of judgment" on Egypt and its gods (Exod 6:6; 7:4; 12:12; Num 33:4). God did not intend the plagues to motivate Pharaoh to repent. Rather, God hardened Pharaoh's heart to prevent repentance, perhaps to demonstrate the sovereign extent of divine power so that the Hebrews—and their descendants—would have absolute confidence that God is in control of history (e.g., Exod 14:4-9).

John uses imagery from the plagues to indicate that God is passing judgment on the Roman Empire in a way comparable to God passing judgment against Egypt. Moreover, the plague motif implies that God is moving towards the New Jerusalem in a pattern similar to the journey of the Hebrews to freedom.

John wants the church, seeing the eschatological plagues being visited upon the Roman Empire, to be faithful to God's commands, even as the Hebrews were faithful to the command to brush blood on their door posts. Beginning with chapter 2, John has called the members of the church who collude with the empire to repent. They still have the opportunity to "come out" of Rome (18:4) and to reach the promised land of the new heaven and new earth.

John writes to the church and not to the empire. While John invites the members of the church to repent, the prophet does not issue a similar invitation to the empire. It appears to me that the opportunity for the Roman Empire to repent has passed, even as Pharaoh passed up that opportunity. Revelation 9:20-21 portrays humankind having foregone repentance. Nevertheless, presumably, individuals outside the church who had cooperated with empire could repent and join the community on the road to the New Jerusalem.

At one level, a preacher can find things happening in the contemporary world parallel to the plagues—that is, things that will ultimately contribute to the downfall of aspects of life today. At another level, however, I disagree with John, who thought the Roman Empire was so far gone that it was beyond repentance. While empire is leading many dimensions of the world today towards the final fate of the plagues, I believe that repentance and renewal are still possible.

A sad irony underlies the plagues, both in Exodus and in book of Revelation. They typically involve things that God meant to support life and community, but the transgressions of empire turn them into things that lead to chaos and destruction. This could be a powerful theme in preaching: exploring how today's empires use things meant for life in ways that lead to chaos and destruction.

Revelation 8:7–13: The First Four Trumpets

8:7. The blast of the first trumpet—hail, fire, and blood—burns up a third of the earth and trees, and all grass.[4] This image is similar to the seventh plague, Exodus 9:23–25, while also calling to mind Ezekiel 38:22, Joel 2:30, and Sirach 39:24–31. In a nuance similar to Revelation 8:7, Wisdom 16:15–24 sees the intermingling of hail and fire as God's instruments in both punishing the wicked and protecting the righteous.

The first trumpet pictures the earth losing the ability to sustain life. Although John may not have had this mind, a preacher could point out that many of today's empire-oriented practices are depleting the capacity of the earth to sustain life, even as the world population continues to grow.

8:8–9. The blast of the second trumpet—a flaming mountain falling into the sea—causes a third of the sea to turn to blood and a third of the living creatures and ships to die and be destroyed. This image combines the first Egyptian plague, in which God turns the Nile to blood in Exodus 7:14–25, with a traditional image that depicts Babylon as a mountain which God sets afire and throws down (Jer 51:25). Scholars also point out that John's listeners would have been familiar with the eruption of Mount Vesuvius in

---

4. The number one-third echoes Ezek 5:2–12, where God passes judgment three times, each on a third of the people. As we note in connection with 6:8, the movement from one-fourth of the earth there to one-third of the earth here is John's way of saying that the time of ending is getting closer.

79 CE, which destroyed Pompeii and Herculaneum with dramatic flames, ash, and lava.

The second plague pictures God returning the Roman Empire—a latter-day Babylon—to chaos. The theme of irony pervades this scene. A mountain in Jewish tradition are sometimes symbols of strength and permanence, yet it is cast into the sea (chaos). The empire presented itself as mountain-like in the sense of claiming to be strong and permanent. It exploited the seas in maintaining its power. But John exposes this falsehood by showing God throwing the mountain into the sea, which becomes especially threatening by turning to blood.

On the one hand, the preacher can easily connect the pretension of Babylon and Rome to similar pretensions in empire today. According to John, pretension pushes the mountain into the sea. On the other hand, the preacher cannot casually connect natural disaster—such as the eruption of Vesuvius—with divine judgment. At the same time, a preacher will want to name environmental abuse by empires that leads to disasters in nature.

8:10–11. The blast of the third trumpet—a star named Wormwood falling from heaven—fouls rivers and springs (sources of fresh water needed for human beings and animals). This image is vaguely reminiscent of the first plague on the Egyptians, Exodus 7:14–25, but depends particularly on Isaiah 14:12, where the falling star represents God dethroning the ruler of Babylon. The name of the star, Wormwood, recalls the plant of the same name, which has a bitter taste. Amos used the figure of wormwood to characterize Israel's unfaithfulness (Amos 5:6; 6:12). Significantly, Jeremiah said that God would make the false prophets eat wormwood because they approved of idolatry, which led to injustice (Jer 23:15; cf. 9:15). Gerhard Krodel sees the star making the water bitter as the reverse of God providing life-giving water at Mara (Exod 15:25).[5]

The third plague symbolizes the Roman Empire as a star whose idolatrous and unjust effect on the world is like wormwood: Rome fouls the human community. Consequently, the fate of Rome will be similar to the way in which it ruled: A preacher could explore how the star of today's empire is falling. The text suggests an especially vivid image: empire as wormwood falling into and fouling the springs that should preserve life. Where and how are communities drinking wormwood water today?

8:12. The blast of the fourth trumpet strikes sun, moon, and stars and causes each one to lose a third of its light, and, consequently, day and night each lose one-third of their light. This image calls to mind the darkening of the heavens in the plagues on Egypt in Exodus 10:21, as well as broader

5. Krodel, *Revelation*, 198.

associations with God's judgment (Isa 13:10; Joel 3;15; Amos 5:20). Beyond that, the heavens will collapse at the apocalypse (e.g., Mark 13:24). According to Genesis 1, the sun, moon, and stars are part of the superstructure supporting the existing, broken world. God created them in the order of day and night (Gen 1:3–5), then sun and moon and stars (Gen 1:14–19). John pictures God dimming them in the approximate reverse order. Moreover, many Romans, like many other peoples around the Mediterranean, looked to the astral entities as gods.

The fourth plague represents God dimming not just the sun, moon, and stars but, by extension, the structures that support the old age. The fourth plague demonstrates that the God of Israel is more powerful than the gods of Rome. Indeed, God shows that they are under divine control by dimming their light, which anticipates God pulling their plugs completely when the fourth bowl is poured. While empire counts on the predictability of the time-table of day and night for its repressive practices, the fourth plague introduces an element of unpredictability into the empire's mindset.

A preacher might point out that John wants the congregation to believe that God is turning down the rheostat on the light of history—that is, to believe that God is diminishing the structures that support the empires of the world. I do not believe that God is doing so, but the light is dimming in many quarters, especially as governments and groups forego the qualities of life that God intends for all—such as love, peace, justice, dignity, freedom, and material security—in favor of promoting special interests according to such things as race, ethnicity, and class. As the book of Revelation makes clear elsewhere, such practices carry within them the germ of their own destruction.

8:13. The appearance of the bird in mid-heaven crying "Woe! Woe! Woe!" before the final three plagues intensifies the listeners' attention to these plagues. Commentators are divided as to whether the bird is an eagle or a vulture since the word *aetos* can refer to either bird. "Eagle" seems more likely since the same word appears in Revelation 4:7, the great throne room, where it would be strange to have a vulture. Moreover, there may also be an element of caustic humor in that Rome used the eagle as a symbol.[6] The eagle in mid-heaven pronouncing judgment thus lampoons Rome for attempting to deceive people by using the eagle in imitation of God. The eagle of God now judges the Roman eagle. The eagle flies in mid-heaven—at a very high point—where all can see and hear it. Where God bears Israel up on eagle's wings in Exodus 19:4, the eagle in Revelation 8:13 announces "Woe" (*ouai*),

---

6. Apocalyptic writers sometimes symbolize Rome as an eagle, e.g., 2 Esd 11:1–12:1; T. Mos. 10:8.

a term that was sometimes used to indicate curse and judgment (e.g., Isa 3:9, 11; Ezek 24:6, 9; Jer 13:27; 48:46; Sir 41:8; 2 Esd 15:47; 16:1, 63, 77).[7] The threefold repetition underscores that the woes are under divine control.

The preacher might turn to the Roman use of the eagle as a substitute for real transcendence as a wedge for opening a discussion about how contemporary corporations and other groups use the language of transcendence to sell products or develop loyalties. The return address label on a package from Amazon, for example, is "Amazon Fulfillment." This practice attempts to deceive people into thinking that receiving a product fulfills life's deep desire for meaning.

Revelation 9:1–12: The Fifth Trumpet

John develops the fifth plague (9:1–12) in more detail than the first four (8:7–12). This is consistent with the identification of the fifth and sixth plagues as "woes," or expressions of judgment resulting in intensified suffering as history swings on the hinge from the old world to the new.

Christians are sometimes put off by the grotesque picture of the locusts in the fifth plague. The preacher might help the congregation identify with this plague by comparing John's locusts to the function of wild figures in science fiction books and films. Commentators universally and rightly point out that John does not envision real locusts, but uses the locusts as symbols to explain the meaning of the human violence that John sees coming to the Roman Empire.

I have alluded several times to John's understanding of the relationship between disobedience and the means whereby God punishes disobedience. The visionary develops that notion explicitly in the fifth plague. The Wisdom of Solomon summarizes thus: God sent punishment upon the wicked "so that they might learn that one is punished by the very things by which one sins" (11:16).[8] The Roman Empire has ruled by violence. Consequently, God will wreak judgment on the empire by subjecting it to violence. According to the fifth plague, destruction will come not from a force external to history (such as an invasion of angels from heaven) but will take place within history. In the sixth plague, John identifies one source of such violence: the Parthian army (9:13–19).

---

7. The first woe comes in pass in 9:1–12, the second in 9:13—11:14. John says the third woe "is coming very soon," but does not specifically mention it again, leaving commentators to debate its occurrence. Since a "woe" is a condemnation, it seems logical to associate it with the final condemnation of Rome.

8. Cf. Wisdom's meditation on idolatry and its effects in 14:12–31, esp. vv. 30–31.

9:1-2. Most commentators agree that the star is an angel. This fallen star is an angel of destruction in the service of Satan.[9]

John uses the imagery of a three-story universe with heaven above, earth in the middle, and an underworld. The bottomless pit (*abyss* in Greek) is a prison-like place in the lower region, a place of chaos (Amos 9:3), the home of the dragon (Isa 27:1), a jail for evil rulers and spirits (Isa 24:21-11; Jub. 5:6-8; 1 En. 10:4-6; 18:11-13). The bottomless pit represents force fields of destruction and violence that oppose God's desire for order and mutual support.

God gives the destroying angel a key, a symbol of control. The fact that the pit is locked indicates that God has limited the punishing forces dwelling within, but they are now being released. The smoke is a symbol of judgment (as in Gen 19:28; Deut 29:20; Joel 2:30). Enoch thinks of the abyss as a furnace of fire (14:3).[10] The darkness recalls the plague of darkness at the exodus (Exod 9:18) as well as wider associations of darkness with condemnation (e.g., Amos 5:18; Hos 6:5; Joel 2:10; Zeph 1:15). God will use the violence accompanying the release of the inhabits of the pit to destroy the violence of the empire.

As noted frequently, the idea that God directly authorizes violence against the human community—even in the name of justice—contradicts my deep senses of the limits of God's power and the nature of God's unconditional love.

9:3-6. John now describes the purpose of the locusts whom the destroying angel, on God's authority, releases from the bottomless pit (9:3). A swarm of locusts can make short work of a crop by loudly devouring it. God set locusts upon Egypt as the eighth plague (Exodus 10:1-20), and they devoured vegetation. Joel 1:2-2:20 famously depicts God sending divine judgment in the form of a vast army of locusts (cf. Wis 16:19; Sir 39:39). John envisions super-locusts who have power like scorpions.[11]

However, the destroying angel turns the locusts away from consuming vegetation and focuses the locusts on torturing human beings "who do not have the seal of God on their foreheads" (9:4). As we saw in connection with 7:1-8, the "sealed" ones are the faithful and true who experience this period of violence, but do not give up their witness.[12]

---

9. The angel of destruction here is a kind of counterpoint to the angels of the churches in Rev 2-3.

10. This smoke signals that the prayers of the saints, offered with smoke, are being answered (8:4).

11. Sir 39:30 mentions that God uses the scorpion to punish the ungodly.

12. The Hebrew slaves fleeing Egypt marked their doorposts with blood so the angel of death would pass by (Exod 12:1-28). Ezek 9:4 speaks of marking people against

Revelation 9:6 puts forward a chilling picture of the work of the locusts. They do not kill human beings, but torment or torture people for five months in the way that the sting of a scorpion torments a person—a bitter bite followed by long and painful swelling. John uses "five months" to represent a long, indefinite period of time. The unremitting pain will be so intense that people will seek death, "but death will not come to them"; i.e., God will not permit them to die so that God can prolong their punishment (9:6).

In seeking death, however, the unfaithful do not quite know what they want. They seek the first death which, for John, seems to mean that the person goes to Hades. The final judgment, and second death, follows, at which time God awakens all for final disposition. Those complicit with Satan and the beast join these figures in eternal punishment (20:6, 13–14; 21:8).

9:7–10. The prophet ends the description of the fifth trumpet blast by detailing the locusts themselves and by identifying the ruler of the inhabitants of the pit. John's locusts are super-animals who are like war-horses. They have crowns of gold and human faces, hair like a woman's, lion's teeth, and scales like iron breastplates, making the same noise as chariots rushing into battle (Joel 2:5).[13] They can sting for five months with their tails, a short but intense time.

These locusts and their powerful stings represent the Roman military system and its effects on the inhabitants of the empire. The sting (violence) comes from the behavior of the army toward its own people. To live in the empire was the same as living with the effects of a sting from the super-locust. The sixth trumpet represents the Parthian army as an external threat of pain caused by military action.

The theme of the domain of Satan imitating the domain of God surfaces as the golden crowns and human face echo the crowns on the heads of the elders and the human face in the throne room (4:4, 7, 10). Values and behavior are keys to determining whether something is of God or Satan.

According to John, then, the rule of the Roman Empire is like an unrelieved scorpion sting that functions like the plagues God invoked on Egypt, but is even more painful. The preacher might use this image to describe the quality of life of many individuals and groups in the early twenty-first century: existence with the feel of an unrelenting, ever-swelling scorpion sting.

The designation "hair like women's hair" is most unfortunate. Many commentators think that this expression was something like a first-century

---

destruction. In imitation, in 13:16, the beast marks its followers.

13. Recalling that Parthian soldiers were noted for long hair, some interpreters see this image pointing to the Parthians. However, a more general reference seems likely since Caesar (and not a Parthian) is the ruler of these inhabitants (9:11), and the Parthians are the subject of the sixth trumpet blast.

idiom referring to long, and perhaps disheveled, hair. Nevertheless, the image reinforces negative associations with women. A preacher should critique the gender-negative aspect of this image.

The prophet's use of the notion of torture goes beyond the specific practices of personal torture used by the Romans to speak of the rule of the empire as itself torture. However, in the early twenty-first century, this preacher naturally thinks both of reprehensible contemporary practices of torture, and of the silence of the pulpit on such practices. The preacher might point out that a culture that tolerates torture—and even legalizes it—sets in motion self-destructive forces akin to those that destroyed the Roman Empire.

9:11. According to Proverbs 30:27, locusts have no ruler. The unusual nature of the super-insects in Revelation is thus reinforced in that they have a leader who can direct their savage power in battle.

This leader is named Abaddon in Hebrew and Apollyon in Greek. Abaddon means "destruction" and is associated with Sheol, the underworld abode of the dead (Job 26:6; 28:22; 31:12; Prov 15:11; 27:20; Ps 88:11). The name Apollyon is from a Greek verb meaning "to destroy" and is likely a pun on the name of the god Apollo, who, among other things, was god of death and destruction. One of Apollo's symbols was the locust. Significantly, the emperor at the time John wrote, Domitian, thought of himself as an incarnation of Apollo. John thus indicates that the Caesar system is responsible for the five months of stinging.

The preacher could amplify the claim of fifth trumpet, playing on the name Abaddon: being under the rule of a Caesar is the same as being dead. Playing further on the name Apollyon, this trumpet reveals that Caesarism, with its idolatry, exploitation, and militarism (highlighted here by the savage locusts), is a means not to security and prosperity, but to death.

Revelation 9:13–21: The Sixth Trumpet

Whereas the fifth trumpet depicts judgment befalling Rome in the form of painful internal condition caused by the Caesar system's policies, the sixth trumpet depicts judgment about to befall Rome from an outside threat, the Parthian army.

9:13. When the sixth trumpet sounds, John hears a voice from the four horns of the golden altar. The horns were horn-like projections at the four corners of the altar, and represented divine power. While John does not explicitly say the voice is from God, the fact that it speaks from the altar gives the voice divine confirmation. God is in charge of the events that

follow. Since the prayers of the saints ascend to the altar, this plague continues God's response (6:10–11; 8:3–5; cf. 5:8).

9:14–15. The voice from the altar relays the message from the four
angels bound at the Euphrates. The great river was the eastern boundary
between the Roman and Parthian empires. The Parthians humiliated Rome
in battle in 53 BCE. Conflict between the two nations often occurred on
the eastern border, leaving the empire ever anxious about a Parthian threat.
God appointed these angels to keep the Parthians in check until "the day,
the month, and the year" for God to deploy the Parthian army to kill a third
of humankind. The references to "day, month, and year" indicate that God
is directly in charge. Since the invasion would kill only "a third of humankind," it would not be the final judgment on Rome.

9:16–19. John now describes the Parthian hordes. While scholars debate whether the translation "two hundred million" is on target, the larger
point is that the size of the army—two hundred million soldiers—would
overwhelm the first-century mind.[14] The entire population of the Roman
Empire at the time of John was only about sixty million.

The Parthian cavalry was known for its brutal skill in combat. Parthian
soldiers could shoot arrows while riding forward, then, when overrunning
the enemy line, turn on the seat of the horse and shoot arrows backward.

While there is some discussion in scholarship regarding whether the
riders or the horses wore the breastplates, the larger point is that the riders
and horses were capable of stomach-churning carnage. Having the heads of
lions, the horses are fierce. The motif of Satan imitating God is again at work
as these lion heads recall the face of the lion in the throne room (4:7) and
the lion of the tribe of Judah (5:5), who is also the lamb.

The breastplates are the colors of fire (red), sapphire (blue), and sulfur
(yellow), and the horses, like the sea monster of Job 41:20–21, shoot fire,
smoke, and sulfur out of their mouths.[15] Things like fire, smoke, and sulfur
are often instruments of condemnation and destruction in Jewish literature.
In Genesis 19:24, for example, God uses fire and sulfur on Sodom.

From a preacher's point of view, the sixth plague is a classic demonstration of the principle articulated above to the effect that punishment for
sin often comes in the very form by which the community has sinned. Rule

---

14. The Greek does not contain an actual number but reads "two myriads times a
myriad." Many interpreters take a myriad to be 10,000, so 10,000 times two times ten
thousand comes to 200 million.

15. In an earlier day, the word "sulfur" was translated "brimstone," hence, the expression "fire and brimstone." John refers to "fire and sulfur" in Rev 14:10; 19:20; 20:10;
and 21:8.

by threat of military violence is one of Rome's sins. God would punish Rome by means of military action at the hands of the Parthians.

The preacher might point out that while the militarism of the fifth and sixth trumpets does not bring about the immediate end of Rome, the omnipresent tension within Rome and between Rome and Parthia corrodes community. While persistent militarism may not immediately bring about the end of a country, John's premise is that those who live by the sword die by the sword (13:10).

9:20–21. The prophet brings the first six trumpets to a sobering conclusion. "The rest of humankind who were not killed by these plagues did not repent" of idols and the murder, sorcery, fornication, and theft that corrupt community in the wake of idolatry. Here again John assumes the principle that human community becomes like the gods that we worship.

Commentators universally point out that this passage is in tune with classic Jewish denunciations of idolatry. Some passages refer to idols being made of materials like gold, silver, bronze, stone, and wood, and note that idols cannot do things like see, hear, or walk (e.g., Ps 115:8–3; Isa 40:18–20; 41:6–7; esp. 44:9–20; Jer 10; Dan 5:4; esp. Wis 13:10—14:21). Some passages directly associate idolatry and the worship of demons (e.g., Deut 32:17; Ps 106:37; Mic 5:12).[16]

Idolatry results in social chaos. John mentions four qualities of idolatrous society as representative of the consequences: murder, sorcery, fornication, and death. Murder is the ultimate disruption of community. Sorcery includes magic, the attempt to manipulate the gods in self-service. The word "fornication" implies exploitative behavior and the breakdown of mutually supportive relationships. Theft violates boundaries and destroys trust. While these qualities are often found in stock lists of vices in the Roman period, they also echo conditions in the empire. The Romans relied on threat of death, exploited others, and effectively stole land through legal processes. Caesar worship was cut from the same cloth as sorcery.

As indicated already, preachers can help congregations wrestle theologically with the conclusion that John's perspective on opportunities for repentance is selective and contains a theologically disturbing element. Repentance is essential to being part of the movement to the new Jerusalem— turning away from idolatry and its values and practices and turning towards God and covenantal faithfulness. The members of the churches in Revelation 2–3 who have accommodated to imperial culture are the only people John directly encourages to repent (2:5, 16, 21–22; 3:3; 19). The preacher can certainly bring this message to congregations today.

16. Paul underscores this theme in 1 Cor 8:5 and 10:20.

In Revelation 9:20–21, the prophet implies that those involved in idolatry should have repented in response to the conditions described in plagues, but they did not do so. At this point in the vision, John has not directly invited the idolatrous inhabitants of the empire to repent, nor does he do so here or elsewhere in the book. Indeed, the plagues on Egypt as the backstory of the six trumpet plagues suggest that John uses Revelation 9:1–19 to help the church understand that these plagues—and the subsequent intensification of destruction in the next chapters—are irreversible punishment on the empire.

While John offers no hope to the empire as empire, it would still be possible for persons entrenched in the empire to convert by turning away from idolatry and the empire and turning to the living God and the community on the way to the Realm. Judaism regularly welcomed converts in this way. As an expression of Judaism, the church did the same. John assumes that some such people are among the great multitude "from every nation, all tribes, and peoples and languages."

On the one hand, the passage makes a point as good today as in the first century. God is utterly opposed to idolatry and its communal consequences (represented by murder, sorcery, fornication, and theft). Moreover, empires today rely upon the threat of death, exploits, and theft. Empire sometimes uses sorcery-like rhetoric to justify these things.

On the other hand, I take the same theological exception to some of the notions in this passage as to similar expressions elsewhere. I do not believe that God has fixed an hour, day, month, and year on which to destroy the empires of today and put in place the new heaven and new earth. While the empires of today engage in murder, sorcery, fornication, and theft, I do not believe they are beyond the possibility of repentance. Moreover, I think it would be exceedingly callous for the church to have access to the possibility of repentance as a means for renewal, and for the church to withhold that possibility from the world today.

Revelation 10:1—11:14: The Bittersweet Vocation of the Prophet and the Prophetic Community

This passage indicates that God will no longer delay the final movement to the new Jerusalem (10:6). In the apocalyptic mindset, the final era of history is especially difficult as the rulers of the present age ramp up their resistance to the coming of the Realm.[17] The purpose of the passage is to deepen

17. Interpreters often refer to Rev 10:1–11:14 as an interlude because it comes between the sixth (9:13–21) and seventh (11:14–19) trumpet blasts. A similar interlude

(and slightly refocus) the community's understanding of the vocation of the apocalyptic prophet and of the church as apocalyptically prophetic community in the season when struggle is heating up. To help the community endure the difficult season of transition, the passage aims to prepare the community for what it needs to do as well as for the hostile response of the empire. The text is both pastoral commissioning and pastoral warning.

Revelation 10:1–7 puts a finer point on the prophetic message: God is ending the delay of the end. Revelation 10:8–11 focuses on the individual prophet (John). According to 11:1–14, the church as community has a prophetic vocation.

The preacher might use Revelation 10:1—11:14 as the starting point for a conversation concerning the vocation of the minister and the congregation. Denominations and movements differ greatly on the vocation of the church and its leadership. Within congregations, ministers and laity sometimes view these things differently. The preacher might sketch different points of view and bring them into dialogue with John's claim that leaders and congregations are prophets in the apocalyptic way.

Revelation 10:1–7: A Mighty Angel Receives
a Little Scroll: No More Delay

10:1–3. John uses the figure of "another mighty angel" as an authority who comes down from heaven to reaffirm the prophetic identity of both John and the community and to deliver a change in instructions. In the book of Revelation, the expressions "another angel" and "mighty angel" typically occur when the writer is emphasizing judgment (5:2; 7:2; 8:3; 14:6, 8–9, 15, 17–18; 18:1–2, 21).[18] This association with judgment and the end-time colors Revelation 10.

John draws on Daniel 10:4–5 and 12:5–9 for much of the description and action of the angel in Revelation 10. The cloud is associated with the presence of God (Exod 16:10; 1 Kgs 8:10). The rainbow signals that the angel has a message of promise, though that message includes a latter-day equivalent to the flood (judgment; Gen 9:13–16; Rev 4:3). The legs—pillars of fire—kindle the memory of God leading the people through the wilderness (Exod 13:21) and, so often mentioned in the book of Revelation, of God punishing

---

(7:1–17) comes between the sixth (6:12–17) and seventh (8:1–5) seals. The designation "interlude" is a little deceptive because the passage is not simply a break in the action but contributes materially to the purpose of the book.

18. Blount, *Revelation*, 188.

by means of fire (Rev 8:5–8; 9:17–18; 11:5; 14:10; 17:16; 18:8; 20:9–15). The description of the angel embodies much of the message of the angel.

The angel sets one foot on the sea and the other on the land. This gesture demonstrates authority over all things that happen in these arenas, especially pointing to Revelation 12:18—13:1, where John reveals that Satan comes from the sea and gives authority to the beast on the land. The angel shouts to demonstrate the power of the message and so that everyone can hear: this angel's message is publicly available to the church. The angel speaks like a lion, denoting power associated with God (Jer 25:30; Hos 11:10; Joel 3:16; Amos 1:2; 3:8). The seven thunders underscore that the words of the angel are the message of God (Exod 9:23–24; 19:16; 1 Sam 7:10; Pss 29:3; 77:18; Isa 29:6; cf. Rev 4:5; 6:1; 19:6)

The little scroll (*biblaridion*) is the occasion of much discourse. Is it the same scroll as the one in 5:1—8:1 (*biblion*), or is it a different scroll? Interpreters today tend to think that John is referring to the same scroll whose opening set in motion the process of moving towards the end, beginning with the seven seals. Since the Lamb opened the scroll initially, it is reasonable to think that the Lamb gave the open scroll to the angel. John thus indicates to the reader that the course set out in the scroll is still in progress.

10:4. After the sensory build-up of Revelation 10:1–3, the next development is a surprise. John prepares to write down what he has seen, as he was instructed earlier (1:11, 19; 2:1, 8, 12, etc.). Why does the voice from heaven direct him to "Seal up what the seven thunders have said, and do not write it down"? Interpreters point to Daniel 12:5–9, where an angel asks a question like one surely in the minds of John's congregations: how long will it be until God accomplishes God's eschatological purposes? Daniel's angel receives an answer, but is told that the answer is to remain secret and sealed. In a similar way, many interpreters surmise, John may have received more specific indication of events leading to the fast-approaching end. This information assures John's listeners that they do not have to endure much longer, yet it discourages them from being distracted by these events. This hesitance is in the spirit of Mark 13:32, where Jesus indicates that only God knows the time of the apocalypse.

I sometimes scan the dial and listen for a few seconds to every FM station from 89.7 to 107.9. I nearly always hear preachers updating the timeline from now to the second coming. This passage gives the preacher a biblical response to such attempts to fix a date. John implies that such knowledge is not for us. The immediate vocation is not to follow the timeline, per se, but to engage in faithful witness. Indeed, fascination with a timeline can distract from witness.[19]

10:5–7. The preceding thoughts are consistent with the message of the angel in vv. 5–7. The angel with one foot on the sea and the other on land raised his right hand to heaven and swore an oath (10:5; see Deut 32:35–40; Dan 12:7). This gesture ascertains the trustworthiness of the angel's message. The preacher might compare this action with a person swearing to tell the truth in today's courtroom, though the angel's action is even more principled.

The angel swears by God, and hence can guarantee the broad movement of history that John foresees in the immediate future (10:6a). The church can count on the angel's testimony in the same way that the human family has been able to count on the things God created—heaven, earth and the sea.[20] Even in the long history of human disobedience, God has used these elements from the structure of the old age to provide the things needed for life and to offer the possibility of blessing.

The message is that "There will be no more delay (10:6b)." The sound of the seventh trumpet will announce the fulfillment of the promise of the "mystery" that God made to the prophets to replace the present world (10:7).[21] The "mystery" is the eschatological transition from the old world to the new.[22] John encourages the congregations to faithful witness during the final struggle by assuring them that time is running out. They will not have to witness long.

This text raises a fundamental issue for the preacher. The promise of the text did not come true in John's day. Indeed, after two thousand years, the world is still in the grip of empire. The preacher can help the congregation consider the possibilities we develop in the introduction: some Christians believe that God has delayed the end for a hidden reason; some Christians believe that God's time is different than our time; some Christians turn away from the idea of an apocalypse believing, instead, that God is omnipresent, inviting participation with God in creating a world with the values and practices of the new heaven and new earth. The preacher might

19. Of course, some Christians do not expect an apocalypse. I am among them. While they are not distracted by trying to calculate the timing of an end, they sometimes give more energy to proclaiming that they do not believe in the end than in pointing to God's renewing lure.

20. For similar oaths, see Dan 12:7, as well as Gen 14:19–22; 22:16; Exod 32:13; Isa 45:43; Jer 49:13; Ezek 20:5.

21. For examples of promises to the prophets, see Jer 7:25–26;

22. For similar uses of "mystery" (*mystērion*), see 1 Cor 15:50–57; Rom 11:25–26.

use the text as a launching pad for a conversation helping listeners clarify their own points of view.

Revelation 10:8-11: John Eats the Little Scroll

The prophet now reemphasizes the nature of the prophetic vocation in the increasing conflict between the old and new worlds. The voice directs the prophet to take the open scroll from the angel standing on sea and land (10:8). When John goes to the angel and requests the scroll, the prophet indicates that he is willing to accept the contents of the scroll and its consequences (10:9). Presumably, John could turn away.

10:8. In a scene based on Ezekiel 2:8—3:3, the angel gives the scroll to John with the instruction to eat it. The eating represents internalizing. The content of the scroll—the revelation that God is destroying the present age and is now moving quickly to set the new age in place—is to become a part of John's identity and purpose. John's life is to serve that transformation.

10:9-10. The scroll is bitter to the stomach. That is, the pain of the destructive phase of the great replacement makes John sick. At the same time, the scroll is sweet as honey in John's mouth. That is, while the news of judgment is painful, it points towards the new Jerusalem.

In Revelation 10:11, "they" (perhaps the seven thunders) clearly state John's mission. John is to "prophesy again about many peoples and nations and languages and kings." To "prophesy" is to announce that the great transformation is taking place, that judgment is even now falling on the unfaithful (those complicit with Rome), that the movement towards the new heaven and the new earth is underway, and that this movement will reach its conclusion without delay. This prophetic ministry is thus both bitter (announcing judgment) and sweet (pointing to the new age).

John is to prophesy to the great diversity of the human family. John typically refers to this family as peoples, nations, languages, and tribes. Here John substitutes "rulers" (kings) for "tribes," perhaps to call attention to the accountability of Caesar-like figures for the common welfare.[23]

This passage seeks to prepare the congregations for prophetic apocalyptic witness. While the prophet's message is ultimately sweet (the coming of a new Jerusalem), the journey is often bitter, for the prophet must also name the judgment as part of that movement. While John does not directly suggest that this bitterness has two parts, they are true for some prophets: (1) the peoples, nations, languages, and rulers sometimes cause prophets

---

23. From the point of view of Ps 72, the monarch is accountable for seeing that justice takes place throughout the community.

to suffer (11:7–10); (2) the destruction of evil, like that described in the six trumpets can be hard to see (8:7—9:21). The prophet may feel the pain of those who are destroyed.

While contemporary prophets often say they speak out of righteous anger, there seems to me to be an element of anguish in John's writing that suggests a shift in communication strategy for some preachers. Many pastors, especially in Eurocentric congregations, speak to the empire present in the persons in the pews. When the preacher begins in anger—especially when directed to the congregation—listeners find it easy to dismiss the preacher, sometimes with their own anger. A preacher may have a better opportunity to connect with listeners by speaking out of the anguish from both witnessing brutal empire behavior and perceiving the judgment that falls upon empire.

Many people today are interested in personal elements in the lives of others. How did the preacher come to ministry? How did the minister become aware of the prophetic dimensions of ministry? What is it like for the pastor to preach in a prophetic mode? To what degree is the preacher's vocation bittersweet? Preachers could engage congregations by sharing their stories in response to these questions, but preachers need to do more than simply report their autobiographies. The preacher would do so in concert with this passage and from other biblical, historical, and ecclesiological sources, with an eye on how the sermon could help the congregation think more deeply and broadly about their own lives and witnesses as vehicles of prophetic witness.

Revelation 11:1–14: The Two Witnesses: Prophetic Community

Revelation 10:8–11 focuses on the bittersweet calling of the individual prophet (John). Revelation 11:1–14 widens the lens to the calling of the church as community which M. Eugene Boring calls "the prophethood of all believers."[24]

Revelation 11:1–3: The Temple as Location of Witness

11:1–2. The passage appears to begin with an excerpt from the *Journal of Architecture* as John is given a measuring rod and told to measure the

---

24. Boring, *Revelation*, 142.

temple. In the ancient world, measuring was a way of indicating that the measured space was under control. Since John acts in behalf of God, the act of measuring indicates that God will protect the temple, the altar, and the worshipers from destruction (11:1). Ezekiel and Zechariah use the motif of measuring to assure listeners that God will rebuild the temple after the Babylonian destruction (Ezek 40:1—44:27; Zech 2:2). Since John is now on earth, the earthly temple is in view. However, John uses the architectural location in symbolic ways to speak about communities. Scholars largely agree that the temple, altar, and faithful worshipers represent the faithful, witnessing church.

John, however, is not to measure the court outside the temple, for that is given over to the nations who will trample the city for forty-two months. Jewish literature often depicts the nations (or gentiles) as idolatrous, unjust, exploitative, violent, and sometimes assaulting Jerusalem and the temple (Isa 63:18; Zech 14:2–3, 12–15; 1 Macc 3:45). Rome is the epitome of this perception of nations.

The empire will trample (harass) the church for forty-two months, a figure John derives from Daniel 7:25 and 12:7 where Daniel indicates that persecution of the faithful will last "a time, two times, and half a time." For Daniel, a "time" is a year, so the violence would be three and half years—that is, forty-two months, or about 1,260 days. This period of antagonism is savage—but its duration is limited: *only* forty-two months.

John thus prepares the listeners for the stark picture of the two witnesses as paradigmatic of the church's ministry in 11:3–13: The congregations should expect brutal opposition. But John assures the congregations that God will ultimately preserve the community and its message. John wants the congregations to develop the courage to continue to witness even when being trampled. This is exactly what happens in 11:3–13.

Revelation 11:1–6: The Two Witnesses

John's use of symbolism continues in 11:3–4 with the ministry of the two witnesses who have authority to prophesy for 1,260 days (the same as forty-two months). The witnesses represent the mission of the church when the nations trample the temple; i.e., when the Romans persecute the church during the great ordeal.

11:3–6. The sackcloth helps interpret the mission of the witnesses. Sackcloth was associated with mourning (Gen 37:34; Esth 4:1), so that prophets sometimes wore sackcloth to represent mourning over the message that God was about to punish the people because of disobedience.

Sackcloth could also signal that the time for repentance has come (Dan 9:3; Joel 8:1, 13; Matt 11:21). Sackcloth is associated with judgment in 6:12.

The two figures at the center of the text are "witnesses" (*marturēs*). "Witness" is here a virtual synonym for "prophet" and refers to persons who interpret what is happening in the world from the theological standpoint of the book of Revelation. They call attention to the sovereignty and community-supporting (covenantal) purposes of God. They expose the disobedience of the empire, and they announce God's coming punishment (8:7—9:21). These witnesses model the witness that John would like for the church to make, but the empire pushes back in the most extreme ways.

John uses the two olive trees and two lampstands as multivalent symbols of the mission of the church. Zechariah 4:2–3 and 11–14 envisions the two lampstands as descendants of David's (ruler) and Joshua's (priestly) lines who point towards the eschatological restoration of Judah. These figures contrast with the comparable figures of Caesar and Roman civil religion in Revelation 13:1–18; the latter lead the way to eschatological destruction. In Zechariah, the one lampstand is God, but Revelation 1:20 uses the lampstand as a symbol for the church, in line with the notion of Israel and church as light of the world (Isa 42:6; 49:6; 51:4; Matt 5:14).

The witnesses have power similar to that of Elijah, through whom God sent fire from heaven in the presence of the prophets of Baal to demonstrate divine sovereignty (Rev 9:5; 1 Kgs 18:20–40), and through whom God shut the sky so that no rain would fall in response to the idolatry of Ahab and Jezebel (Rev 9:6a: 1 Kgs 17:1–7). God will give the witnesses "authority over the waters to turn them into blood, and to strike the earth with every kind of plague" (Rev 9:6b; Exod 7:14–25).

On the one hand, the preacher can find a positive implication here. Many congregations today feel almost powerless in the face of massive need and of international systems of empire. The preacher can help the church think about how the witnesses can be a model for today's church. In our setting in empire, how can we be Elijah-like and Moses-like?

On the other hand, John indicates that the church can use this power to punish those who harm the witnesses (9:5a, 6c). Elsewhere I have indicated that the God of unconditional love and unremitting will for justice would actively seem to inflict pain on others. It follows that the church should not inflict suffering on others or support those who do.

Revelation 11:7–10: The Empire Murders the Witnesses

11:7. When the witnesses—the church—have testified, the beast will come up from the bottomless pit, make war on them, and kill them. The beast from the bottomless pit is the Roman Empire (Rev 13:1).[25] Since, to our knowledge, Rome did not persecute the church in a widespread way in the late first century, John wants to alert the church to expect that Roman antagonism will magnify as the tribulation increases. John imagines forty-two months during which Rome treats the church harshly, even putting some witnesses to death.[26]

11:8. The ancient world placed great importance on showing respect for the dead, including appropriate burial practices. Rome reveals its dissipate character by allowing the dead bodies to lie unburied in the streets (9:8). The community that disrespects the dead also disrespects the living. This dissolute behavior is not limited to the Roman government, but includes "peoples and tribes and languages and nations" who "gaze at their dead bodies and refuse to let them be placed in a tomb."

Scholarship debates the identity of the "great city that is prophetically called Sodom and Egypt." The two leading candidates are Rome and Jerusalem. The immediate answer would seem to be Jerusalem since that is where Jesus was crucified (11:8b). However, John elsewhere calls only Rome "the great city" (16:19; 17:18; 18:10, 16, 18–19, 21). John sees God invoking the plagues upon Rome, as God did Egypt (9:1–19). Some writers contemporaneous with John associate Sodom with the same kinds of sins that John attributes to Rome (2 Pet 2:6; Jude 7; 3 Macc 2:5; 2 Esd 2:8). John typically evaluates Jerusalem positively (3:12; 11:12; 21:2, 9–10; 22:19); he does not depict Jerusalem as resisting God. While Jesus was crucified in Jerusalem, the Roman governor sentenced Jesus, and John has just spoken about Rome killing witnesses to Jesus' life. In my view, John portrays Rome as reaching its bloody fingers around Jerusalem, even as it squeezed the life out of Jesus.

11:9. The "peoples and tribes and languages and nations" let the bodies lie in the street for three and a half days. That is not only disrespectful, but it also creates a health hazard. The three and a half days recollect the three and a half years of their prophecy (11:1–3), but the time differential indicates that the bodies will lie in the street only a short time. With this small touch, John signals that the end-time is not far off.

11:10. Recollecting the fact that people in the Roman Empire gave one another gifts (for reasons ranging from expression of emotion to creating

---

25. On the bottomless pit (*abyss*), see Rev 9:1–11; 20:1–3.
26. The motif of war against the saints recurs in Rev 12:17; 13:5–7.

beneficial relationships), the "inhabitants of the earth" (those who collude with Rome) gloat over the deaths of the witnesses and exchange presents. I once heard someone speak of this as "Christmas in reverse," as people give presents to celebrate death.

This text invites a sermon on how empire manifests disrespect. While the text focuses on how empire disrespects aspects of the church, the preacher could extend the topic to how the empire disrespects the purposes of God across many people, languages, tongues, and nations.

The preacher might explore the degree to which Rome reaches its hands into Jerusalem today and imposes its death-dealing ways. By Jerusalem today, I have in mind communities that seek to represent God's will for people to live together in covenant. Empire today sometimes celebrates carrying out atrocities and calls upon the church to bless them. Indeed, while John may not have been thinking of Christmas, the preacher might note that in some churches, Christmas and gift-giving express ethnocentrism and nationalism that reinforce the old heaven and the old earth.

Revelation 11:11–13: God Vindicates the Witnesses: They Stand on their Feet

The beast (Rome) did its worst: it killed the witnesses and left their bodies in the street. The power of death is the empire's greatest power. To put a person to death and then to disrespect the body demonstrates Rome's depravity.

11:11. The nations trampled the witnesses for three and a half years—a long but limited period—but the corpses of the witnesses lay in the street for only three and a half days before God breathed life into them again. The image of God breathing life comes from God's similar action restoring the valley of dry bones in Ezekiel 37:1–14—a vivid representation of God bringing the community dead from the Babylonian conquest back to life. John believes that God will restore the witness of the church in a similar way. The image of God breathing life also echoes God creating the first persons (Gen 2:7) and the resurrection of Jesus.[27]

The fundamental difference between God/Jesus/church and Satan/Caesar/empire is that Satan uses the threat of death to exploit communities for Satan's self-service, whereas God gives life through Israel and the church to create mutually supporting, life-affirming community. The preacher can use these contrasting purposes as norms to identify the degree to which a

---

27. In one of the most striking instances of Satan imitating God, the beast gives life to a Caesar who had been murdered (13:15).

person, community, movement, practice, or value serves more the purposes of Satan or of God.

The residents of the earth who saw the witnesses restored to life were terrified. If Satan and the beast can raise repressive rulers from the dead (13:15), then the empire can proceed with its horrible predictability. Although the reappearance of witnesses with their message of the new heaven and new earth interrupts that expectation, few people know how to live into the new possibility. Indeed, sometimes people would rather live with the familiarity of the painful known rather than risk the liberating possibility promised by an unknown.

11:12. John redoubles the vindication of the witnesses as the voice from heaven invites them to "Come up here," the same words which invited John into the heavenly world in Revelation 4:1. Just as Christ was true and faithful unto death, and God brought him into heaven, so the witnesses were true and faithful, and God responded in the same way.

Here as elsewhere, John does not predict a specific chronology of opposition to the witness of the church, but uses the story of 11:4–13 to say that the church should be prepared for Rome to try to "trample" the church. But, if the congregations remain steadfast, God will prove faithful.

11:13. As we have noted, John thinks that the time for the Roman Empire as empire to repent has passed. Punishment is inexorably ahead. But this passage is the clearest in the book that individuals (and, presumably, smaller communities) can repent. Some people in the city are part of the events of 11:4-12. Presumably, they hear the testimony. They see the empire murder the witnesses. They see that God raises the witnesses from the dead. They see the witnesses ascend. After these things many people are terrified and give glory to God—i.e., they repent (13:13). However, the city continues in its old-age ways.

Preachers and congregations today sometimes become discouraged when their efforts seem to bear little fruit. Empire seems to go relentlessly forward with few individuals or groups repenting and turning towards a Realm-like life. This passage is John's way of saying, "Despite the refusal— and hostility—of many in the Empire, the testimony of the church can bear fruit. Keep witnessing, even in the most discouraging circumstances. Some people will repent." The preacher might use this passage as a prompt to remember or identify positive witness to the Realm in the contemporary world that can encourage the congregation to continue testifying.

As long as the lure of the Realm is present, then a greater manifestation of the Realm is possible. From the standpoint of process theology, that lure is present in every circumstance.

Revelation 11:14–19: The Seventh Trumpet

John uses 11:14 as a transition from the meditation on vocation in 10:1—11:13 into a hymn that contains one of the inspirations for one of the most well-known pieces of Christian music (11:15–19). This passage invites the church to continue its witness in order to join the saints gathered around the throne.

Revelation 11:14: The Third Woe

11:14. Having described the first and second woes, the visionary says, "The third woe is coming very soon," but it does not specify that woe (11:14). The angel in mid-heaven who announced the woes tied them to the trumpets (8:13). It follows that the third woe is the seventh trumpet, and everything that follows until the new Jerusalem comes down from heaven (14:7—20:14). The final condemnation is ahead, and the faithful need to be fully prepared.

Revelation 11:15–19. The Dominion of the World Has Become the Dominion of God

In Revelation 11:15–19, John again assumes the idea, previously articulated, that events in heaven are prototypes for events in the world. John pictures loud voices in heaven celebrating an event that is yet to occur in the world: the final and full manifestation of the Realm. Since the Realm is guaranteed in heaven, the congregations can witness in the confidence that the Realm will soon appear in the world.

11:15. Before focusing on the third woe with its increasing conflict and violence, John prepares the faithful for this woe by offering them a vision of the ultimate future. John hears loud voices in heaven singing "The [realm] of the world has become the [realm] of our [God] and of [the Messiah] and [God] will reign forever and ever." The "world" is the present broken age under the heel of empire. John envisions the day when God has replaced the world with the new heaven and the new earth. The verb "has become" is in the perfect tense, which means that the action of manifesting the new Jerusalem is complete, and its effect will abide. The church can live in the present as if the new world is already here.

In *Messiah*, G. W. F. Handel set Revelation 11:15 and 19:6 to music in the "Hallelujah Chorus," which is, for many Christians, a sensory prolepsis of the eschatological world.[28] When the preacher addresses this text, the congregation could sing the "Hallelujah Chorus."

11:16–18. The twenty-four elders represent the same qualities as they do in Revelation 4:4, 10; 5:8. By falling on their faces and worshiping, they turn their power to the service of God and they turn away from Caesar (11:16). God is "Almighty" (1:8; 4:8) in contrast with Caesar's limited power. They give thanks because God has taken God's great power and begun to reign, ending the anguish of life in the empire and bringing God's purposes of peace, justice, and abundance into every person, situation, and community. Whereas they previously described God as "who is, who was, and who is to come" (1:4; 8; 9; 4:8), they now omit "who is to come" because in this vision of the future God has come and established God's rule (11:17).

In response to God's activity, the nations rage (11:18). This expression echoes Psalm 99:1, where the nations rage similarly against God, but God is still enthroned and working to establish justice, equity, and righteousness (cf. Ps 2:1–6; Exod 15:14, 18). In keeping with the plagues of Revelation 9:1–20, the reference from Exodus recalls that God liberated the Hebrew slaves even when Pharaoh raged. John's community should not be surprised when the empire rages, nor should they be surprised that God ultimately rules.

The time has almost come for final judgment, the moment when God judges all who have lived on the degree of their faithfulness (20:11–15). God will then assign the final destination of all—the great and the small, those who are powerful and in the upper echelons of the social pyramid and those who are powerless and in the bottom strata (11:18). The wealthy in the empire (and beyond) are no longer protected by power and privilege. The poor and powerless are also accountable.

God will reward God's servants, including the prophets, the saints, and "all who fear God's name"—i.e., the faithful. The reward is a place in the new Jerusalem. By contrast, God will destroy those who destroy the earth. Ultimate destruction is the lake of fire (20:7–15).

11:19. The last verse in this chapter describes a multimedia event in which God opens the temple and the people see the ark of the covenant, as well as lightning, rumbling, earthquake, and hail. This scene functions as a divine stamp of approval on the immediate context (11:15–18) and the larger narrative of the book. This is John's symbolic way of assuring listeners that they can have confidence in this book. The opening of the temple and the visibility of the ark indicate that God's purposes are clear: people can see directly into the temple, including the Holy of Holies where the ark

28. Handel, *Messiah*.

of the covenant had once resided in darkness. The ark vanished when the Babylonians destroyed the temple, but some Jewish communities expected it to reappear in the unfolding of the eschaton (e.g., 2 Bar. 6:5–10; 80:2). Moreover, the ark functioned as a palladium—a sacred symbol that preserved the safety of community. Despite the distress of the great transformation, God will preserve the faithful community. The geophysical events indicate theophany: God is present and acting in the way John interprets those things in the book of Revelation.[29]

John may offer the preacher an important pastoral model. The plagues of 9:1–18 (and the earlier seals) are violent. In 9:19–20, they come to a sad moment: no one has repented. The meditation on vocation in 10:1—11:14 is heavy: the witness of the church can result in persecution and death (albeit with the promise of resurrection). Revelation 12:1 returns to sobering themes and the penultimate scene of the book, the final cosmic battle.

Revelation 11:15–19 offers preachers and listeners a welcome change of pace. For this text is a prolepsis of the resolution of conflict between God and Satan, and the great thanksgiving in response to the complete and final manifestation of God's rule. Via their imaginations, listeners join the twenty-four elders around the throne. This approach gives listeners a congregation of the Realm to help them through the struggle of witness.

---

29. On theophanic associations here: for lightning, Exod 19:16–18; Hab 3:3; on rumblings, Ps 47:5–6; on thunder, Isa 30:30; Ps 18:13; on earthquake Pss 46:6; 68:8; on hail, Isa 30:30; Ps 18:13.

Revelation 12–14

Revealing Why and How
the World Is So Broken

O ne of the most important functions of religion is to help people make theological sense of life. People want to know why things are the way they are. In a Bible study, for instance, a woman asked, "How did the world get in such a mess? What is God going to do about it? And what are we supposed to do?" Preaching should help the congregation come to clear and confident answers.

Revelation 12:1—14:20 explains why and how history reached the nadir of John's day.[1] Revelation 12 reveals a conflict in heaven between the dragon (Satan) and the angel Michael that resulted in the dragon being thrown down to earth, where it sought to do violence against the witnessing community before John's time. Revelation 13 explains John's immediate context: the dragon vested its power in the first beast, the Roman Empire. The second beast, the imperial cult, supports the first beast. Revelation 14 foresees John's time as the climactic conflict between God and the dragon and anticipates God defeating Satan for the final time.[2]

John employs a flashback motif in Revelation 12. Because this device is so common in contemporary television and film, a preacher could play on it when explaining this material.

---

1. The Introduction suggests that preachers think of Rev 12:1—14:20 as the prelude to the major vision that begins at 1:16. However, in a sermon series or Bible study series, the preacher might *begin* with 12:1—14:20 to set the stage for series.

2. Along the way, John adapts the Ancient Near Eastern combat myth shared in different versions by many people in antiquity. The standard discussion can be found in Collins, *Combat Myth*, 61–85, which catalogues many versions of the myth.

Revelation 12:1–6: The Dragon Attacks
the Witnessing Community

John explains the way things are by using two figures to represent two fields of force in the world—a woman and a dragon. In 12:1–2 and 5–6, the focus is on the woman, and in 3–4, the focus is on the dragon.

12:1–2. While a common interpretation of the pregnant woman is Mary (the mother of Jesus), the details of v. 6 (fleeing into the wilderness for 1,260 days) do not fit into the story of Mary. While interpreters have proposed other identities for this woman, it seems most plausible to see her as a symbol of the community that offers God's way of life and blessing to the world—the faithful of Israel and the church.[3] The references to the woman in Revelation 12, then, include both the community of witness prior to John's time as well as the one in John's own day. Both the dragon's attack and the promises of God to the community came before John's time.

The woman's dress—the sun, "with the moon under her feet, and on her head a crown of twelve stars"—has both polemical and affirmative dimensions. As observed previously, many Romans regarded the sun and the moon as deities. Caesar looked particularly upon Apollo, a moon god, as a patron. By contrast, by making the sun and the moon part of the woman's dress, John reminds listeners that God made the sun and the moon to serve God's purposes of blessing. The crown indicates power, which is supposed to be used constructively for community (2:10; 3:11–12; 4:4, 10; 14:14).[4] The number twelve, as we have already observed, bespeaks completeness in community.

The preacher has a delicate opportunity here. It is difficult to imagine a more empathetic and generative image than a pregnant woman with which to depict the community whose mission is blessing. Yet the preacher needs to explain this image in ways that do not stereotype or drift into other forms of misogyny, and that respect the full personhood of women.

12:3–4. Here the visionary refers to Satan by means of the traditional image of a dragon as an enemy of God (e.g., Ps 74:14; Isa 27:1; 51:9; Jer 51:34; Ezek 29:3; 32:2) and turns to Daniel 7:7 and 20–24 for the ten horns (which, in Daniel, represent ten rulers of oppressive empires). The seven heads probably come from Ancient Near Eastern traditions that associated multiple heads with sea monsters such as the Canaanite god, Lotan, who

---

3. Modifying Murphy, *Fallen is Babylon*, 282–84. Israel is sometimes portrayed as a woman who births community (e.g., Isa 13:8; 21:3; 26:16–21; esp. 66:7–9; Mic 4:10; 2 Esd 13:32–38) and as a mother (e.g., Isa 54:1; 1QH 3:1–11; 2 Esd 10:7).

4. For destructive uses of the crown, see Rev 6:2; 9:7.

Baal defeated in creation.[5] The dragon intends for the seven heads to deceive people, as seven is a number associated with God. The diadems represent rule. John uses these symbols to say that Satan is currently represented in the world through the Roman Empire.

The dragon reveals its power when its tail sweeps a third of the stars in the crown down to earth.[6] This is a pictorial way of explaining how the dragon attracts people who have been part of the community of witness (in the stars) into the service of the dragon: they were caught by Satan's tail—that is, they bought Satan's deception.

John uses the image of the dragon confronting the woman—seeking to devour the child at birth—as a way of indicating that Roman opposition to the community of witness is nothing less than Satan's continuing attempt to exterminate that community.

John makes two important points for preaching here. One is that the dragon has real power, so much so that the sweep of the dragon's tail can move people from the community of salvation to the community of the condemned. The other is that the dragon sometimes conceals that power by operating through deception—offering things as good that are actually destructive. Indeed, anyone could recognize a dragon; hence, the dragon cunningly operates in the world through empire, which seems to offer peace and security when, in fact, it offers chaos and threat.

In the emerging multicultural world, the preacher may want to remind the congregation that different cultures use dragon symbolism in different ways. In some Asian communities, for instance, the dragon is a positive symbol.

12:5–6. John interprets the purpose of the ministry of Jesus as ruling the nations with a rod of iron (cf. 2:27; 19:15). This language comes from Psalm 2:9, a royal hymn used when Israel crowned a new monarch. The purpose of the rod of iron is to shape the world into a community that brings God's purposes to life, a task that calls for discipline. According to Psalm 2:10–11, all rulers are accountable to God for the degree to which they serve God's purposes. When Jesus announced that the time for the great accountability had come, the dragon attempted to devour Jesus, but God "snatched" Jesus out of the mouth of the dragon and elevated Jesus to the throne room of heaven. The verb "snatched" (*harpadzō*) implies conflict and dramatic action.

John now depicts the situation of his community. The woman—the community of witness—is then in the wilderness for 1,260 days. The meaning

5. Leviathan has multiple heads in Ps 74:14.
6. Here, as elsewhere, John uses the word "earth."

of Revelation 12:6 is essentially the same as that of 11:3: the church is in a long but indeterminate period of witness in the midst of struggle—described here as being in the wilderness—awaiting the final transformation. God is working with providence and nurtures the community. The wilderness is a potent symbol in Jewish literature as a place of great threat, and yet a place where God's providence is revealed. For example, God preserved the community in the wake of the exodus from the empire of Egypt (Exod 15:22—17:7). God preserved the prophet Elijah in the confrontation of Jezebel (1 Kgs 17:1-7; 19:1-18).

Preachers and traditional congregations today sometimes feel as though we are in a wilderness. So many things previous generations have assumed about the church are changing. Contemporary culture itself sometimes feels like a wilderness. John here reminds the preacher of two things. The first is that even in the midst of wilderness conditions, the church has a mission. The second is that God promises to preserve the witnessing community. The preacher needs to help the congregation discern the mission and identify points of provision.

Revelation 12:7–12: Michael Defeats the Dragon in Heaven

The preacher could use the encounter with this text as an illustration of the importance of reading a text for what the text itself says and not simply reading for what we think it says. For a long time, I thought this passage describes the origin of evil as a fallen angel: an angel in heaven rebels against God, causing God to cast them down to earth. Such versions of the story occur in Jewish literature—e.g., 1 En. 6:1—16:4; 54:6; 2 En. 29; 31:1-8; with echoes in Jude 6 and 2 Peter 2:4.

However, Revelation 12:7-9 tells a story with a different nuance for a different purpose. This passage describes the defeat of Satan in heaven as prelude to Satan being on earth. To think of it one way, the passage encourages faithfulness by warning the community that Satan (the power behind Rome) is already defeated. All who ally themselves with Satan will share that defeat. To think of it another way, the passage encourages faithfulness by assuring the faithful that they are committed to the side that will prevail.

12:7–9. Two groups of angels fight it out. When Satan confronts the woman in 12:1-6, Michael and other angels respond by making war against Satan (12:7-9). Michael was well known in Jewish literature as a leader among angels (e.g., Dan 10:13, 21; 12:1; Jude 9; T. Mos. 10:2; T. Levi 5:6; T. Dan 6:2-3; 1QM 17). The dragon and its retinue fight back, but Michael and the heavenly host defeat them. The passive voice of the verb ("was thrown down") indicates that God then cast Satan and company down to earth.

The fight appears to be one of brute force, but John reframes the means and significance of this defeat in 12:11 by saying that it takes place by the "the blood of the cross." One form of power (brute force on the part of Satan) is defeated by another form of power (complete commitment to the values and practices of God).

In this passage, John uses five names by which Satan is known: dragon, ancient serpent, devil, Satan, and deceiver of the whole world. While Genesis 3:1–21 pictures a serpent tempting the first couple, Genesis gives no indication that the serpent is Satan. However, later literature sometimes makes that identification (e.g., Wis 2:24). The last designation reveals how Satan works: by deceiving.

John uses this mythological image to indicate why he believes the tribulation is at hand. Satan has been cast down to earth, where he is making a last-ditch effort to maintain influence in the world (12:12b).

12:10–12. A loud voice—so everyone can hear—interprets the significance of what has happened. According to 12:10, salvation, power, the Realm, and the authority of the Messiah have come. This combination of terms, as in 11:15, is a way of saying that the rule of God is established in heaven and will soon be fully revealed on earth. As we note at 11:15, each of these terms contrasts with Rome.

These things are possible because the accuser (Satan) has been thrown down. Satan functions as a kind of prosecuting attorney in the divine court in Job 1:11, 2:5, and Zechariah 3:1. Moreover, as M. Eugene Boring points out, the faithful were in danger of being taken to Roman court for prosecution.[7] Satan sought to deceive people into cooperating with the Roman Empire. Satan engages in this activity "night and day." Evil is relentless.

Revelation 12:11 reprises the theology of 5:9 and 7:14. At those points, we noted that Jesus defeated Satan by believing that the values and practices of God supersede those of Satan and by trusting in the promises of God, even in the face of Satan's worst. The resurrection put Satan (and the empire) on notice that their days are numbered. Revelation 12:7–9 adds a reciprocal mythological dimension: Satan's defeat in heaven verifies that Satan is indeed defeated by the blood of the lamb. The faithfulness of Jesus and the community confirms the reliability of the myth.

The church (the comrades of 12:10) conquers Satan when the community follows the path of Jesus by being faithful in the face of the threat,

7. Boring, *Revelation*, 165.

and by testifying in court and beyond. To conquer is not to overwhelm by raw force but is to live by the values and practices of God.

Revelation 12:10 invites the heavens and their inhabitants to rejoice over these developments, even as it warns the earth and the sea to prepare for an increase in conflict and suffering. Satan is pulling out every stop in a last-ditch effort to preserve the empire.

Revelation 12:13–17: The Dragon Intensifies Its Attack

John continues to use highly symbolic language to expand on two themes introduced in 12:1–11. First, the dragon is now intensifying the attack upon the community of witness. Second, God provides the resources to sustain the community when the dragon attacks.

12:13–14. The dragon now targets the community of witness on earth (12:13). God has given the woman "the two wings of the great eagle" so the woman can fly to the wilderness (per 12:6) for nourishment for the time, times, and half a time (1,260 days, as in 12:6 and 11:2, a long but limited period of struggle). The term "eagle's wings" hearkens to God using eagle's wings to carry the Hebrew slaves out of the Egyptian Empire and through the wilderness (Exod 19:4; Deut 32:10–13). It also resonates with Isaiah's promise that the exiles will "rise up on eagle's wings" out of the empire of Babylon (Isa 40:31). The community does not fly to the wilderness as escape. Rather, as in 12:6, the eagle's wings provide the community with strength to witness within the wilderness.

12:15–16. There is no single text in Jewish literature that backgrounds the dragon attempting to destroy the community by opening its mouth and spewing forth a great flood. Here John draws on representations of water as a threat to order and survival (e.g., Gen 1:1–2; Pss 69:2; 88:17; Exod 14–15). Daniel depicts the enemies of Israel behaving like floods (Dan 9:26; 11:10; 11:40 in reference to the end-time). The use of this imagery is John's way of saying that the dragon intends to return the community of witness to chaos through the agency of Rome.

At the same time, this reference to water evokes the idea that God delivers people through water. God can bring the community safely through this chaos as God opened the Red Sea (Exod 14–15; Pss 74:13; 77:16; 124:4–5), the Jordan (Josh 3:1–17), and made a way through the waters of Babylonian exile (Isa 43:2, 16).

Indeed, the earth itself opens its mouth and swallows the river as it swallowed the Egyptian army (Exod 15:12), the participants in Korah's rebellion (Num 16:31–35; 26:10), the disobedient in the Deuteronomic version of the wilderness rebellion (Deut 11:6; cf. Ps. 106:17). While the earth has a destructive side, John reminds listeners that nature contains structures of providence that support the witnessing community.

12:17. In Revelation 12:17, the dragon escalates the war against the community of witness. "The rest of her children" is the church of John's own day "who keep the commandments of God and hold the testimony of Jesus." God and the community have frustrated the dragon by their persistence. But rather than give up, the dragon grows more angry.

A fair number of people in congregations today are not aware of the nature and function of mythological language in the Bible. This chapter provides the preacher with an opportunity for a teaching sermon on these things, using Revelation 12 as a case study.

More specifically, the chapter opens the door to contrast myths then and now. The preacher can identify myths—narratives—that communities today use to justify empire. Several examples: national exceptionalism, racial superiority, gender dominance, and religious exclusivism. In each case, the preacher could expose the story that powers the aberration and, inspired by Revelation 12, emphasize why and how things came to be as they are. The preacher is called to critique such things in light of the values and practices of the Realm of God.

This chapter is one of several in the book of Revelation from which the preacher could help the congregation think critically about the figure of Satan. The preacher could trace the development of Satan from prosecutor in God's court to direct enemy of God. On the one hand, I do not believe in Satan as a distinct entity in the world. With many others, I see this figure as a personification of the experience of evil. On the other hand, the figure of Satan reminds us that evil in the world is more than individuals doing bad things. Destructive forces in the world are often systemic in character.

A sign of optimism in contemporary culture is the number of people who hope for transformation in the church and world. Revelation 12 offers a dramatic reminder: evil is tenacious. Indeed, the more possibility God offers, the more entrenched and fierce the dragon becomes. The preacher may need to help the congregation see that change is often a slow and painful process. More is needed than a protest march and a new piece of legislation. The prophetic community needs to be prepared for a long haul.

12:18—13:10: The Nature and Purpose of the Beast

The chapter and verse divisions of the Bible are sometimes misleading. This is the case with Revelation 12:18, which directly posits the relationship between the dragon and the beast. The meaningful units of interpretation are 12:18—13:10 (revealing the nature of the beast) and 13:11–18 (revealing the nature of the imperial cult and those represented by it). John echoes a theme in apocalyptic literature that a sea beast and land beast will appear in the end-time (2 Esd 6:49–52; cf. 1 En. 60:7–9; 2 Bar. 29:3–4). This vision continues the cosmic drama of 12:1–18, indicating that for John, the tension between the beasts and the church is a manifestation of the cosmic conflict.

12:18—13:3. The dragon "takes a stand" on the seashore. The sea, of course, represents the threat of chaos. At creation, God redirected much of the energy of the primeval sea from random expression of energy into relationships of mutual support (Gen 1:1—2:4), but the chaotic potential was still present, so, according to Job 38:8–11, God drew the boundaries for the sea at the shore. By standing on the seashore, Satan seeks to release into the world the very chaos that God restrained. Some commentators note that the Roman proconsul for Asia Minor traveled by sea.

The beast comes from the sea as an agent of chaos.[8] The ten horns, seven diadems, and blasphemous names identify the beast as the Roman Empire. John adapts the beast images from Daniel 7 where they represent four empires that oppressed Israel (as discussed at Revelation 12:3). The ten horns symbolize ten rulers (17:12). The seven heads stand for Rome (seven hills and seven Caesars; 17:9). The diadems represent power and illustrate another way the beast imitates the things of God (cf. 19:12). The reference to blasphemous names comes from the Caesars and the imperial cult claiming attributes and authority that belong only to God. For example, many emperors were deified after their deaths. The famous Priene Calendar Inscription (dated about 9 BCE) indicates that Augustus Caesar was known as "son of God," the "savior," and his birth was the beginning of "good news" (gospel).[9] Some interpreters think that Domitian, emperor during John's day, approved of the title "Lord and God" for himself. The Caesars not only trample the divine name, but also make decisions that dishonor God's name.

The beast is like a leopard with the feet of a bear and the mouth of a lion. These details are modified from Daniel 7:4–6, where each animal stands for a different empire. The fierce qualities of these animals suggest the ferocity of the empire, as if Rome is a concentrate of the evils represented in the empires of Daniel's time.

The dragon gave its authority to the beast. The beast represents the qualities of the dragon in a way similar to the church being the body of

---

8. If the preacher uses a big screen, the preacher could project some visual representations of the beast (e.g., paintings or line drawings).

9. The reference to blasphemy reaches ahead to 13:8.

Christ. The beast has the power to do the chaotic things the dragon does in 12:1–17.

When speaking of the mortal wound to one of the heads that healed, many scholars think that the prophet alludes to a story in Rome that Nero, an emperor who took his own life in 68 CE, came back from the dead. Nero was the first Caesar who persecuted the church. Many people in John's day thought of Domitian as a revived Nero. John thus suggests that persecutions are ahead that will be similar to those in Nero's day. Bringing a dead being back to life is yet another point at which the dragon and the beast imitate God and Jesus, but this revival has a brutal aspect. The revival of an emperor means that imperial savagery comes back to life.

John engages in rhetorical hyperbole in saying that the whole earth follows the beast in amazement. John uses a word for "amazement" (*thaumadzō*) that often describes how people respond to the miracles of Jesus. This theme is especially important in 13:13–15. To use a contemporary expression, many people find the beast "amazing," but they do so with uncritical amazement.

While North Americans treasure democracy, the report that the "whole earth" was amazed and followed the beast is a caustic reminder that the majority can be wrong. Any group—from a national election to a church board—can think that the shiny objects of Satan are the things of God.

13:4. As we have pointed out, worship is a central theme in the Revelation. A community takes on the values and practices of the deity that the community worships. When people worship the beast, they worship the dragon, hence, they worship Satan. Worship in this context refers to participating in the imperial cult (see 13:11–18).

Historians of ancient culture point out that a sense of fatalism gripped many people in the Hellenistic age. That is the spirit of the question "Who is like the beast, and who can fight against it?" This is a statement of resignation. Worship under threat leads people to feel powerless and to resign themselves to the way things are.

13:5–8. The beast exercises its rule for forty-two months, that is, a long but limited period, and is the season of tribulation (11:2). In this period, the beast utters haughty and blasphemous words (similar to those of Antiochus Epiphanes IV in Daniel 7:8, 11, 20; 8:11). These haughty words and blasphemies are in the same as those in 13:2 (see above). In the ancient culture, a name often revealed identity. To honor God's name is to order life according to God's purposes. To blaspheme God's name is to deny the values and practices of God.

To blaspheme God's dwelling is not, as one might expect, to blaspheme the temple, but is to blaspheme "those who dwell in heaven."[10] The latter designation is multivalent. It includes the mythic heaven-dwellers of 12:1–17, the faithful who have and will perish (6:9–11), as well as the faithful church living in the present on the basis of the values and practices of the future.

Here, as so often in this last book of the Bible, the passive voice indicates the activity of God. The Almighty has the power to halt the blasphemies, but does not do so at this point in time. In John's theological worldview, God permits these things to continue because they are among the means by which punishment takes place. Blasphemy creates a destructive social order that will collapse upon itself.

But why, according to John, does God allow the beast to make war on the saints? As we have said, apocalyptic theology typically anticipated a period of suffering preceding the great transition. This movement often includes the unfaithful dominant culture exercising violence against the faithful, as in John's figure of the beast making war against the saints. From this perspective, the beast making war against the saints is part of this scenario: it needs to happen on the way to the end. It may seem arbitrary to today's congregation, but it is part of the otherness of the text.

As we said earlier, the empire appears to be a picture of diversity since it contains every tribe, people, language, and nation. While cultural diversity is present, it exists with empire qualities. For the empire exploits the resources of the diverse communities for the empire's self-serving ends.

While most of the inhabitants of the earth worship the beast, one group does not: those whose names "have not been written from the foundation of the world in the book of life of the Lamb that was slaughtered." We consider this book and its relationship to the eternal destiny at 3:5 and 20:11–15: the book records the names of those who will be part of the new Jerusalem. For now, it is enough to note that its immediate purpose is to motivate the congregations to witness faithfully by assuring them that when they witness faithfully, the lamb will record their names in the book of life.

On the one hand, this text invites several positive conversations for the sermon. One is about the possibility that similar kinds of blasphemy are taking place today in the world and perhaps in the church. In the dangerously polarized climate of the early twenty-first century, another conversation is about the degree to which empires today are at war with the possibilities of a new heaven and new earth. A third is assurance. Whereas John used the image of names being written in the book of life as a way of

10. The Romans had already blasphemed the temple in Jerusalem by destroying it in 70 CE and setting a Roman ensign in its ruins.

assuring people that they would have no doubt about their future when they witness faithfully in the war with the empire, what theological ideas might the preacher use today?

On the other hand, many preachers will want to help the congregation consider the possibility of rejecting the determinisms presupposed in this passage. Along with many other Christians, I do not accept the idea of a fixed apocalyptic timeline, much less one that includes God sitting idly by while Christians and others suffer. The preacher can help the congregation consider alternative ways of thinking about how history unfolds and God's relationship to that process.

A preacher can also lead the congregation in imagining theologically appropriate strategies for witnessing in our polarized contexts. Of special consideration: how a congregation should relate to other Christian bodies who make war on the congregation because of practices related to differences on the theological interpretation of the meaning of life. For example churches today are at polar opposites regarding the interpretation (and acceptability) of ending pregnancy and affirming LGBTQAI life.

13:9–10. John now picks up themes from Jeremiah 15:2 and 43:11 in a two-part theology of intent and consequence. Each part articulates a principle that is manifest in John's world.

The principle of the first line helps the congregation make sense of their immediate experience: "If you are to be taken captive, into captivity you go." If God determines you will go into captivity, that will happen. John anticipates that some members of his community will be imprisoned. John uses this slogan to help such captives (and others) recognize that captivity is under divine control. This insight should enable captives to endure imprisonment.

A minister does not have to accept the idea that God is in control of the details of a situation to commend the underlying point of this passage. In many situations, captors (servants of empire) think they can control the outcome of the situation to the benefit of the empire. But members of the witnessing community can have a liberating critical perspective within the situation. For they can believe that God will ever work with the world to lead it beyond Empire towards the values of the new Jerusalem. Thus informed, they can regard captivity as an opportunity for witness.

The principle of the second part of the theological statement both helps the community make sense of things happening in the broader social world and nuances a strategy for witness: "If you kill with the sword, with the sword you must be killed." This statement is a specific formulation of the broader notion that a community is punished by the very means that the community is disobedient.[11] Since the empire rules with violence, it will be destroyed by violence. The violence taking place in the Roman Empire is nothing less than the empire being punished by the means by which it ruled.

Given the language of war and violence permeating this vision, the congregations could easily think its "fight" with the empire involves fisti-cuffs, spear, and sword. Yet, elsewhere John makes it clear that the community conquers by giving faithful testimony in the face of opposition. Here the prophet reminds the congregations that if they take up the sword, they too will be killed by the sword. They should fight not with the implements of war, but with acts of witness.

We have already noted several points at which a preacher could use this principle to interpret developments in the contemporary world. Empires of all kinds that rule on the basis of raw power and self-service can expect their demise through those very means.

The final line is one of the most significant expressions of the mission of the church in John's vision (13:10d). The church is to endure with confidence. Endurance (*hypomonē*) is not passively bearing the situation. It means continuing to do what the community is called to do—make a faithful and true witness—even in the teeth of opposition.

The final line sets a significant agenda for preaching today. For the church confronts powerful social forces, destructive and exploitative, with resources beyond the imagination of the typical congregation that struggles to pay its utility bill. The church also confronts internal conflict that saps its energy and confidence. When preaching, the preacher needs to ask, "What can I say that will help the church endure—not simply as an institution, but as a community of witness?"

Revelation 13:11–18: The Imperial Cult Promotes Worship of the Beast

The Roman Empire was a collection of many peoples with different histories, cultures, and religions. The empire allowed many deities and cults to exist alongside one another. Indeed, the empire practiced a kind of religious freedom. At the same time, Rome formulated religious stories and practices to give the impression that the gods created and maintained the Roman state, including the office of emperor. The empire assimilated many historic deities, especially from Greece, often giving them Roman names and adapting their stories to serve Roman ideology. As a sop to local cultures, the empire allowed many traditional religions to continue.

11. Wis 11:15–20 offers an exceptionally clear statement about this principle.

In the spirit of religion serving empire, Romans created and used the imperial cult to generate loyalty to the empire by leading people to believe that devotion to the emperor (and, hence, devotion to the empire) was devotion to the gods.[12] Many Romans believed that the practice of the cult was necessary to maintain the good will of the gods so that the empire would survive. The cult had its own priesthood and liturgical life, including making sacrifices before a statue of Caesar and pledging loyalty (making a confession of faith) to Caesar. The Roman establishment came to consider participation in the cult as a test of loyalty to the empire.

In this book, the imperial cult refers to two things. Obviously, it refers to participating in the things that happen in the cultic space. Beyond that it is a symbol for values, and behaviors that exemplify the empire. Roman imperial religion is a classic (if regrettable) instance of people becoming like the gods they worship.

Having revealed the nature of the beast in 13:1–10, the visionary now reveals the nature of the Roman imperial cult. John's critical theological evaluation is that the Roman imperial religion facilitates the deception of Satan and the beast: the cult of the emperor imitates God and Jesus. The prophet seeks to help listeners learn how to distinguish true (and life-promoting) religion from false (and death-dealing) religion.

13:11–12. Both the larger empire and the Caesar cult are beasts. The empire comes directly from the sea—chaos. The second beast came from the earth—that is, the empire itself created imperial worship to give the appearance of divine sanction. Such religion is a form of idolatry.

The theme of imitation surfaces when John centers the imperial cult in a lamb with two horns. This lamb is strikingly similar to the lamb of 5:6–10. Caesar worship thus purports to offer Caesar as an agent of salvation. However, the imperial lamb reveals that it serves the increase of chaos when it speaks in the voice of a dragon. Visual appearance alone is misleading. The character of the second beast becomes clear only when it speaks in complicity with the first beast.

The imperial cult has the "authority of the first beast" behind it, thereby inviting devotion not simply to the Roman Empire, but to Satan. The imperial cult "makes the earth and its inhabitants worship the first beast." The reference to "the earth and its inhabitants" indicates the scope of the imperial cult: to have access to the good things of the Roman Empire, people had to worship the beast.

The motif of deception is again at work when John speaks of one "whose mortal wound had been healed." As noted at 13:3, John refers here

12. John soon refers to this religious life as "false prophet," 16:13: 19:20; 20:10.

to the story that Nero had died and come back to life, with the effects of his career extending into the reign of Domitian.

13:13–15. According to John, the imperial cult can perform miracles that are as impressive as those in the Bible. John cites two examples of miraculous demonstrations through the cult. In the first example, in the same way that Elijah called down fire from heaven (1 Kgs 18:20–80), so the cult causes fire to come "down from heaven to earth in the sight of all." From John's point of view, the imperial cult can do things as dramatic as the prophet calling down fire from heaven.

The second example expands 13:3. Imperial religion made "an image for the beast that had been wounded by the sword and yet lived." Roman civil religion "was allowed to give breath to the image of the beast, so that the image of the beast could even speak and cause those who would not worship the image to be killed." The expression "to give breath" recalls God giving breath to the first person (Gen 3:7), and especially God giving breath to the valley of dry bones (Ezek 37:1–14) and, of course, resurrecting Jesus. From John's point of view, again, the imperial cult can do things as dramatic as raising as bringing the dead back to life.

John points to a preaching issue. For John, the capacity to work miracles is not itself authoritative,[13] but authority derives from the use to which the community puts the miracle-working power. Imperial religion may resuscitate Caesar, but Caesar uses that fresh opportunity to "cause those who would not worship the image of the beast to be killed." The irony is bitter. Caesar uses the power for life to put people to death.

In the spirit of the movement towards the new heaven and earth, Dawn Ottoni-Wilhelm of Bethany Theological Seminary (Richmond, Indiana) describes the purposes of God as "life-giving." Here is an essential criterion for discerning whether a preacher can speak of a particular event as miraculous: the degree to which it serves the purposes of the empire of Satan or the realm of God, the degree to which it points to death or promotes life.

Some Christians do not believe miracles occur regularly today in the sense of events violating what moderns call the laws of nature—such as fire coming down from heaven or raising the dead. The reason is that if God has the power to intervene in history in that way but does not do so, then God is not truly loving and good. Per process theology, such Christians believe, instead, that God does not have the power to do such things. They believe that God, ever-loving and desiring only good, seeks to lure participants to the highest possible good in light of the circumstances.

---

13. For similar views, see Deut 13:1–3; Mark 13:21–22; 2 Thess 2:9–10.

From this point of view, a preacher might invite the congregation to consider stories of the miraculous in the Bible as figures that prompt the congregation to be open to the divine lure and as patterns of what happens when we respond to it. In a homiletical move familiar to many, preachers might look for an analogy. Instead of looking for occurrences of the raising of corpses, for instance, the preacher might cite a group whose dream of freedom appeared to be dead, but then came back to life as the result of people in the situation responding to the lure for freedom. In Ottoni-Wilhelm's phrase, the preacher looks for circumstances that embody God's life-giving purposes.

I continue to be surprised at how often members of Bible study groups that I lead in congregations ask about whether miracles occur today. A preacher might use this text as a beginning point for a consideration about what people today might believe about the nature and purpose of miracles and modern stories about them.

13:16–18. The mark of the beast is a biblical image that is large in popular consciousness. I have encountered people who will not read page 666 of a long novel or who associate the beast with social security numbers and other such things. Often people identify the mark of the beast without reference to any source other than popular religious radio or their own imaginations. John's perspective both silences the mischaracterizations and gives us something important to say.

Antiquated religions sometimes provided marks that identified people as belonging to those religions. Such marks helped the people who wore them remember that they belonged to (and were responsible to) particular deities. Sometimes the marks reminded the deities of who belonged to them. Many people in antiquity, for example, wore necklaces made up of the amulets of their gods. John assumes this custom.

The mark of the beast is inclusive. It spans the social pyramid of antiquity. It applies to "all, both small and great, both rich and poor, both free and slave." People received the mark of the beast when they participated in the imperial cult. John says that all will be marked on the right hand or the forehead, and that "no one can buy or sell who does not have the mark, that is, the name of the beast or the number of its name." There is no record of the imperial cult applying a physical mark: John has in mind an invisible one. The mark is the name or the number of the first beast, which is explained in 13:18 as the number 666 (cf. 14:11; 15:2; 17:5). The mark is worshiping at the imperial cult and participating in the values and behaviors of the empire.

The beast again imitates God: the faithful are also marked on the forehead with the name of God and the Lamb (3:12; 14:1; 22:24). This mark, too, is invisible. For example, immersion (baptism) is invisible after the water dries.

In this setting, buying and selling is probably not just a reference to commercial transactions, but a symbol for access to the good things of the Roman Empire. The range of possibilities for buying and selling (acquiring things) varied according to social class, with people in the upper echelons having access to considerably more than those below.

The number of the beast, which reveals its name, is 666. Scholars almost universally agree that this number refers to Caesar. Neither Hebrew nor Greek languages had numerals. In addition to spelling out numbers (as in 666), they assigned numerical values to particular letters. The numerical values of the name Nero Caesar in Hebrew adds up to 666. Whereas the number 777 would indicate something of God, the number 666 points to an imitator. M. Eugene Boring points out that in the visions with six elements, the sixth element is always one of judgment: aligning with Caesar is inviting punishment.[14]

In this context, the mark of the beast is the act of manifesting the values and practices of the Roman Empire, epitomized by participating in the imperial cult. The mark that one is sealed to God is that one becomes a witness in the movement to the Realm of God.

How, then, would the beast identify the faithful against whom to take recrimination? The faithful reveal themselves by not participating in the imperial cult and the world it represents. Adella Yarbro Collins proposes that members of the church might have refused to use the Roman coins that bore images indicating divine authorization of the emperor,[15] or to participate in forms of public life that idolized Caesar.

Social pressure was incredibly powerful in the communal cultures of antiquity. Many people believed that a community would be safe from chaos only if it appeased the gods. People would quickly report others who threatened the security of the community by not worshiping the gods and by not participating in the wider society as expected. Authorities could then intervene.

The preacher, then, could consider the mark in the text as a lens for helping today's congregation consider the mark they wear—the seal of the faithful or the mark of the beast? Furthermore, although John did not use the "mark" in this way, it would be in John's spirit to help the church today think about the mark we are making in the world. And what mark would we like to leave?

14. Boring, *Revelation*, 162–63.
15. Collins, "Political Perspective," 252.

Revelation 13:11–18 provides the preacher with a dramatic opportunity to think with the congregation about the purpose of worship. Many Christians think of worship as little more than what happens in the liturgy on Saturday night or Sunday morning. Many Christians today think that the aim of liturgical worship is to generate a religious feeling and provide a few helpful hints for living. In this vein, I once heard a preacher say that the aim of preaching is "to make 'em laugh, to make 'em cry, and to make 'em feel religious." In this atmosphere, it is impossible to overemphasize the importance of the sermon helping congregations come to a *critical* understanding of these things.

Revelation 13:11–18 provides the preacher with an opportunity to help the congregation consider an appropriate relationship among church, worship and culture. For Rome, the purpose of worship (and religion more broadly) was to prop up the state. In traditional Judaism and among the followers of Jesus, worship at its best represents the values and purposes of God that the community is to live. The prophet is an ombudsperson, one who evaluates the degree to which worship and the broader life of the community are consistent with the expectations of the tradition. The prophet helps the community identify inconsistencies and consider corrective action. The preacher is supposed to perform this role in the congregation. The congregation is supposed to carry out this role in the culture.

Throughout chapter 13, John calls attention to ways that Satan and the beast imitate God and Jesus for the purpose of deceiving people. In an oral form or on the big screen, the preacher might make a side-by-side comparison of ways that the dragon and the beast imitate God and Jesus.

Revelation 14:1–5: The 144,000 Redeemed Who Do Not Lie

In 12:1–17, John uses a traditional mythological worldview to describe the cosmic nature of the conflict between the dragon and God. In 12:18—13:10, the prophet explains that the conflict will take place in the historical dimension of John's day between God and Satan's immediate agent, the Roman Empire. In 13:11–18, the prophet interprets the imperial cult (and the approach to life that it symbolizes) as a particular instrument whereby the dragon operates. In chapter 14, John shows the situation of the church as it will be (14:1–5). In 14:6–13, the prophet uses messages from three angels to envision the contrasting destinies of those in league with Satan and with God. In 14:14–20, John reveals what God will do to the unfaithful.

14:1. John now directly contrasts the rule of God and Jesus (and the community associated with them) with the dragon and the beast (and the community associated with them). John images Jesus as a Lamb. It is hard to imagine a greater contrast with the dragon and the beast. Whereas the beast came from the sea (chaos), the Lamb came from heaven and is now on Mount Zion, God's stronghold. From this mountain, God judges and punishes (Isa 10:12; 29:8; 2 Esd 13:33–38), engages in battle with evil forces, and restores community (Isa 4:5; 37:32; Joel 2:32). The mount has eschatological overtones (Isa 24:23; 2 Esd 13:33–38), used by the prophet as a figure for the eschatological fulcrum in history.

The Lamb has the 144,000 with him—the faithful and true witnessing community (7:1–8)—who bear the names of God and the lamb on their foreheads. Per our discussion at 13:16–17, this mark is a sign that God has sealed them, and it contrasts with the mark of the beast. Like the mark of the beast, it is not a physical mark, but the daily witnessing of those faithful to God and unaccommodated to empire.

14:2–3. John now hears a sound that comes not from the 144,000 on Mount Zion, still in the midst of conflict, but it comes from heaven—those "gathered before the throne and before the four living creatures and before the elders." Their "new song" sounds like three things in heaven—the waters of 1:15 and 19:6, the thunder of 4:5; 6:1; 8:5; 10:3–4; 11:19; 16:18; and 19:6, and the harps as in 5:8; 15:22; and 18:22. These images communicate that the song is powerful and its origin in heaven underlines its trustworthiness.

The sound is the "new song" of 5:9: a hymn recognizing that God is effecting the apocalyptic transformation of the world through the slaughtered Lamb and is creating a witnessing multicultural community whose life represents—in a priestly way—the transformed world. In contrast to the empire, the priestly community serves the purposes of God.

The prophet's statement is provocative: "No one could learn that song except the one hundred forty-four thousand who have been redeemed from the earth." When people are enthralled by empire, they do not see alternatives, much less one defined by a slaughtered Lamb. The question for a sermon could be, "How are individuals and communities today so blinded by empire that they cannot see the alternative God poses?"

14:4–5. John's continued description of the 144,000 is difficult both exegetically and hermeneutically, as John indicates that they "have not defiled themselves with women, for they are virgins." Commentators universally insist that John cannot intend the text literally, as that would mean that women are excluded from the Realm and that sex (even in marriage) is defiling.

Since John routinely uses metaphors from the Torah, Prophets, and Writings to interpret the situation of church and world, it is natural to think that John does so here. Jewish literature uses the image of harlotry—a defining form of sexual defilement—to speak of idolatry (e.g., Jer 3:2; 13:27; Ezek 16:15–18; 21:1–49; 43:7; Hos 5:4; 6:10). Moreover, some commentators call attention to the holy war tradition that required warriors to abstain from sex so they would be fully prepared for combat (e.g., Deut 20:1–9; 23:9–10; 1 Sam 21:4–5). The Jewish theologian Philo speaks of women and men who do not engage in idolatry as virgins.[16] John uses the images of abstinence and virginity to mean that those who can learn the new song are those who have not engaged in idolatry and to say, further, "They prepared themselves fully for conflict with the empire, and they remained faithful during the battle."

The prophetic community (the 144,000) "follows the Lamb wherever he goes." They do not lie and they do not blaspheme—that is, they do not participate in the idolatrous attitudes and lifestyles that emanate from Caesar and empire worship. They are the "firstfruits" for God—the first pieces of a crop to ripen. They demonstrate that the plant is alive and growing, and the harvest is ahead. The faithful church is the firstfruits of the new heaven and the new earth. However, the final harvest is yet to come (14:14–20).

On the one hand, the preacher can easily summarize John's purpose in 14:1–5 and apply it to today. The church that wants to be part of the movement to the eschatological world must prepare for conflict as it renounces the idolatry of empires today. The preacher can further help the church recognize the firstfruits of renewal wherever they appear in our culture, and can encourage the congregation to think about how to bear such fruit.

On the other hand, the preacher should think critically with the congregation about the masculine exclusivity and gender discrimination against women in the notion that they "have not defiled themselves with women." While some scholars think John is misogynistic, John is not entirely negative in portraying female figures. For example, the woman in chapter 12 appears in a positive light. Nevertheless, John appears to participate in the sexism that is so much a part of male life. But even if John did not intend to cast women in a bad light, the image has the effect of not only reinforcing the secondary status of women, but implying that they are dangerous.

A preacher might take a three-prong approach. The preacher could (1) explain the situation of John's congregation and the purpose of this text, (2) critique the destructive effects of the picture of women in the text, and (3) pose ways of expressing the intent of the text that are gender neutral or gender affirmative.

16. Blount, *Revelation*, 269.

Revelation 14:6–13: Eternal Gospel
in Contrast with Fallen Babylon

14:6–7. John sees an angel flying in mid-heaven (the highest point of heaven so that everyone can hear; 8:13). The angel announces an "eternal gospel." The contrast with the empire continues. Caesar's proclamations were sometimes known as gospel. From John's perspective, however, Caesar's gospel is false and temporary. God's gospel condemns the empire, even while promising the true and eternal new heaven and new earth. Just as the empire embraces "every nation and tribe and language and people," so God intends the eternal gospel for all.

The idea of the eternal gospel can open a window for the preacher. In today's society, the eternal gospel offers certainty and direction that speaks so much anxiety and confusion. However, "eternal" does not have to mean permanent in the sense of being one-dimensional and set in stone. To make a hermeneutical move, the good news is that God ever and always (eternally) offers the possibility of the new heaven and new earth.

A loud voice—so that everyone can hear—then states the purpose of human life: to fear God and to give God glory. The hour for judgment is at hand. Worshiping God means not worshiping Caesar. To worship means both liturgically and ordering life in God's way. Hence, in this setting, to fear and worship God includes two dimensions: (1) it means to reverence God and to live according to God's direction; (2) given the gruesome punishment for not reverencing God in this book, it also means to be afraid of divine punishment.

John grounds both the eternal gospel and the call to reverence in God's work as Creator of heaven and earth, sea and springs of water. God has authority because God made the structures that support creation. Caesar did not create in this way. Moreover, while the sea may be a source of chaos (and the womb of the beast), the sea is ultimately under God's control.

For a preacher, Revelation 14:7 points to the answer to one of life's most penetrating questions. What is the purpose of life? In particular, "What is the purpose of *my* life?" This text offers a significant starting point for discussion. That purpose is to reverence God and to give God glory.

14:8. A second angel, inspired by Isaiah 21:9 and Jeremiah 51:7–8, uses the name Babylon as a cipher for the Roman Empire to forecast its destruction: "Fallen, fallen." Babylon has fornicated (committed idolatry) and made "all nations" join with her. Babylon offered wine to the nations, but the wine that appears to offer pleasure leads to destruction. Too much wine causes people to lose their senses and to do things they might not otherwise do.

This statement is a pastoral warning to those who accommodate to empire: you should stop accommodating, or you, too, will fall. At the same time, it is an assurance to the faithful: you can continue to witness, confident that Rome, who appears to be a latter-day Babylon, is living on borrowed time.

While John uses the word "wine" metaphorically and does not directly intend to discourage using alcohol, his language does provide the preacher with an opportunity to issue such a warning. While drinking alcohol appears to offer pleasure, many people find that the first drink is the first step into alcoholism. Because of the breadth and depth of this problem, I unapologetically recommend temperance.

14:9–11. A third angel particularizes what will happen as history moves towards its apex by recalling 13:1–18, esp. 11–18: those who worship the beast and bear its mark "will drink the wine of God's wrath, poured unmixed into the cup of [God's] anger." Wine in the ancient world was so strong that people typically mixed it with water. God is so angry with Rome that God will not dilute the divine wrath.

Those who think they are drinking the best wine will discover something else in their glass. "They will be tormented with fire and sulfur in the presence of the holy angels and in the presence of the Lamb. And the smoke of their torment goes up for ever and ever. There is no rest day or night for those who worship the beast and its image and for anyone who receives the mark of its name."

At one level, this image is easy to explain. John uses traditional symbols for punishment—fire and sulfur—for the fate of those who collude with Rome.[17] In contrast to the praise rendered by God day and night in 4:8, this torment goes on day and night. While John uses metaphor extensively, the widespread belief in hell in the first century prompts me to think that John believes directly in such punishment.[18]

At another level, these verses, like much of 14:14–20, raise the question of the degree to which it might be theologically appropriate to think that the holy angels, Jesus, and God actively promote such vicious behavior, even in response to the mega-sin of the empire. Because this question permeates 14:14–20, I take it up at the end of the chapter.

14:12. As in 13:10, John sees endurance as the mission of the church. Here, too, the "commandments of God" refer to God's covenantal purposes

---

17. For examples of fire and sulfur together in this way, see Gen 19:14; Ps 11:6; Ezek 38:22, as well as Rev 9:17–18; 19:20, esp. 20:10; and 21:8.

18. For examples of punishment beyond death see, e.g., 1 En. 1:13; 18:9–16; 48:8–10; 90:26–27; 100:7–9; 103:7–8; 108:4–7; 2 En. 40:12; Jdt 16:17; 2 Esd 7:26–38; 2 Bar. 59:5–12; 85:13–15.

and particularly to God's command to "come out" of the empire (18:4). Scholarship is divided regarding whether the English expression "faith of Jesus" means "faith in Jesus" (believing in Jesus), "the faith that Jesus had," or "the faithfulness that Jesus demonstrated." Given the fact that John does not typically speak of believing in Jesus, but often holds up faithful witness of the Lamb, a combination of the last two options seems most likely. In any event, endurance means continuing with witness so that one will not fall with Babylon into the fire and sulfur.

14:13. The beatitude here, as at 1:3, presumes that the blessed are part of the movement to the Realm of God. This beatitude speaks of the first death—that is, the end of this life beyond which one waits for the apocalypse, the final judgment, and for some, the second death. Those who die in the Lord—that is, those who die at the end of a faithful life and await the new heaven and new earth, are already blessed. Their deeds (faithful witness) lead them to an eternity of rest.

This passage, like so many, invites listeners to ponder the degree to which they will be faithful from the perspective of the final consequences. Today's preacher might think about the question, "What positive reasons can I offer the congregation for wanting to make the difficult witness to the Realm in our empire society?"

When I lead Bible studies in local congregations, the issue about which I am most often asked is eternal life. "What can I believe about life after death?" While the visionary does not deal with this question as a systematic theologian, the text does present the preacher with an occasion on which to begin with the view of eternal life in the text, and then bring that view into dialogue with other perceptions.

Revelation 14:14–20: The Winepress of the Wrath of God

The flashback/fast-forward of 12:1—14:20 concludes with the fast-forward of vivid final scenes of judgment. John introduces the agent of judgment in 14:14 and follows with two scenes: vv. 14–16 and vv. 17–20. These short pieces anticipate the story that is fully revealed in 15:1—22:5. Revelation 14:14–20 picks up the imagery of sickle, grain, and grapes from Joel 3:13, which is itself a judgment scene (Joel 3:9–16).[19]

14:14. John sees the ascended Jesus (described in language reminiscent of 1:16–20) as the agent of the final judgment. Jesus is seated on a white cloud, signaling that he is from heaven in the manner of Daniel 7:13–14,

19. Scholars of the Torah, Prophets, and Writings are divided on whether Joel 3:13 refers to both a grain and grape harvest or simply the latter. John seems to think Joel has both in view.

and wearing a golden crown, indicating power and rule (as in 4:4). The sickle evokes judgment (Joel 3:13; Jer 50:16).

14:15–16. The background of this scene is a grain harvest. An angel from the temple announces a directive from God, the hour for reaping (the final judgment): "the harvest of the earth (history) is fully ripe." The language of harvest to speak of the apocalyptic turning point implies ingathering the good grain (entering finally and fully into the Realm) and separating the chaff (punishment).[20]

The ingathering includes struggle and separation, represented here by the violent cut of the sickle. This scene assures those who stand with the Lamb through the tribulation that they can be included in the ingathering and, indeed, are among the firstfruits (14:4).

14:17–20. The background of this scene is a winepress. The worker placed the grapes in a vat, pit, trough, or other hard surface, and crushed the grapes to get the juice out.

John now sees two more angels. The first comes with a sickle from the temple. The second angel, who has authority over fire—that is, over punishment—comes from the altar and commands the first angel in a loud voice (so everyone can hear) to gather the clusters from the grape vine because the grapes are ripe.[21] The motif of ripeness functions here, as in 14:15–26, as a figurative way of saying the final judgment is at hand.

With the sickle, the angel gathers "the vintage of the earth" and throws it "into the great wine press of the wrath of God." John taps Joel 3:13, Lamentations 1:15, and especially Isaiah 63:3–6, where the prophets use the winepress for an image of God visiting catastrophic judgment on Israel's enemies. God's desire for vengeance is so permeating in Isaiah that God tramples down the Edomites in the press, "their juice splattered" on God's garments, and God "poured out their lifeblood on the earth." In an even more chilling magnification, John sees the blood flowing "from the wine press, as high as a horse's bridle, for a distance of about two hundred miles."[22] John describes the effect of this flow by referring to its height on a military horse, thus possibly suggesting that a means of judgment begins with military violence.

While the English phrase "two hundred miles" gives contemporary readers a reasonably accurate sense of distance, that expression obscures the symbolism of the Greek "1,600 stadia," a number made up of multiplying

20. Scholars call attention to passages like these to emphasize ingathering: Matt 9:37–38; Mark 4:26–29; Luke 10:2; John 4:35–38. Other passages emphasize the separation, e.g., Matt 3:11–12; 13:24–43.

21. On fire as punishment: Rev 3:18; 8:5–8; 9:17–18; 14:10; 15:2; 19:20; 20:10; 21:8.

22. 1 En. 100:3 similarly describes a horse walking through the blood of sinners as deep as the horse's chest.

forty by forty (referring to the four corners of the earth). This is a way of saying that the whole world—from every corner—will fall under judgment.

"The wine press was trodden down outside the city." The empire sought to end the threat posed by Jesus by putting him to death outside the city. Soon, in the model of sinners being punished by the way they sinned, God will put the empire to death.

As mentioned above, the images of punishment in 14:14–20 are theologically problematic in the extreme. John pictures the holy angels and Jesus presiding over eternal torment. Insofar as I believe God is unconditional love, it is inappropriate for them to approve of the active administration of pain. To be sure, it is important for people to confront the consequences of our misdeeds and to take responsibility. While the unrepentant can bring suffering upon themselves, the eternal extent of the torment means that there is no opportunity for repentance and restoration. As so often indicated in this book, I disagree with John: I believe there is no situation that is utterly void of some degree of promise

The preacher might turn to a hymn and a novel for case studies and conversation partners. Julia Ward Howe, an abolitionist, visited a camp of Union soldiers outside of Washington DC in 1861, after which she wrote "Mine Eyes Have Seen the Glory"—inspired, in part, by Revelation 14:19–20, which she paraphrases as God "tramping out the vintage where the grapes of wrath are stored." She looked upon the Union army as God's sword of judgment over slavery.[23] While I cannot believe that God initiates or sanctions war, I can hope that the omnipresent God always offers the invitation to the qualities of the new Jerusalem.

In *The Grapes of Wrath* (1939), John Steinbeck pictured the attitudes and behavior of banks, landowners, and other powerful social interests as greedy, self-centered, and heartless, directly resulting in the suffering of migrant workers. Steinbeck imagines judgment falling on these exploitative interests through historical process. "In the eyes of the hungry there is a growing wrath. In the souls of the people the grapes of wrath are filling and growing heavy, growing heavy for the vintage."[24] To be sure, eighty years after Steinbeck, and two millennia after John of Patmos, empire—so often greedy, self-centered, heartless, and violent—is still entrenched. Perhaps the preacher can see the lure of God in the fact that some people are still not resigned to empire, but hope and work for change.

23. Howe, "Mine Eyes Have Seen the Glory," 705.
24. Steinbeck, *Grapes of Wrath*, 367.

Revelation 15–16

Revealing the Digits on the Clock:
Ticking towards Midnight

While interpreters sometimes refer to 12:1—14:20 as an "interlude," these three chapters function as a kind of prelude to the main vision of the book, with 12:1—13:18 flashing back to reveal how the situation in John's day came about, and with 14:1–20 flashing ahead to the final events of history. When listeners turn to 15:1, then, they return to the forward movement of John's narrative from 11:19.

Revelation 15:1–8 reveals that the plagues (bowls of wrath) of 16:1–26 will be the end of the outpouring of the wrath of God. Furthermore, Revelation 15 reveals (again) the nature, purposes, and power of God. God's main purposes are to conquer the beast and bring about the eschatological promised land. God has the power to accomplish these things. Since God is by nature just and true, the congregation can keep God's commandments and testify to Jesus in the coming season of tension and suffering with confidence that the new Jerusalem lies beyond.

Revelation 15:1–8: The Last Plagues
End of the Wrath of God

John has signaled the congregation that history is moving towards its culmination by increasing the extent of the damage of God's punishment from one-fourth of the earth (and pertinent inhabitants) through the seven seals (6:1—8:5) to one-third through the seven trumpets (8:6—11:19). Now, with the bowls (15:1—16:22), John reveals that the clock of history is about to strike midnight. The final strike will include the final events of 17:1—22:8.

Revelation 15:1: Relating the Last Plagues to 17:1—22:5.

Revelation 15:1, a transitional verse, points to the vision of the seven bowls of wrath ahead. Seven angels appear with seven plagues. The number seven, of course, shows that these things come from God. The mention of the plagues calls to mind the plagues of the Exodus and the fact that God used the plagues as part of the process of freeing the Hebrew slaves from slavery to the Egyptian empire. God will similarly free those who keep the commandments of God and the testimony of Jesus from the Roman Empire and from the brokenness of the old age.

Significantly, John says that the plagues of 16:1–21 will be "the last." Since punishments continue from 17:1 to 20:15, hearers may wonder, "How can they be the last in sequence?" Commentators largely agree that Revelation 16:1–21 offers a symbolic theological framework for interpreting the meaning of 17:1—20:14. Like the seals (6:1—8:5) and the trumpets (8:6—11:19), the vision of the bowls does not describe one event following another, but is a collage whose individual elements contribute to a larger theological picture. From this point of view, the descriptions of Revelation 17:1—20:14 are more specific visions of the historical implications of the outpouring of the bowls of wrath—the final destruction of the empire, with which "the wrath of God is ended."

A preacher or teacher could use the difference between taking "last" sequentially and, in the sense explained earlier, as an illustration of the importance of interpreting biblical material in light of its own meaning. This material could also give a preacher or teacher an opportunity to compare the broad chronology of the Revelation and the specific timelines of popular premillennialism.

Revelation 15:2: The Conquerors in Heaven

John now sees a sea of glass mixed with fire. The sea of glass from 4:6 represented the chaos associated with the sea. That body of water is now calmed under the aegis of God; indeed, it is turned into a thing of beauty. Perhaps inspired by the stream of fire as part of God punishing the arrogant beast (Dan 7:10–11), those who have conquered the beast stand beside the sea. To conquer is to continue to be faithful when confronted by the image of the beast (a reference to the idols erected in behalf of Caesar; 13:14–15; 19:20; 20:4), as well as by the number of its name, which is blasphemous (13:1, 5–6; 17:3).[1] They hold harps, which John mentioned earlier in heavenly set-

1. On conquering, see Rev 2:11, 17, 26; 3:5, 11, 21; 5:5; 12:11; 21:7.

tings (5:8), and which he connects with the 144,000—the faithful and true witnesses—in 14:2.

Revelation 15:3–4: The Song of Moses and the Lamb

3–4. The community in heaven sings the song of "Moses, the servant of God," and the Lamb. The presence of Moses reminds listeners that the work of God through the Lamb is continuous with the earlier work of God through Israel.[2] Since John reports the text of only one song (15:3b–4), it appears that the song of Moses and the song of the Lamb are the same. The work of God through the Lamb is similar to the work of God at the Exodus, but different in degree.[3] God liberated the Hebrew slaves from the Egyptian Empire, and now God is liberating the world from the grip of Satan operating through the Roman Empire. The prophet does not model the song of Moses and the Lamb on a particular preceding song, but creates this new song by sewing together a series of expressions that evoke deep resonance from Jewish tradition.

A purpose of this song is to inspire the witnessing community to continue faithful testimony, even as the beast shows its teeth. The song sparks listeners to contrast the power and promise of the Lord God Almighty with the pretension and brutality of Caesar. Yet, the song also leaves the preacher with a theological enigma.

The first part of the song fits straightforwardly into the theology of the book of Revelation. The deeds (works) of God are great and amazing. These expressions call to mind divine sovereignty, God delivering the community from danger, and divine judgment.[4] John frequently uses combinations of the words in "Lord God Almighty" to call attention to the absolute sovereignty and world-shaping power of God (1:8; 4:8; 11:17; 16:7; 19:6; 21:22).

God's ways are just (righteous) and true.[5] While "just" is a plausible translation of *dikaios*, "righteous" is better. In popular English today, the words "just" and "justice" often denote punishment, as when a murderer receives capital punishment, and the family of the victim says, "Justice has

2. John uses the word "servant/s" for both the church contemporaneous with him (1:1; 2:20; 6:11; 7:3; 19:2, 5) and for figures from the Torah, Prophets, and Writings (10:7; 11:18).

3. Note broad thematic similarities between two of the most dramatic songs of Moses (Exod 15:1–8; Deut 30:30—31:47) and Rev 14:3b–4.

4. As, for example, Pss 92:5; 98:1; 111:2; and 139:14. For the references in this note and the following, I draw on Reddish, *Revelation*, 293.

5. For example, see Deut 32:4; Ps 145:17.

been done."[6] The words "right" and "righteous" come closer to the heart of
dikaios. While this notion does include God rendering fair judicial decisions,
it goes much farther, including God doing what is right in the full arena of
life. The righteousness of God includes vindicating the oppressed, acting to
save, and fostering right (supportive) relationships in community (e.g., Isa
41:10). Isaiah 45:20–23 stresses that the idols cannot save Babylon. To be true
(*alēthinos*) means not only to be correct, but to be trustworthy and real in
contrast to that which is untrustworthy and false, especially life under the
aegis of idols (e.g., 1 Chr 15:3). God does not deceive (Deut 32:4).

God is sovereign over all nations, which means that (1) God has final
power over all nations and (2) all nations are accountable to God.[7] To say that
the works of God are great and amazing is to say those works are righteous
and true—that is, the works will vindicate (save) the witnessing community
and condemn the empire. For the works of Rome are unrighteous (they destroy right relationship) and false, including the way the empire bestows divine honor upon Caesar. The emperor purports to be the ruler of the nations,
when (according to John) the emperor's rule is already condemned.

The latter part of the song moves toward a theological issue for the
preacher. John asks a question of God suggested by Jeremiah 10:7, "Who
will not fear and glorify your name?"[8] Jeremiah 10:6–16 compares the idols
with the living God and concludes that Israel is in exile because of idolatry.
Although Jeremiah does not use the word "repent," Jeremiah implies that
the exiles should do so. Presumably John envisions the nations repenting
and, consequently, reverencing and glorifying the name of God.

God alone is holy. John usually employs the word *hagios* for holy, but
here uses the word *hosios*, which occurs in the book of Revelation only twice:
here and at 16:5.[9] It refers to integrity in relationship. God does what is right
because God must do so to maintain divine integrity. Listeners, therefore,
can trust that what God does is right.

John anticipates that "All nations will come and worship before [God],"
for God's "judgments have been revealed."[10] The idea that "all nations will

---

6. I refer here how I hear "justice" in many conventional Eurocentric communities.
To be sure, in many progressive ecclesial circles, the cry for justice in solidarity with
people of color and other oppressed peoples is often much closer to the heart of the core
meaning of *dikē* than the popular meaning of retribution.

7. For example, see Jer 10:7.

8. Reddish, *Revelation*, 293 also points to Ps 86:9, 12; 99:3; Mal 1:11.

9. Reddish, *Revelation*, 293 cites 1 Sam 2:2; Pss 99:3; 111:10.

10. Reddish, *Revelation*, 293 cites "All nations will come and worship before you"
which is similar to expressions in Ps 86:9; Isa 2:2; 66:23; Jer 16:19, "Your judgments
have been revealed" is similar to Ps 98:2.

come and worship" is an assertion that parallels the earlier question, presupposing the answer "Everyone will worship." The English expression "your judgments" masks the fact that "judgments" translates *dikaiōma*, which is related to *dikaios*. *Dikaiōma* denotes righteous actions. These acts include passing judgment according to the right criteria, but more comprehensively, these acts include setting all things in right relationship. God has revealed the full scope of *dikaiōma*. These revelations should be a lure to the nations to come and worship.

The preacher could certainly use the text in accord with John's purpose, namely to hold out its vision as an encouragement for the congregation to worship God in liturgy and in life. This involves turning away from the worship of the empire and Caesar and turning towards God and salvation. John holds out this vision at a time much like our own, when history is taking a turn towards chaos, and we need to make theological sense of it and to witness accordingly. The church is to join the song of Moses and the Lamb, who are already in the processional on the way to the finale of history.

Yet, as pointed out above, there is an enigma here. On face value, Revelation 15:4 is a statement of universal salvation—that is, the salvation of everyone.[11] Yet, to this point in the book of Revelation, John has given no indication that the nations will repent and come to God *en masse*. Indeed, at the final judgment, not only are the devil, the beast, and the false prophet thrown into the lake of fire, where they will be tormented forever (20:10), but all those whose names are not written in the book of life are also thrown into the fire of torment (20:14–15).

Scholars have tried to resolve this enigma in several ways. One solution is to think that John thinks those consigned to eternal condemnation will repent after the second death. However, the prophet gives no hint of this possibility. On the contrary, the reference in 20:10 to eternal torment suggests final disposition. A related solution is to think that John quoted an existing hymn that presumed post-death repentance, but that text—if it ever existed—is lost to us. Yet another solution is to consider that the nations do not truly worship God, but only acknowledge God's sovereignty and rightness. However, this conclusion cannot withstand the emphasis in 15:4 on reverencing and glorifying God's name. A better solution, as already suggested, is that John speaks of "all" in a hyperbolic way, typical of some Jewish writers of the time. Matthew, for example, says that "all Jerusalem" was frightened with Herod at the birth of Jesus (Matt 2:3) and that "all Judea" was going out to be immersed by John (Matt 3:5).

---

11. According to Boring, Jewish tradition contains contrasting streams, one that sees the nations condemned—e.g., Ezek 38–39; Joel 3:2; Zech 14:2; and Ps 2:1–2; another stream envisions the conversion of the nations—e.g., Isa 2:1–4; 19:24–25; Ezek 16:52–63; Mic 4:1–4; Ps 86:9–10 (Boring, *People's New Testament*, 806).

Regardless of the preacher's exegetical perspective on this enigma, a preacher could raise the question of the degree to which the congregation today believes in universal salvation. The preacher cannot casually justify universal salvation on the shaky possibility that just one text may voice that conviction. But the preacher could begin with this text to a wider doctrinal consideration of what the congregation might believe about salvation—limited or universal.

Three of the big themes in this passage could form the spine of a sermon on the doctrine of God by considering the divine nature, purpose, and power: (1) God is by nature "just and true"; (2) God's main purposes are to conquer the beast and to bring the community into the eschatological promised land; (3) God has the power to accomplish these things.

Revelation 15:6–8: Authenticating the Seven Bowls of Wrath

In a scene whose purpose is reminiscent of 8:3–5, John now reinforces the idea that God is the moving force behind the seven plagues that will take the world into the last confrontation with Satan. John uses images to create a multimedia certificate of authentication.

John mixes two things when speaking of "the temple of the tent of witness in heaven" (14:5a). John typically uses "temple" (*naos*) in heaven to denote the authorizing presence of God (e.g., 3:12; 7:15; 11:1–2, 19; 14:15, 17; 16:1, 17). In the new heaven and new earth, a temple is no longer needed (21:22). By relating the "tent of witness" to the temple, John invokes the "tent of meeting," the portable tabernacle, that the people carried with them in the wilderness wandering (e.g., Exod 33:7–11; 40:34–38; Lev 1:1–2; Num 17:7; 18:2). The tent contained the "tablets of witness," the Torah, that represented the covenant and articulated the core of God's principles for living in community (Exod 32:15; 34:29). God punished the people when they violated those principles. The tent of meeting represented God's presence traveling with the community. John thus assures hearers that the authority and presence of God represented by the heavenly temple is with them as they wander through the final wilderness.

The seven angels emerging from the temple with the seven plagues are dressed "in bright linen with golden sashes across their chests." The linen is the dress of priests and angels (e.g., Exod 28:5, 39; 39:27; Lev 16:4; 1 Sam 2:18; 1 Chr 15:27). The golden sash—similar to the one ones 1:13 and Daniel 10:5—underscores the fact that the angels will soon act in behalf of the One who rules heaven and earth.

The writer underscores the divine origin of the plagues by having one of the four creatures of 4:6–8 give the seven angels the "seven golden bowls."

Israel used bowls, sometimes golden, in worship to remove ashes and fat after sacrifices burned on the altar (Exod 27:3; 38:3; 1 Chr 28:17; 2 Chr 4:8). These bowls are "full of the wrath of God," an image closely related to that of the cup of wrath that God prepared for the disobedient (e.g., Ps 78:5, 22; Jer 25:15–29; 49:12). Isaiah 51:21–23 envisions God preparing the cup of staggering—the bowl of wrath—for Babylonian idolaters to drink. The latter-day Babylon, Rome, has persuaded the people of the earth to get drunk on the false values of the empire (17:2, 6). The time is at hand for Babylon to drink a much-deserved cup of condemnation.

Immediately the temple fills with smoke "from the glory of God and from [God's] power." Such smoke can denote the presence of God (e.g., Exod 19:18; 40:34; Isa 6:4) to enact judgment (e.g., Deut 29:20; Ps 18:8; Isa 34:10; Joel 20).[12] This smoke may be the same smoke from the incense of the prayers of 8:3–5, which recollect the cry of the martyrs of 6:9–11.

The appearance of these last seven bowls to convene the final battle is God's response to the bowls holding the prayers of the saints (8:3–4)—that is, the plea for vindication from those under the altar (6:9–11). Recalling the theme of God being right and true from 15:3–4, God will do what is right by punishing the disobedient and ultimately setting things right for the faithful witnesses.

John next concludes this part of the vision: "No one could enter the temple until the seven plagues of the seven angels were ended." The Jewish tradition mentions only a few other times when the presence of God was so intense that people could not enter the temple, including Moses, who cannot enter the tent of meeting because the glory of God filled it (Exod 40:34–35), and the priests who could not enter the temple at its dedication for the same reason (1 Kgs 8:10–11, cf. 2 Chr 5:11–14). These incidents demonstrate that God alone determines the things that emanate from the tent and the temple. God alone decides what happens next.[13]

As we have noted several times, authority is one of the most vexing issues in the early postmodern twenty-first century. In Bible studies in local congregations, I often hear questions along the lines of "Why do you think I can believe thus-and-so?" John intends for Revelation 15:5–8 to give authority to the subsequent visions of the book. A preacher could use this instance to introduce a wider critical evaluation of what sources today's congregation regard as authoritative and why. If the evaluation reveals inconsistencies or

12. This association is present in Rev 9:2–3, 17–18; 14:11; 18:9, 18:18.

13. Aune, in *Revelation 6–16*, 882, surveys other attempts to explain why no one could enter the temple, including the view that the time has passed for intercession, intended to persuade God to be less wrathful. However, as Beale points out, no characters in the book of Revelation make such a plea. The saints under the altar have put forward the main request, namely that God vindicate them (6:9–11), a plea that God is now answering by sending the final plagues (Beale, *Book of Revelation*, 807).

weak points in the congregation's structure of authority, the preacher might pose more satisfactory alternatives.

Revelation 16:1–21: The Seven Bowls

The bowls contain the last seven great plagues that end the wrath of God. Like the seals (6:1—8:1) and the trumpets (9:1—11:19), the vision of the plagues is not a prediction of direct events that will take place. Instead, John uses the symbolism of the elements of the vision to offer a theological interpretation of the conditions of the late first century as he perceives them in the present, and as he anticipates they will unfold in the future. As noted in the prior discussion of the word "last" (15:1), the bowls provide the theological framework for interpreting the events in 17:1—20:15. The latter are not separate from the bowls, but complete the picture of history whose final movement began with the seals (6:1—14:20).

The plagues that come from trumpets (8:5—11:19) and the bowls are similar. John uses the plague motif with the bowls in much the same way as the plagues function with the trumpets. While the specific manifestations of each plague differ in the two series, they follow the same general order and subject matter, showing that these visions do not focus on separate sections of a timeline, but speak in similar ways about the same period of history.[14]

The seven plagues that come from the bowls differ in intensity from the seven plagues that come from the trumpets (8:5—11:19). As noted in our remarks about the word "last" (15:1), while the trumpet plagues damage a third of the things they afflict, the bowl plagues afflict more—e.g., the first plague affects all those who bear the mark of the beast, the second and third

---

14. Murphy notes similarity in order and content as follows. See his *Fallen is Babylon*, 337.

Trumpets	Bowls
1. On earth	1. On earth
2. On the sea	2. On the sea
3. On rivers and springs	3. On rivers and springs
4. On sun, moon, and stars	4. On sun
5. Abyss opened	5. On the throne of the beast
6. Angels held at Euphrates	6. On the Euphrates
7. Realm comes accompanied by dramatic geophysical phenomena and destruction of destroyers	7. On the air, dramatic geophysical phenomena, destruction of Babylon

plagues affect the entirety of the sea and the rivers. John escalates the sizes of the afflictions to signal that the end is here.

The bowls do not add new themes to the book. Rather, John uses some fresh images from the plagues on Egypt to reiterate the big idea: the last era of history is at hand, and the congregation needs to prepare to live through the final conflict between God and Satan in the form of the destruction of the Roman Empire. These final bowls annihilate the very structures of life that make it possible for the empire to exist. The pouring of the bowls transforms the empire into a chaos so that the empire that sought to rule in coalition with the ruler of chaos (the dragon) is undermined by its own alliance with chaos.

Revelation 16:1–11: The First Five Bowls

As in the cases of the seals and the trumpets, John gives brief descriptions of the first bowls. The descriptions of the later bowls are fuller and speak more deeply to John's situation.

16:1 A loud voice directs the seven angels on the earth to pour out the bowls of the wrath of God. The voice is almost certainly that of God, in the tradition of Isaiah 66:6, thus underlining God's control of these and subsequent events.

16:2. The first bowl echoes the sixth plague on the Egyptians (Exod 9:8–12) as the bowl pictures "a foul and painful sore" on all who have the mark of the beast and worship its image (see 13:11–18). "This punishment is a form of ironic justice: those who have the 'mark of the beast' now have a new 'mark'—the affliction of painful sores all over their bodies."[15] Moreover, such sores are among the curses that the Deuteronomic theologian sees God meting out to the disobedient (Deut 28:27).

16:3. The second bowl recalls the first plague on the Egyptians (Exod 7:14–25) as the bowl pours "into the sea, and [the sea] became like the blood of a corpse, and every living thing in the sea died." While the Revelation often associates the sea with chaos and the domain of the dragon, the sea was also a source of food—especially "living things" such as fish. Indeed, the sea teems with life in Genesis 1:20–23. The sea was a means of transportation, notably for agricultural products needed to feed the empire and for moving officials and military personnel. In contrast to Genesis 1:20–23, the second bowl makes the sea as a place of death; it is useless for transportation as it becomes clotted blood, an especially gruesome figure.

15. Reddish, *Revelation*, 303.

16:4. The third bowl also reverberates with the first plague on the Egyptians (Exod 7:14–25) as the bowl pictures the rivers and the springs of water becoming blood. The third bowl ups the ante from the second bowl, since rivers and springs are sources of the fresh water that is absolutely necessary for life. Not only is the sea clotted with blood, but other sources of water are fouled.

16:5–7. The prophet now inserts a doxology that gives John's interpretation of the reason for the plagues and, indeed, for history ending with such brutal punishment for the empire. The hymn is based on the conviction that God is just (righteous), holy, and true.[16] John invokes a version of the formula introduced in 1:4, 8 describing God as "who is, who was, and who is to come." In the same vein as 11:17, John here omits "who is to come" because the prophet believes that God is coming in final judgment and redemption in John's moment in history.

God has judged the empire and rendered the verdict that the empire deserves. The empire "shed the blood of saints and prophets"; consequently, God has given "them blood to drink." Again, we see the principle in action that a community is punished by the very means by which it sinned. The empire literally murdered and, hence, the empire itself would be murdered. Some apocalyptic literature imagines measure-for-measure punishment— that is, punishment that has an appropriate size and weight (so to speak) for the sin. A pound of sin deserves a pound of punishment. Here, however, the empire killed (or would kill) a relatively small number of people, while the entire empire falls to violence. The image of drinking blood was particularly loathsome to the Jewish community. Blood outside the body creates a condition of uncleanness.

After hearing this bracing announcement, the altar affirms its correctness (16:7). To have the altar speak is a way of referring to the saints under the altar—the martyrs of 6:9–11. They cried out for vengeance. John believes that God is responding to their cry through the developments in the book that eventuate in the denouement of the present age.

A preacher may turn to 6:9–11, where my discussion offers a fuller critical reflection on the theology at work there and in 16:5–7. In short, I find John's theology on the issue of recrimination deeply problematic, as I do not believe that a God of unconditional love who operates by lure would directly seek to inflict the kind of pain symbolized by giving the inhabitants of the empire blood to drink. To be sure, perpetrators need to be held accountable, and their attitudes and actions may create the circumstances of their own demise. An empire that rules by violence will likely meet a

16. The notions that God is true, just, and holy are discussed at 15:3–4.

violent end which it brings on itself. A preacher might help a congregation recognize that, even when such developments result in more just conditions, violent destruction is cause not for celebration, but for lament for the pain involved.

16:8–9. The fourth bowl is a riff on the ninth plague on the Egyptians (Exod 10:21–29). John's fourth bowl causes the sun to scorch people by fire. That the visionary has the empire in view is clear in the Greek, where John uses the word "blaspheme" (which the NRSV unfortunately translates as "curse"). The followers of the beast blaspheme in 13:1, 5–6.

The scorching caused by the fire of the sun is serious and painful. But it is only a pale pain compared to the eternal torment in fire that ultimately faces those who do not repent (20:9–10, 14–15). To use a comparison that is not really in the text, God sends the serious sunburn of 16:8 as a pastoral warning intended to promote repentance so that people can avoid the ultra-serious pain of the lake of fire.

Whereas Pharaoh ignored God's command to release the slaves, John portrays the Romans going a step further and directly blaspheming God. They fail to repent, and they withhold glory from God.[17] Had they repented, they would have joined the faithful in a situation in which "the sun will not strike them, nor any scorching heat" (7:16).

16:10–11. The fifth bowl also echoes the ninth plague on the Egyptians (Exod 10:21–29) as the bowl pours wrath on the "throne of the beast, and its kingdom was plunged into darkness." Losing their light, "the people gnawed their tongues in agony, and cursed the God of heaven because of their pains and sores, and they did not repent of their deeds." The angel pours the wrath directly on the throne which Satan had given the beast in 13:2. Whereas God created light as the first step towards blessing in Genesis 1:3–5, God takes away light among the last steps of invoking curse. Moreover, the light allows people to perceive. This is consistent with Jewish tradition, which often uses light as a symbol for understanding. Light also makes it possible for plants to grow. By contrast, darkness represents misperception and disobedience and takes away some things necessary for life.

In addition to darkness causing the people to be unable to see, the bowl causes people to gnaw their tongues in agony. The pain that a person feels accidentally biting the inside of her check is a feint feeling of this agony. However, so entrenched is the commitment of the state to itself that those in the nerve center will not repent of what they have done.

17. Their response is the exact opposite of the purpose of life as summarized in Rev 14:7 and 11—namely, to revere God and to give God glory.

The throne reminds listeners of the power center of the empire, the collusion of dragon and beasts to use power for their own self-serving ends. While Caesar's particular throne was in Rome, the power of the throne was enforced in hundreds of local offices, as in 2:13 and the omnipresence of the imperial cult (13:10–18). By particularly mentioning the throne, John emphasizes that the people and institutions directly connected with the government of the empire will feel the effect of this bowl. The privilege of being in the upper strata of the Roman social world cannot prevent this agony. Revelation 16:10b indicates that the rest of the population of the Realm will also feel the agony, the sores, and the pain.

Revelation 16:12–21: The Final Two Bowls

The descriptions of last two bowls are longer than those of the first five bowls. They are also more specific with respect to situations ahead.

Revelation 16:12–16: The Rulers from the East

16:12. The sixth bowl pours out "on the great river Euphrates, and its water was dried up in order to prepare the way for the kings from the east and brings "three foul spirits like frogs" from the mouth of the dragon." The drying up of the Euphrates does not echo a plague from Egypt, but the drying up of the Red Sea (Exod 14:1—15:20). The frogs bring to consciousness the second plague on Egypt, the frogs (Exod 8:1–15).

The drying up of the Euphrates echoes the drying up of the Red Sea with a bitter ironic twist. The drying up of the Red Sea opened the way to freedom. In 16:12, the drying up of the Euphrates opens the way for punishment. The Euphrates marked the eastern border of the empire, beyond which was the territory of the Parthians. As we noted at 9:13–19, the Romans feared the Parthians because they had a crack military. As in 9:13–19, the prophet intimates in 16:12 that a Parthian invasion could be part of God's punishment on Rome.

The preacher could use this development in the text as a reminder that the Roman Empire is punished by one of the very means by which it ruled—violence. Moreover, the prophet expressly said, "If you kill with the sword, with the sword you must be killed" (13:10), an idea that underlies 17:1—20:15.

16:13–14. In Exodus 8:1–15, the frogs completely covered the land and made ordinary life impossible, and the land stank when the frogs died. But in Revelation 12:13–16, the character of the frogs and their activity is more heinous as the prophet sees "three foul spirits like frogs coming from the mouth of the dragon, from the mouth of the beast, and from the mouth of the false prophet. These are demonic spirits, performing signs, who go abroad to the monarchs of the world to assemble them for battle on the great day of God the Almighty." Just as Moses's frogs covered the land and made it impossible to live, so the frogs in the form of foul spirits cover the earth with deception and twist life towards a terrible end.

For John, the frogs are figures for foul spirits who come from the dragon (Satan, 12:18—13:1), the beast (the Roman Empire, 13:1–10) and the false prophet. The latter is a new designation in the book of Revelation for Roman imperial religion and those it represents (13:11–18). The language of "foul spirits" is a way of speaking about demonic spirits (as they are specifically named in 16:14a) who operate in the world with real force to cause things to happen that disrupt God's intentions for love, justice, peace, and abundance.

When John says that the foul spirits "go abroad to the monarchs of the whole world, to assemble them for battle on the great day of God the Almighty," the meaning is that the foul spirits use the deceptive character of the empire to assemble a coalition of nations "for battle on the great day of God the Almighty." Seeking allies, the empire deceives and lies.

In the background is Zechariah 14:12, which pictures "all the nations" gathered against Jerusalem for battle. Initially, the nations appear to have success against Jerusalem (Zech 14:2), as the Roman Empire appears to be having against God and the church in John's time. But God intervenes with a show of might that splits the Mount of Olives (14:4–5), and eventually results in the painful destruction of the armies of the nations (14:12–14) and in the manifestation of God's rule over all the earth (14:6–11, esp. 9).[18] John thus implies that conflicts involving the Roman Empire in the present and future are part of this transformation of circumstances.

16:15. The prophet interjects a statement from the ascended Jesus. "See, I am coming like a thief! Blessed is the one who stays awake and is clothed, not going about naked and exposed to shame." The main point of the interjection is clear. Jesus will return suddenly from heaven, without warning, in a way similar to the unexpected arrival of a thief (cf. Mark 13:32–37; Matt 24:36–44; Luke 12:35–40; 1 Thess 5:2; 2 Pet 3:10). If the community is to be blessed—that is, if they are to be part of the final movement into the new heaven and new earth—they must stay awake and be clothed when Jesus arrives.

---

18. For similar apocalyptic battles, see Joel 3:2; Zeph 3:8.

As noted at 3:2 and 3:4–5, staying awake and remaining clothed are expressions for continuing faithful witness. In the ancient world, to be seen naked was shameful. Isaiah says metaphorically that Babylon's nakedness will be uncovered; in John's day, those in league with Rome (the latter-day Babylon) share in that reprehensibility.[19] In the shame/honor culture of antiquity, shame was not simply personal embarrassment, but a fundamental violation of the values of community and cause for judgment. Some of the prophets correlate idolatry and shame with judgment (e.g., Isa 20:4; Ezek 16:36; 23:9; Nah 3:5).

Revelation 16:15 seems to interrupt the natural flow of the text. The reason John inserted 16:15 at its present point is not fully clear, a fact that prompts some debate among scholars. However, interpreters tend to agree on two things. For one, the insertion discourages speculating about the timing of the apocalypse. God will conclude this age and the coming to the next according to God's own time. For the other, the insertion also makes explicit an underlying purpose of the immediate vision (16:12–16) and the larger context (16:1–21), which is meant to motivate hearers to be ready for the unknown timing of the apocalypse.

16:16. The discussion of the sixth bowl concludes with one of the most famous places in popular biblical consciousness today. "And they assembled them at the place that in Hebrew is called Harmagedon," a place-name that is more often translated Armageddon. This word occurs only once in the Bible. It probably comes from two Hebrew words—*har* and *mĕgiddôn*, meaning "Mount of Meggido"—though, in point of fact, there is no actual mountain at Meggido. Likely, John had in mind Ezekiel 38:8; 39:2, 4, 17, which describes God defeating many nations on "the mountains of Israel." Moreover, John associated that place with Meggido and the many battles and life-shaping events that took place there (e.g., Judg 5:1–31, esp. 19; 2 Kgs 9:14–29, esp. 27–28; 23:28–30; Zech 12:11). If the preacher displays a map on the big screen locating Megiddo, the congregation can quickly see its strategic location.[20]

Critical commentators are united in declaring that John did not foresee a literal battle taking place at the non-mountain Megiddo. John uses this imagery to suggest that military violence ahead for the Roman Empire is part of the climactic confrontation of history.

Hermeneutically speaking, Harmagedon is not a single event, but a battle that occurs over and over. A preacher might give the name "Harmagedon"

19. For nakedness as cause for judgment, see Isa 3:17; Mic 1:11; Nah 3:5; Hab 2:15.

20. Megiddo has been excavated archaeologically, and today it is a UNESCO World Heritage Site. A preacher can easily find line drawings, maps, and pictures of the site suitable for the big screen.

to circumstances today where forces of empire exercise violence to preserve their self-interest as they do battle with God's desire for the world to become more of a new heaven and new earth. The battle of Harmagedon can take place in such scenarios as a police officer pulling someone over on an urban street corner for no other reason than the color of their skin; a governing body regarding legislation that can restrict—or expand—human life; or regarding practices that are repressive or liberating among nations.

Revelation 16:15–16 gives the preacher a natural opportunity to think critically with the congregation about efforts to construct timelines of events leading to the end and attempts to locate our period of history on that timeline. The preacher could use the reference to Harmagedon as a case study. Premillenialism is noted for its efforts to construct timelines for the end of history. A sermon could describe such efforts and interpret why people continue to construct such timelines when, generation after generation, the timelines have not come true.[21] For congregations that anticipate a final and full transformation, John's guidance is still apropos: the community should concentrate on faithful testimony and not on calculating the end. The text reminds communities who are hesitant about an apocalyptic pinnacle that their priority, too, is faithful witness. They never know when opportunities for giving testimony will appear in their midst. Indeed, such opportunities may come like a thief in the night.

Revelation 16:17–21: "It Is Done" and Babylon Does Not Like It

16:17–21. The seventh bowl, in part, recalls the seventh plague on the Egyptians (Exod 9:19–35) as the bowl pours out lightning, rumblings, peals of thunder, a violent earthquake, and devastating hail. Befitting the seventh and last bowl in the series, a loud voice from the temple (probably God) says, "It is done." Here is another case in which an event in heaven is paradigmatic for what will happen on earth. Although the process of destroying the power of the dragon, the beast, and the false prophet, described in detail in 17:1—20:15, is still in process on earth, John describes this state of affairs with the expression "It is done." While the final punishment and the new heaven and the new earth are actually still in process, the fact that God has guaranteed the outcome means that John speaks as if the transformation has already taken place. As far as the congregations are concerned, "It is done."

To make an analogy, the election is over. The dragon, the beast, and the false prophet have been voted out, but they are still in office as lame ducks

21. The preacher who uses a big screen could display a sample premillennial timeline.

until the date their terms officially end, and the new legislature is sworn in. However, lame ducks have some power and can do a lot of damage.

The announcement "it is done" is followed by dramatic signs in nature—lightning, rumblings, thunder, and violent earthquakes of unprecedented destructive magnitude. John regularly uses such theophanic events to indicate that the things depicted in the vision are trustworthy. These events are like an imprimatur assuring the reader that God acts through them.[22] Furthermore, prophetic and apocalyptic visions often include God using cosmic elements for punishment, destroying the world as it is in order to begin the process of recreation (e.g., Isa 13:10; 29:5–6; 30:30; 34:4; Ezek 32:7–8; Dan 12:1–2; Joel 2:10, 31; 2 Esd 5:4–5; Mark 13:19, 24–27; Matt 24:21, 29; Rom 8:18–25). The size of the earthquake—"such as had not occurred since people were upon the earth"—emphasizes the magnitude of the destruction. The power of Rome will be utterly destroyed.

God divides Babylon, "the great city," into three parts. God dismembers Babylon-Rome in the same way that God dismembered the great sea dragon so its parts cannot work together again (e.g., Ps 87:10; Isa 51:9–10).[23] The cities of the other nations allied with Rome fall. By felling the cities with whom Rome was allied, God disrupts the system with which the empire worked with other idolatrous powers. In doing these things, God gives them "the wine-cup of the fury of [God's] wrath."[24]

The islands are affected, as they often are in times of judgment (e.g., Isa 20:6; 23:2, 6; 24:15; Ezek 26:15, 18). Mountains disappear, as they also do in seasons of judgment (e.g., Ps 97:5; Isa 42:15; 54:10; Ezek 38:20; 2 Esd 15:42).[25] While hail appeared in 11:19, the hail in 16:21 is mega-size (the hailstones weigh between sixty and one hundred pounds). Hail is an instrument of judgment, not only in Exodus 9:19–35, but in many other places (e.g., Josh 10:11; Isa 28:17; Ezek 38:22; Hag 2:17).

Revelation 16:21 puts the preacher in a difficult position. The response of those associated with the empire is to curse (blaspheme) God, as at 16:9–11, and they do not repent. John does not even mention repentance at 16:20–21. G. K. Beale suggests that the absence of repentance here means "no room is now left for repentance."[26] This viewpoint is consistent with my

22. See discussion at 4:5; 8:5; 11:19. These phenomena can have overtones of judgment.

23. Isa 30:7 and Ezek 29:3; 32:2 regard Egypt as Rahab.

24. On drinking the cup of God's wrath, see 14:8.

25. Caird proposes that John referred to islands since the Romans use of islands for detention. For Caird, the mountains refer to Rome with its seven hills (Caird, *Revelation*, 209). The islands and the mountains and their oppressive functions will pass away.

26. Beale, *Book of Revelation*, 845. This restriction must apply only to those in the

similar earlier conclusion. While prophetic and apocalyptic voices typically stress the possibility—even necessity—of repentance, there are exceptions. For example, Amos 8:2 says flatly, "The end has come upon my people Israel." The opportunity to repent has passed.

As I commented in connection with 9:20–21, while John may have believed the opportunity for the empire to repent had passed, today's preacher does not have to share that conviction. According to John, time had run out. As one who does not believe that God will (or can) orchestrate a single moment that concludes this age, I believe that the door to repentance is still open.

With respect to the theme represented by the confidence that "It is done," the preacher faces a conundrum that is similar to one we have identified in connection with several other passages. On the one hand, at the level of poetry described above, the notion "It is done" is quite evocative. John believes that empire is already defeated. The transformation of the world into the Realm is underway. Many preachers and congregations continue to believe this.

On the other hand, the brutal fact is that conditions in the world are not much different than they were in the first century, except that the scale of oppression is much larger. The contemporary Babylons are not dismembered. Islands and mountains (symbolically speaking) are not disappearing. Blasphemy of the kind John has in mind is rampant. To be sure, the contemporary world is shot through with violence that may bring about the self-destruction of some empire-like nations along the lines of communities inviting judgment upon themselves through the means whereby they sin. But if past performance is one of the most reliable predictors of future results, then the past two thousand years suggest that today's empires will be replaced by those of tomorrow.

A preacher who shares my skepticism about the degree to which "It is done" might also be able to make a theological and hermeneutical move that John did not intend, but which plays off John's language. The resources necessary for the Realm—a world shaped by the values and practices of God's desire for mutually supportive community—are already available. God's lure to use them for the Realm is relentless and omnipresent. "It is done" not in the sense of the process being finished, but in the sense that we already have the resources. What is needed is not more stuff out of which to make a new Jerusalem. What is needed is for individuals and communities to repent of collusion with empire and to join God.

---

empire who continue to blaspheme, since John encourages repentance on the part of those in the church who drift in the direction of accommodation to the empire—e.g., 2:5, 16, 21–22; 3:3, 19.

Revelation 17:1—19:10

Revealing the Fall of the Empire

S ome Christians think that Revelation 17:1—19:10 adds another series of events to the events on the timeline of the book. The discussion of Revelation 15–16, however, joins the contemporary movement in scholarship that sees Revelation 17–18 expanding the picture of the consequences of the bowls of wrath and the last plagues of Revelation 16. While the analogy is imprecise, it is as if a preacher makes a big point in Revelation 16 and then fills out the point with additional information in Revelation 17:1—19:10. Indeed, Revelation 17 gives more background on why God sends the bowls of wrath, while Revelation 18 uses a funeral liturgy to depict the effect of the final bowls of wrath.

An über-problem bedevils interpretation of Revelation 17. John uses the image of "great whore" to represent Babylon (the Roman Empire).[1] The image of a woman as a way of speaking about a community that has become unfaithful is rooted in Jewish tradition (e.g., Lev 17:7; 20:5–6; Deut 31:16; Judg 8:33; Isa 1:21–23; Hos 4:13; Jer 3:1–3; Ezek 16:1–63; Hos 1:1—4:19; Mic 1:6–7). But whether John (or the wider tradition) consciously intended it, this text reinforces the notion that women are the responsible party in disobedience. Moreover, referring to a people by the image of someone who prostitutes herself casts a negative light over women more broadly. While John may not have intended to license male abuse of women, the fact that the woman (the empire) is beaten severely, so to speak, in Revelation 18 participates in an abuse paradigm.

Christians sometimes respond that John balances this negative view with the new Jerusalem "as a bride adorned for her husband" (21:2). Yet the image of the bride casts the woman in a role defined by the highly patriarchal culture of antiquity. The bride (and wife) in antiquity had little agency in conventional social circles. Moreover, both the picture of the woman engaged in

1. See especially Pippin, "Heroine and the Whore," 127–45.

prostitution and that of the woman on a wedding day reduce the experience of women to the dimension caricatured by these two roles.

I propose at 14:4 that a preacher might respond to this difficulty with a three-step movement. (1) The preacher could explain the function of the image of the woman in the text, (2) critically reflect on that image with an eye towards how the image contributes to the continuing repression of women, (3) and propose other ways of speaking about the woman. In this chapter, for instance, I refer to the woman seated on the waters as an "alluring, idolatrous personified city," thinking not so much of the physical city of Rome as of Caesar and the network of leaders of the empire.

Revelation 17:1–6a: Alluring, Idolatrous City on a Scarlet Beast[2]

In Revelation 17:1–18, the prophet describes the alluring, idolatrous city in visceral images. In the remainder of the chapter, John interprets the symbols.

Revelation 17:1–6a: Describing the Alluring Idolatrous City

17:1–2. The angel's stated agenda is to show John the punishment of the alluring, idolatrous city, Rome (17:18). Before showing the punishment itself (which is revealed in 18:1–24), the angel reveals more of the identity, values, and practices of this idolatrous city (17:1–17). John draws extensively in this chapter from Jeremiah 50–51, in which God pronounces harsh judgment on the original Babylon. As God did what God threatened once before, so God can do it again.

The city is seated on "many waters," which John identifies as "peoples and multitudes and nations and languages" (17:15), a multicultural populace that imitates God's dominion (5:9; 7:9). In the multivalent symbolism of John, the waters represent the empire's dependence upon controlling the waters for commerce (especially food distribution) and military deployment. The waters are chaotic and they facilitate chaos. Rome imitates God as God rules the waters (Ps 29:3).[3]

The rulers of the earth have fornicated with Rome. Here fornication is a figure for making political alliances that violate God's hopes for human

---

2. On the sin of idolatry see, e.g., Ezek 16:15–17; Jer 1:21; 13:27.

3. In Jer 51:13, the waters include canals that carried water to fields for irrigation. Babylon controlled these waters with political ends in view.

community (e.g., Isa 23:17; Nah 3:4). As noted previously, the phrase "inhabitants of the earth" in this book refers to those who cooperate with the dragon and the beast (2:13; 3:10; 13:8). Recalling Jeremiah 51:7, John indicates that the rulers of the earth have become drunk through the wine of fornication. A drunk person can no longer perceive clearly and act faithfully as when sober. John thus explains why, drunk with Rome, the rulers of the earth now share Rome's punishment.

17:3–6a. The angel carried John away in the spirit, which means that John entered into an ecstatic state in which he received the next phases of the vision (cf. 1:10; 4:2; 21:10). He was in a wilderness—a multifaceted place of revelation, providence, and punishment. As God punished Israel with forty years in the wilderness, so God is punishing the empire and its partners. The wilderness is Babylon's fate (Jer 51:26, 29, 43).

The alluring, idolatrous city is sitting (enthroned) on a scarlet beast, a color similar to that of the red dragon (12:3), thus implying continuity with the dragon.[4] Moreover, the color scarlet was associated with wealth. John explained the blasphemous names, the seven heads, and the ten horns in 12:18—13:8 as the Roman Empire. The empire has made Caesar and its own life into an idolatry. The personified city and the beast are distinguishable, but inseparable and interconnected. The city is the nerve center of the beast.

The alluring, idolatrous personified city is clothed in scarlet and purple (expensive and associated with the upper class). The presence of gold, jewels, and pearls is the definition of excess. The alluring one holds "a golden cup full of abominations and the impurities of her fornication." Drawing loosely from the golden cup in Jeremiah 51:7 that held God's wrath, the prophet means that, while the city held out an attractive golden cup to the earth, it was deceptive in that its contents lead to punishment. For the cup contained abominations and impurities. The abominations were presaged in Daniel 9:27, where it refers to a statue of Zeus that Antiochus Epiphanes IV erected in the temple when conquering Jerusalem (cf. Dan 11:30; 12:10). John earlier identified fornication as abusive political alliances. Rome invited others to drink of a golden cup that actually contained a theological poison.

The city has a name on its forehead along the lines of 13:16 and 14:9.[5] The name is a "mystery" less in the sense that it is inscrutable and more in the sense that having a mystery also imitates God, who also has the big mystery: the news of the great apocalyptic transformation (1:20; 10:7). God's mystery is life-giving. The city's mystery is death-dealing.

4. The Greek words for "red" (12:3) and "scarlet" (17:3, 4; 18:12, 16) are different, but the symbolism of the red/scarlet color is the same here.

5. The mark on the forehead is another point at which the beast imitates God, who seals the faithful in this way: 7:3; 9:4; 14:1; 22:4.

Not only has the alluring city persuaded others to drunkenness, but the city itself is drunk on its own sense of self-importance. The city is "drunk with the blood of the saints and the blood of the witnesses to Jesus." The idea of drinking blood is repulsive. John likely has in mind martyrs under the altar (6:9–11), Antipas (2:13), and those from the wider community, for whom murder is ahead.[6]

John does not have alcohol addiction in mind, but that phenomenon is a model of what often happens in empire. People are attracted to the golden cup—literal alcohol. It tastes good. It loosens them up. It gives them a buzz. It increases their sense of self. For many people, alcohol addiction sets in before they know it. Alcohol becomes a bottled Caesar. Serious treatment— including giving up alcohol—is often the only way out.

The preacher could help the congregation see how empire offers its own values and behavior in a golden cup. But the cup is filled with "abominations and the impurities of . . . fornication"—that is, idolatries and other disobediences that may be fun for a moment, but set in motion processes that lead to ruin.

Revelation 17:6b–18: I Will Tell You the Mystery

17:6b–8. John reacts to the vision of the alluring, idolatrous city with great amazement (*thauma mega*), a response to something dramatic. While "amazement" is often a positive sense of awe, as in the wake of the miracles of Jesus and other wonder-generating events (e.g., Matt 8:27; 15:31; Mark 5:20; Luke 8:25; 9:43), it can also include incredulity, perplexity, negative surprise, or suspicious curiosity (e.g., Mark 6:6; 15:44; Luke 1:21; 14:38; John 3:7; 4:27; Acts 2:7; 3:12). The latter is in view as if to say, "When I saw her, I was incredulous: how could anything this bad come about?"

The angel then performs one of the most important functions in religion by making sense of what the listener sees and hears. In so doing, the angel provided the title for this commentary. "I will tell you the mystery." The word "mystery" (*mysterion*) occurs in its technical use as Babylon's mystery (cf. 13:5).[7] The angel will explain how the alluring, idolatrous city and its larger empire fit into the final drama of history. Moreover, this state-

---

6. Many interpreters think that John has just one group in mind. The word "and" in the expression "the blood of the saints and the blood of the witnesses to Jesus" functions epexegetically—that is, so that the second clause explains the first: "the blood of the saints, that is, the blood of the witnesses to Jesus." The choice of conclusion does not materially change the point.

7. This mystery is in imitation of God's mystery: 1:20; 10:7.

ment is a key to how to interpret the book of Revelation. While the book is not a simple allegory, its images do evoke associations. John has already given the identity of the alluring city, as well as the beast with seven heads and ten horns that carries the city.

The preacher might take a clue from the latter expression—"carries the city"—which suggests that forces around the Mediterranean basin consciously collude with the city to enforce empire. The sermon could explore who "carries" empire today. How do individuals and communities who are not directly part of the nerve center of today's empires nevertheless help keep those empires in place? For example, who votes for political candidates who in turn stand for empire?

John has earlier described God as one "who is and who was and who is to come," with emphasis on God coming to open the way to the new heaven and new earth (1:4, 8; 4:8). The prophet now plays on the motif of Rome imitating God by describing the empire in an expression with a decisive difference: "it was and *is not* and is to come." Many interpreters take the references "it was, is not, and is about to ascend" and "it was and is not and is to come" to refer to the Nero myth (discussed at 13:3). Nero was murdered ("he was and is not"), but many believed he would return to recommence his reign of terror ("is to come," "is about to ascend"). Few interpreters think that John expected Nero to return literally; most think that John used the return of Nero as a figure for an increase in the brutality associated with Nero.

John denotes the meaning of "the inhabitants of the earth" as "those whose names have not been written in the book of life from the foundation of the world."[8] They "will be amazed" (surprised, incredulous, perplexed) in the most negative way when they see the beast on its way to destruction. Moreover, they are even more surprised when they realize they will accompany it.

For a Bible study or sermon, this passage provides an easy way for the leader to let the book of Revelation offer its own guidance in how to interpret it. The leader could begin with the interpretive principle of 17:7 and illustrate that principle from this passage and other passages.

A preacher and a congregation might identify with John's expression of incredulity (17:6b). Through the revelation that began in 1:20, the prophet has seen the dragon and the beasts for what they are. But John's statement of surprise suggests that aspects of the alluring, idolatrous city only now become as clear, as when someone says, "I knew it was bad, but I

---

8. On the book of life, see the comments on 3:5; 13:8; 20:12, 15; 21:27; 22:9–10; 22:18–19.

did not realize how bad." A pastor might identify circumstances in today's culture of which the same might be said. For example, many Eurocentric people, especially in the middle, upper middle, and upper classes, do not understand the distorting power of racism.

In 17:8b, "The inhabitants of the earth . . . will be amazed," John seeks to look at the final judgment from the perspective of the followers of the empire. The preacher might help the congregation try to imagine how the "inhabitants of the earth" today (those enrolled with empire) interpret—or misinterpret—signs that empire is under judgment. Many people today rationalize the importance of maintaining empire and recommit themselves to threat and violence as the means. How might the church try to appeal to such folk to take a second look at their own perspectives?

Revelation 17:9–14: Current Events in the World of John

John now explains selective elements of the vision of 17:1–8 as representing reigns, events, or conditions that have recently taken place, are currently happening, or will soon occur. John points to these things as indicators that the final transformation is underway.

17:9–10. I have had a lot of fun with John's opening remark, "This calls for a mind that has wisdom," by quipping, "You bet it calls for a mind that has wisdom." Wisdom is the capacity to interpret and respond to life from God's perspective. In the apocalyptic movement, wisdom comes from the revelation of John.

At one level, according to John, the seven heads of 13:7 are the seven hills of Rome. In 71 CE, the Romans minted a coin with Vespasian (the Caesar at the time) on one side and the goddess Roma seated on seven hills on the other side.[9] The reference to "seven hills" is both a geographical reference and a theological indictment, as the seven hills imply Rome imitating God.

At a more difficult level, the seven heads are seven Caesars, five of whom have fallen, one of whom is living (and presumably on the throne), and one more is still ahead (though this last monarch will reign only a little while). This is a way of indicating that Caesarism does not have long to live.

17:11–13. "As for the beast . . . it is an eighth, but it belongs to the seven, and it goes to destruction." Commentators sometimes become engrossed in attempting to identify the specific Caesars mentioned here.[10]

---

9. Aune, *Revelation 17–22*, 920–22.

10. For an exceptional summary of possibilities, see Aune, *Revelation 17–22*, 947.

While I admire these detailed investigations, preachers can get John's over-arching theological point without absolute resolution of such matters.

Consistent with John's use of the number seven to represent divine control, the line of seven probably signifies that, while Caesars and imperial life may have been idolatrous and unfaithful, they are under God's rule. The first five emperors typify Caesars who have died. The sixth is Domitian, the one who is alive at the time of John and whose replacement will rule only a short time. The eighth and final figure "was and is not." John believed that the end-time would be short, but the reference to the Nero myth reminds listeners that it would be violent.

With Daniel 7:7:8, 20, and 24 in the background, John envisions ten horns as ten lesser rulers. As in the case of the seven Caesars, the specific identity of these rulers is unclear. While they have not yet assumed power, they are included in the rulers "of the whole world" of 16:14. They are "horns," which means they have real authority, but their rule will be brief, since the denouement of the current age is fast approaching. John may have in mind client rulers, as well as other officials and citizens whose power is tied to the system of the alluring, idolatrous city. The Parthians might be in view, as they had an uneasy truce with Rome.

This group of rulers represents—again—systemic opposition to the values and practices of God. The lesser rulers join with Caesar in making war on the Lamb. While the final eschatological battle for the empire is in view here, a war has long been underway in the form of persecution as the empire has used its power to try to silence witnesses (on this point, see for comparison Rev 19:9).

17:14. John reaches a new rhetorical height in describing Jesus as "Lord of lords and King of kings." Although this transcendent phrase oc-curs often in Christian hymnody, liturgy, and preaching, it occurs in the book of Revelation only here and in 19:16.[11] In a delicious reverse parody, the ruler of ancient Babylon had been known as "ruler of rulers" (e.g., Ezek 26:7; Dan 2:37). Drawing on its use in Judaism (Deut 10:17; Ps 136:3; Dan 2:47; 2 Macc 13:4; 1 En. 9:4; cf. 1 Tim 6:15), the title affirms both the abso-lute sovereignty of God operating through Jesus over all over rulers and the accountability of all nations, peoples, languages, and tongues for how they have made use of God's gifts.

On the one hand, the Lamb conquered through his witnessing death (5:5). The faithful conquer through the same means (12:11). On the other hand, while those things release the possibility of the Realm into the

11. In *Messiah*, Handel conflates Rev 19:9/1 Tim 6:15 with Rev 7:15 to get the ex-alted musical phrase at the center of the "Hallelujah."

bloodstream of the world, the cure awaits. The patient (the world) is still sick. Something more is needed: final victory.

The "called and chosen and faithful" are with the Lamb. The three terms (called, chosen, faithful) denote the one community of Jesus' followers (14:1–5). Elsewhere John calls Jesus "faithful" (1:5; 3:14; 19:1L). The church, consequently, is to be faithful in the same way as Jesus, who continued his witness to death, as did Antipas (2:13; cf. 2:10). To be faithful is to continue to witness in the face of the ultimate threat.

The role of the called, chosen, and faithful community in the final eschatological conflict is not clear. They are "with" Jesus. While John does not actually describe a battle, listeners are surely to suppose that one takes place. and that the faithful who are called and chosen are present. Commentators sometimes surmise that John imagines the church being actively involved as combatants. However, nothing here or in 19:11–19 *directly* suggests this.[12] The church seems to be present, but in a role similar to that of observer, while the Lamb carries out the defining transformation.[13]

I indicated at the outset that one of my disappointments in the book of Revelation is that it does not vest real authority for social transformation in the called, chosen, and faithful. While they participate in the final eschatological struggle, the Lamb is the real agent of change.

The preacher could venture from this text into a sustained discussion of these matters. To the degree that the contemporary world might become more like the new heaven and the new earth, many preachers agree that human agents need to take an active role, even while recognizing that the divine lure makes their work possible. As indicated elsewhere, at the level of contemporary theological authority, I reject the idea that the called, chosen, and faithful are "with Jesus" in order to inflict pain onto others.

12. Some commentators note that apocalyptic literature occasionally envisions the faithful taking an active role in the final destruction of the wicked (e.g., 1 En. 38:5; 91:12; 96:1; esp. 98:12). However, John has left no tripwire in the text to suggest that he envisions the faithful fighting in this direct way. Moreover, I contend that at 19:14 and 19 the army with Jesus is made up of hosts from heaven.

13. Aune, *Revelation 17–22*, 957, notes that apocalyptic literature contains models of both passive and active engagement on the part of the faithful in the final battle. He thinks that the active model is reflected in 7:1–9; 14:1–5, and 17:4. But, as noted in discussion at the pertinent passages, I think that the relative silence of these passages on active roles suggests that such participation is not part of John's theological system.

Revelation 17:15-18: God Put It in Their Hearts
to Carry Out God's Purpose

17:15. The angel continues to unfold the mystery. The waters on which the alluring, idolatrous city sits are the "peoples and multitudes and nations and languages" of the Roman Empire (17:1).

17:16. The book contains no more vivid demonstration of the principle that a community is punished by the means by which it disobeys than 17:16. The city—the governing nerve center of the empire—practiced exploitation and ruled by threat and violence. John anticipates the group represented by the ten horns will develop a hate for this city. He does not speculate on a reason for this pathology. But, according to the Nero myth, the resuscitated emperor could lead the Parthian armies to attack Rome. Beyond such a specific proposal, it is easy to imagine that people in the empire outside of the immediate ruling classes grow tired of being exploited.

Having been ruled by violence on the part of Rome, the ten horns respond in kind by launching a civil war, leaving the city desolate and naked.[14] Listeners would hear John applying Ezekiel 23:25–29 to the first century: divine judgment on a city by means of fire and by stripping the city bare.[15] John envisions the rebels eating the city's flesh. They burn the alluring city with fire, thus anticipating aspects of 19:20; 20:9, 10, 14–15.

John makes a direct theological move in 17:17, explaining what is really at work in the process of destruction: "God has put it into their hearts to carry out [God's] purpose by agreeing to give their [dominion] to the beast, until the words of God will be fulfilled."[16] The punishment of God takes place through conflict until Babylon is destroyed. God does not come from outside the world with condemnation, but acts through forces in history.

On the one hand, a preacher may be attracted to the overlapping notions of punishment taking place through the means of disobedience and judgment taking place through things that happen in history. A preacher might point to these very things taking place in relationship to empire in the early twenty-first century.

On the other hand, preachers and communities can let our perceptions become functional idols. We sometimes interpret historical circumstances in ways that serve our limited, self-serving aims. Furthermore, a preacher should never celebrate destruction by violence, even under the

14. For nations turning on one another, see Ezek 38:21 and Zech 14:13.

15. On nakedness and fire as figures for judgment, see 3:18 and 16:15; see also Isa 3:17; 47:3; Jer 13:2; 34:24; Lam 1:8, Ezek 16:37–41; Hos 2:5; Mic 3:3; Nah 3:5.

16. On God effecting judgment by working through historical process, see Isa 5:25–30; 9:8–12; Jer 5:10–17; Ezek 16:35–43; Hab 1:5–10.

rubrics above. Even when a violent person or community may beget its own end by violence, I believe the preacher should lament that violence. Even when violence destroys evil, the violence itself is to be lamented.

Revelation 18:1–24: Dirge Over Babylon

Although John employs four literary forms in Revelation 18:1–24, this passage in its present form and location has the broad feeling and function of a funeral dirge: lamentation over the fall of the city, even while recognizing that the collapse of the city relieves the world of a node of evil and opens the way for reconstructing a just community.[17] In a sense, John conducts a funeral liturgy for the empire while it still appears to rule. This suggests a possibility for worship and preaching. The service of worship could be organized as a funeral service for empire today, and the sermon could have the character of a funeral homily. The preacher might describe the future of North America or the local community in the way John describes Rome. This might help the congregation envision the outcome of present patterns of disobedience.

The passage falls into four main sections that might form the outline of a sermon. (1) 18:1–3 announces the occasion for the lament—the fall of Babylon; (2) 18:4–8 guides the community in how to respond ("Come out of [the city]"); (3) 18:9–19 focuses the dirge on the end of the activity of rulers, merchants, and sailors; and (4) 18:20–24 concludes with an angel making a dramatic prophetic gesture—throwing a stone into the sea.

Revelation 18:1–3: Babylon is Fallen

The liturgist, so to speak, is an angel from heaven. John underscores the reliability of the liturgy by describing the angel as authoritative, illuminating the earth, and speaking in a mighty voice. Although Rome is a fully functioning empire at the time the angel speaks, the angel announces that the empire is dead.[18] The angel is proleptic in assuming that the empire has

---

17. The types of literature are (1) prophetic taunt song adapted to serve a dirge, vv. 1–3; (2) directive to flee the situation, vv. 4–8; (3) formal funeral dirge materials, vv. 9–19; (4) prophetic gesture (symbol). These parts form the structure of the sermon suggested in the next paragraph.

18. John joins other prophets in adapting elements of the taunt song to funeral practices that lament the death of cities, e.g., Isa 14:4–23; Lam 1, 2, 4; Amos 5:1–3 Ezek 26:15–28; 27:1–8, 26–36.

already expired. To those with antagonistic relationships with the empire, this perspective is consoling. "You do not have to fear this city any longer."

The angel explains what has happened to the empire in language borrowed from Isaiah 21:9, where Isaiah announces the death of Babylon. Where once Rome had been a lively city, it is now a dwelling place of demons, "a haunt of every foul spirit," and every foul bird and hateful beast. The demons are Satan's assistants. The birds and beasts are "foul" or unclean (*akatharos*).[19] In Judaism, clean and unclean refer not to the presence or absence of dirt and filth, but to the degree to which things were in a place to contribute to community. While the particular assignments of clean or unclean might seem arbitrary today, the presence of the unclean creatures here means that the city is no longer capable of sustaining community.[20]

Recalling 14:8 and 17:1–6, the angel explains why the empire has fallen. The nations have drunk of the wrath of her fornication—i.e., an idolatrous, exploitative, violent way of life. The rulers of the earth—rulers of client nations, officials and leading citizens of the empire, and/or leaders of the imperial cult—have fornicated with Rome—that is, they have joined in the empire's idolatrous, exploitative, and violent way of life. The merchants grew wealthy by networking with Rome, while most of the population lived in economically tenuous circumstances, in squalor, and many were enslaved.[21] Caesar and the imperial clique are the demons and foul spirit, unclean birds and beasts. They make the community a foul place to live. What individuals and groups play such roles today?

A preacher could join John in anticipating such a future that already has roots.

Revelation 18:4–8: Come Out of Her!

18:4–5. Isaiah and Jeremiah called people to flee from the original Babylon before God destroyed it (e.g., Jer 51:6; Isa 48:20; 52:11). Continuing to update aspects of the earlier prophets, John hears God plead, "Come out of [the Roman Empire], my people."[22] What does it mean to "come out"?

19. On conditions like these, see Isa 13:20–22; 34:10–11; Jer 50:39; 41:37.

20. For examples of cities God punished similarly: Isa 13:19–22; 34:11–15; Jer 9:9–11; 51:37; Zeph 12:13–14.

21. The word *strenuous* can be translated "luxury," as in the NRSV. But a better rendering in 18:3b is "arrogance," as in 2 Kgs 19:28. The merchants grew wealthy by taking advantage of the power of Roman arrogance.

22. Scholars debate whether the speaker is God, Christ, or an angel. The text does not directly say. But God speaks in the passages from the Prophets, on which John models this plea (Jer 51:6; Isa 48:20; 52:11).

Commentators seem to universally agree that it does not mean to physically leave the Roman Empire. The immediate context (18:3) indicates that those under judgment (1) commit fornication (engage in idolatry) and (2) grow wealthy from the city's luxury by exploiting others economically and socially (cf. 18:9–19). "Coming out" thus seems to mean at least two related things: refusing to participate in the imperial cult (cf. 13:11–18) and refusing to participate in the network of relationships represented by the imperial cult. To "come out," members of the church may need to learn to work and live off the imperial grid. Because many trade unions and social groups in Roman society included rites and foods derived from the imperial cult, church members may need to find alternate ways to make a living (see 2:14, 20).[23] Furthermore, many economic activities sanctioned by the imperial order exploited people below them in the social pyramid. Refusing to participate in imperial relationships might include refusing military service—for those who kill with the sword will be killed by it (13:10).

John regularly warns the community that suffering is part of the faithful life. In the Letter to Smyrna, the prophet cites consequences that befall those who "come out": they suffer affliction; they are slandered; they are victims of legal action; and they are impoverished, perhaps because they have "come out" of aspects of the economy that depend on the imperial system (2:9–10).

The two reasons for coming out of the city are intimately related: "so that you do not take part in her sins and so that you do not share in [the city's] plagues." Those who participate in the practices of the empire take part in sin. Those who sin will be punished with the empire via the plagues. The proviso "so that you do not share in [the city's] plagues" does not mean that the congregations will not suffer during the season of suffering as a result of God destroying the city. Rather, Jesus' followers will not be condemned with Rome and fall victim to God's final punishment of the empire.

The faithful should take special care to exit the city because the city's sin is heaped as high as heaven (cf. Jer 51:8–10; Gen 11:1–9). Mountain-sized sin requires mountain-sized punishment. When Israel felt forgotten, biblical writers stress that God remembered the promises God made (e.g., Gen 8:1; Exod 2:24; 6:5; Ps 98:3). Nor does God forget sin.[24]

While the punishment for the empire may be irrevocable, individuals (especially in the churches) still have time to "come out."

---

23. Blount, *Revelation*, 58–59, 63, 326.

24. God will not forget the cry of the martyrs (6:9–11). On God remembering sin, cf. Ps 25:7; 137:7.

18:6–7. This is a new wrinkle in the language of rendering to the city what the city rendered to others. God will repay the city double for its misdeeds and will prepare a double draught in the cup the city has mixed—the wine of the wrath of the city's fornication. Scholars acknowledge ambiguity in interpretation—it is not clear whether John means that the empire will literally receive double punishment, or whether the expressions "double for her deeds" and "double draft" are idioms meaning that the empire will receive everything it deserves.[25] Because John suggests that the city should receive "a like measure of torment and grief" (18:7b), and because double punishment would seem unjust in a world of *lex talionis* (punishment in proportion to the crime), I agree with those who think the meaning is that Rome will receive the full measure of punishment (not double).[26]

The question also arises regarding the agent to whom the command "Render to [the alluring city" is given. While occasional interpreters think John has the church in mind, this is most unlikely, since John does not elsewhere present the faithful in this role. In other places, John envisions angels or groups operating within history as God's instruments of punishment (e.g., 16:12–16; 17:15–17).

As listeners know from 13:1–5, 11–18, and 17:1–6, the city glorifies itself instead of glorifying God. The NRSV renders the verb *strēniaō* as "lived luxuriously," but that word could also be rendered "lived arrogantly" (as with the noun *strēnos*, "arrogant," in 18:3). Indeed, this arrogance surfaces when the city declares that it sits on the throne as royalty and will never see grief. According to Isaiah, the first Babylon had said much the same thing (Isa 47:8).

The city reinforces an aspect of social discrimination of the time by declaring that it is not a widow, a figure representing the most vulnerable people in antiquity. The city assumes that widowhood, with its grief and survival anxiety, will be an ongoing, everyday part of life, in contrast to God, who looks forward to a transformed world free of things that make for grief and tears (e.g., 7:17; 21:4).

18:8. The empire lived without reference to God. For a long time, self-glorification and self-serving behavior on the part of the ruling classes appeared to protect their power, as well as insulate them from the survival anxiety that daily dogged many in the empire. Consequently, the city will receive the same "measure of grief and torment" that the city administered

25. These expressions are inspired by Isa 40:2 and Jer 16:18; 17:17. Scholarship on these passages has not reached a consensus on whether the prophets meant double punishment or used this expression to mean everything deserved.

26. On proportional punishment, see Exod 21:23–25; Lev 24:17–20; Deut 19:21; Isa 34:8; and Ezek 9:10.

to others. The grief and torment will come upon the city "in a single day," in the form of plagues (pestilence, mourning, and famine—e.g., Rev 6:8; 14:10; 16:16; 18:11, 15, 19) and fire (8:5–8; 9:18; 16:8; 19:20; 20:9, 10 14). These things refer to destructive social conditions, to which John soon turns to show the results of this judgment from the mighty God.

The end will come quickly. It will involve disease from pestilence, mourning over the dead, and famine. The city will burn as even the temple in Jerusalem burned. Indeed, the conditions and fate of Rome will be similar to those of Jerusalem and the temple in 70 CE.

Rome, however, does not perceive the desperation of its situation. Self-awareness and God-awareness are serious problems for the empire. A preacher could use this text to help the congregation think about how important it is for the larger culture and the congregation to develop self-perceptions that are informed by critical theological analysis. Arrogant self-glorification on the part of Rome left the city unable to process the very information that could prevent the plagues and fire from coming upon the city.

Revelation 18:9–19: Three Laments over Fallen Babylon

John now recites the lamentations of three groups who are particularly grieved over the fall of the empire. By participating in the empire, they all received money, power, control, and social standing. The demise of Rome means the demise of their privileged world. These groups are the rulers, merchants, and the seafaring industry.

The groups represent three key elements in the Roman system: (1) political officials, who control and profit from government and military; (2) merchants, who control and profit from buying and selling agricultural products and other goods; and (3) the seafaring business, which controls and profits from transportation and communications that take place over the sea.

John models these laments on Ezekiel 26:1—28:19, where Ezekiel announces judgment against Tyre and portrays them as a great ship, loaded with a large inventory of goods, merchants, and sailors. The ship docks at every significant port on the Mediterranean. But a great storm sends the ship to the bottom. John's message: what happened to Tyre is happening to Rome.[27]

A preacher can identify contemporary analogies to each category— the ruling class, merchants, and the transportation and communications

27. Note that rulers, merchants, and seafarers appear in Ezek 27:35, 26, 29.

industries—whose money, power, control, and social standing derive directly from contemporary empire. In addition, the preacher can criticize the ways in which these groups comprise a system with various parts depending on one another and other parts of the system in places that serve them.

On January 17, 1961, outgoing President Dwight D. Eisenhower warned the United States that a military-industrial complex was moving towards "unwarranted influence," which would result in "the disastrous rise of misplaced power." Over the years, the military and industry have expanded and changed, so that the "military-industrial complex" is now a much more wide-ranging empire involving governments, transnational corporations, financial industry, and political/racial/religious/economic ideologies.

Revelation 18:9–11: Rulers Weep Over the Fall of Babylon

The rulers in view here are likely client-monarchs, including government officials and the ruling classes. They committed fornication—bought power and benefit based on participation in idolatry, exploitation, and threat. When they see the city fallen, and they smell the smoke of its funeral pyre, they engage in traditional customs of mourning—weeping and wailing. The cry of "Alas" or *ouai* is a double entendre, as it is primarily a cry of mourning (e.g., 1 Sam 4:7–8; Jer 10:19) while sometimes spoken at judgment (Isa 3:9, 11; Ezek 24:6; Luke 6:24–26). However, rather than help the empire in its distress, this network of rulers stands far off, afraid that they will be caught up in the torment afflicting the alluring, idolatrous city.

Rome had a negatively circular relationship with these rulers: the empire offered them power and luxury, but coerced them if they did not participate. Now, the empire is helpless, and the rulers abandon it. In view of their commitment to one another, the alluring city and the rulers receive the punishment they deserve.

Revelation 18:11–17a: Merchants Weep Over Babylon

The merchants also "weep and mourn" in traditional expressions of grief because "no one buys their cargo anymore." The merchants are in a co-dependent relationship with Rome, as are the rulers. As often happens, when one part of a system fails, the system fails as a whole. The merchants' lamentation has two parts: vv. 11–14 and vv. 15–17a.

18:11–14. In 18:11–14, the angel lists goods in eight groups. Most of these wares were for the upper classes: (1) precious metals and stones—gold, silver, jewels, pearls; (2) fine cloth—fine linen, purple and scarlet cloth, and silk; (3) things made from scented wood and from ivory; (4) products made from costly wood, brass, iron, and marble; (5) spices and fragrances—cinnamon, spice, myrrh, and frankincense; (6) wine, oil, fine flour, and grain; (7) animals and transportation equipment for the upper class—cattle, sheep, horses, and carriages; and (8) human beings, or slaves. About 20 percent of the population of the empire was enslaved. Slavery was a key to the prosperity of the upper classes. The empire treats a slave—a human being made in the image of God—as nothing more than a piece of cargo.

John plays on the word fruit: "The fruit (*opōros*) for which your soul longed has gone from you." In Jewish tradition, "fruit" (*karpos*, a synonym for *opōros*) can literally refer to produce from the tree or vine, but can also figuratively refer to the life of an individual or community (e.g., Jer 17:10; 21:14; Hos 10:1; Amos 6:12; Mic 7:13). The merchants desired material rewards. But the real fruit of their life is judgment. By contrast, those who join the movement towards the Realm of God will eat fruit from the tree of life (22:2).

In the third seal, John intimated a shortage of basic goods (such as wheat and barley) for the lower classes, while fine goods were still available for the wealthy (6:5–6). Not only are "the dainties and the splendor lost, never to be found again," but as empire dies, all social classes are deprived of the basic resources.[28]

Revelation 18:15–17a follows the same general structure. The merchants bemoan the city. They connect the elite goods (and the approach to life they represent) to the empire by recalling the description of the city in 17:4–5, mentioning fine linen, the colors purple and scarlet, gold, jewels, and pearls.

Revelation 18:17b–19: Seafaring Industry Weeps Over Babylon

The Mediterranean Sea was a Roman lake. The third lament involves those in the shipping industry: owners, managers, and laborers. As we have noted, ships transported agricultural goods, manufactured products, and people (including government officials, the military, and slaves). Like rulers and merchants, shipmasters and others in the industry stand far off and watch the burning city. The water on which they made their living could help extinguish the fire, but they make no effort to put out the fires. Instead, they weep and moan and throw dust on their heads—all customary gestures of lamentation.[29] The sea-based commerce on which they grew wealthy has ended.

28. A preacher who uses a big screen could develop a PowerPoint of these items.

29. For throwing dust on the head, see Josh 7:6; Job 2:12; Lam 2:10; Ezek 27:30.

Their question has an air of resignation. "Who was like the great city?" The scene reminds me of arriving to preach at a large downtown church building, now occupied by twenty-five worshipers on a Sunday morning, and someone says, "Oh, you should have seen the crowds we used to have."

The rulers, merchants, and those in the shipping industry do not "get it." They think of Rome as having been a "great city." They do not recognize it was disobedient to the point of no return. They lament the fall of the city because of what they lose in its fall. They do not recognize that the fall of the city is the judgment of God on both the city and their part in it. Rome is now fully exposed for what it is, and so are the ruling classes; they are complicit.

An imaginative preacher might let the form and function of the text shape the form and function of the sermon on the dirges. The preacher could identify groups in our culture who are in contract with contemporary empire, and who are or will be in distress as aspects of empire weaken and fall and prepare a sermon as a dirge for them. A preacher could begin with the categories suggested by text itself—government officials and those in the wider ruling classes, merchants (commercial enterprises), and the transportation and communication industries.

For preaching, this situation is both a cautionary tale and prompts a pause for contemplating positive potential. The cautionary tale warns against entering into relationships based on empire. Such relationships are self-serving and self-destructive. A household, congregation, or wider community that buys into empire is laying the fire that will create the smoke signaling its collapse. At the same time, when seeing the smoke signaling the burning of the old, the preacher might look for signs of a new Jerusalem in the space cleared by the burning.

The rulers of the earth had plenty of warning regarding the nature and final disposition of the city. Indeed, Revelation 6:1—18:8 is essentially thirteen chapters of red alert. A preacher could help today's congregation recognize warning signs in our own culture.

Revelation 18:20: The Final Verdict in Favor of the Faithful

With the cry for the vindication of the martyrs, Revelation 6:9–11 is in the background of 18:20. John explains again that God has honored that cry. In 18:20, an unidentified voice—presumably from heaven—draws on the model of Jeremiah 51:58 to call for the saints, apostles, and prophets, and those in heaven, to rejoice over the scene they have just witnessed (the eschatological defeat Babylon). The saints are the faithful who have come out of Rome. The figure of the apostles likely represents the twelve whom Jesus chose, and the stream of faithful from their day into the time of John. While the prophets could be the figures from the Torah, Prophets, and Writings, they are more likely the prophets of the early church—figures, including John, who transmit messages from God and who point the community to the importance of faithful endurance (1:3; 19:20; 22:7, 9–10, 12–15; 1 Cor 12:28; Eph 2:20; 3:5; 4:11).

John employs a courtroom image to explain the reason for the rejoicing. "God has given judgment for you [that is, for the saints, apostles, and prophets, as well as the martyrs] against [the alluring idolatrous city, and the empire]." While the book of Revelation contains a dossier of the crimes of Babylon, John specifies the worst of these crimes in 18:24 as murdering the prophets and saints (cf. 6:9–11; 16:5; 19:19). Rome is guilty of something like premeditated murder in the first degree.

The prophet may have in mind actual Roman prosecution of the saints, apostles, and prophets taking place in John's moment or in a coming season. The preacher might bring to mind Christians today whose public witness prompts empire to embarrass, discredit, or disempower them. Some witnesses are jailed when engaging in civil disobedience or prophetic action-symbols of the kind discussed in 18:21–24.

As John speaks, the prophet is still in the mode of future vision. In real time, Rome is still in power. But this scenario of rejoicing reinforces those who have already come out of Rome and encourages those who have hesitated to do so before the final gavel comes down on history.

A preacher who can avoid becoming hokey might develop a sermon around the image of legal proceedings taking place before the *real* supreme court in which God is the chief justice. John has amassed reasons for the guilt of the empire. The preacher can easily amass similar evidence from today's world.

A preacher might also play on the contrast between the circumstances and mood of the rulers, merchants, and sea-farers, and the alluring, idolatrous city with those of the saints, apostles, and prophets. The former lived in deceptive luxury and appearance of power that left them feeling insulated and safe. In fact, those very things were their downfall. Now they are exposed and grieving. At the same time, the city persecutes the saints, apostles, and prophets so they experience discomfort in the present. However, at the apocalypse, God will change that discomfort to rejoicing.

Revelation 18:21–24: The Eerie Silence of Defeated Babylon

John ends this part of the vision with a dramatic prophetic action. The prophet acts out the message (e.g., 1 Kgs 11:29–32; Isa 8:1–4; Jer 19:1–13). A mighty angel (the presence of which underscores the importance) picks up a stone similar to a large millstone and throws it into the sea as a symbol of what will happen to the latter-day Babylon on the model of Jeremiah 51:63–64. The power of the empire will disappear just as the millstone disappears into the water.

John lists five things that will not come from the city anymore:[30] (1) the sound of harpists and minstrels and of flautists and trumpeters, (2) an artisan of any trade, (3) the sound of the millstone, (4) the light of a lamp, and (5) the voice of bridegroom and bride. These things are important for the life of a community to go on—flour ground by the millstone, furniture and other things made by artisans, families promulgated by the bridegroom and bride, and joy signaled by the musicians. However, they will be no more. G. K. Beale points out that just as Rome took these things from the saints, so God will take them from Rome.[31] The result will be the equivalent to today's desolate city block.

The prophet then articulates three reasons God is casting the empire into the sea. First, the merchants were the magnates, the "great ones," whose activity has already been revealed. They exploited workers to create expensive goods for the ruling class while the workers themselves lived in poor conditions (6:5–7; 18:11–17).

Second, the late, great city deceived other nations of the earth by sorcery (*pharmakeia*, from which we get our word "pharmacy").[32] Sorcery attempted to manipulate situations in one's favor. Rome manipulated other nations to buy into the Roman worldview by means of the deception of idolatry (9:20–21). Rome could have used every single one of the things in the previous list for God's purposes of blessing, but instead used them to deceive other communities into thinking that alliance with Rome and idolatry (rather than covenant with God) was the pathway to them.

Third, the empire is responsible for "the blood of prophets and of saints, and of all who have been slaughtered on earth." John has earlier charged the empire with the murder of the martyrs (6:9–11; 16:6; 17:6; 19:2). The prophet now extends that charge: the empire is responsible for the murder of "all who have been slaughtered on earth," that is, all whom the empire has

---

30. Jer 25:10 may inspire this list.

31. Beale, *Book of Revelation*, 920.

32. For negative judgments on sorcery and deception, see Isa 47:9, 12; Nah 3:4–5.

put to death in order to enforce its will.[33] Rome—and all such bodies—are finally accountable to God for what they do with the resources for life that God provides. Here it is again explicit, "If you kill with the sword, with the sword you must be killed" (13:10b).

Revelation 19:1–10: Heaven Sings Over the Defeat of Babylon

Revelation 19:1–10 is a response in heaven to the command of 18:20 to rejoice over the defeat of the alluring, idolatrous city. The response is initially in the form of hymns sung by different voices with distinct nuances of meaning (19:1b–8). The three bodies of hymnic celebration in (a) 19:1b–3, (b) 19:4–5, (c) 19:6–8, sound a counter-melody to the three dirges of 18:9–19. The celebration modulates towards the eschatological banquet (19:9) and a pastoral reminder to worship God alone, a reminder that opens a window into an issue in John's congregations (19:10).

Although the celebration in this passage reaches an ecstatic height, the defeat of the Roman Empire is the penultimate word on the present era of history (17:1–19:10). The ultimate word is the destruction of the beasts and the dragon in Revelation 19:11–20:15. Only then does John reveal the new heaven and the new earth in its transformed splendor.

Revelation 19:1-4: God's Judgments Are True and Just

The language describing the great multitude here and in 7:9 suggests that the crowds in 7:9 and 19:1 are the same: a vast crowd in heaven.[34] If so, the great heavenly multitude now has the satisfaction of seeing something in progress (the final steps towards the new Jerusalem) that they celebrated proleptically in 7:9.

19:1. The multitude exults, "Hallelujah," transliterated from Hebrew, and meaning, "Praise Yah [Yahweh/God]." John uses "Hallelujah" for the first time here, perhaps because the prophet saved this signature exclamation for a high moment.[35] Salvation, glory, and power come from God, not

33. Jer 51:49 charges Babylon with deaths of the people of Israel and of all other deaths that Babylon has caused.

34. Some scholars see the great multitude in 19:1 as a choir of angels, as, perhaps, in 5:11 or 7:11.

35. This expression is particularly associated with the psalms that celebrate God as sovereign of the universe as revealed through enthronement or victories (e.g., Pss. 24, 29, 96, 97).

from the now decimated alluring, idolatrous city. Moreover, these qualities point not just to immediate victory but to the revealing of the new heaven and new earth yet to come.

The early twenty-first century is a world of rhetorical overstatement. It is hardly "awesome" to place an order for a soft drink and have the server respond with that word. Advertisers promise existential equivalents of salvation, glory, and power through wearing particular brands of clothes and driving certain automobiles. The preacher might reflect with the congregation on when they would *really* say "Hallelujah" (or, perhaps, "awesome").

19:2. The hymn gives three reasons for exulting in "Hallelujah." John has developed all of these reasons earlier. (1) God's judgments are true and just (or right) (16:7). (2) Since God judges truthfully and rightly, God condemned the alluring idolatrous city who corrupted the earth with fornication (18:1–6). (3) In so doing, God avenged the blood of the servants (6:9–11; 16:6; cf. Deut 32:43).

Preachers who are attracted to three-point sermons could use the three "points" of this hymn as the outline for a sermon. The preacher could fill out each point with supporting material from elsewhere in the book.

19:3-4. The same multitude continues singing in 18:3–4. They raise a "Hallelujah" over the smoke of the city. Again they celebrate the final smoke—18:8, 9, 18—as they proleptically did in 14:11. Evidently the punishment never ends. For the fire of the burning Babylon never goes out: "smoke rises up forever and ever."

As if zooming a camera into a close-up, John shows the twenty-four elders and the four living creatures falling down in worshiping God who is on the throne, as they did in 4:1-11 (Cf. 5:6–10, 11–14; 7:11–12; 7:15–18). In their earlier appearances, the elders and the creatures pointed to God's awesome liberating power. With the defeat of Babylon, God has proven that power is trustworthy.

The preacher might join John in asking the congregation, "Do you want to come down on the right side of history?" John's vision foresees the fall of Babylon, even though its actual fall is yet to come. The congregation can choose whether it becomes part of the smoke rising Babylon or sings with the heavenly choruses.

Revelation 19:5: A Voice Calls the Small and Great to Praise God

19:5. A voice from the throne invites God's servants, that is all who fear (reverence) God, to praise God. The invitation includes small and great, thus offering an implicit critique of the social pyramid in antiquity. In that social world people lived in classes with fairly rigid barriers between them. Here, people from across the pyramid join in praise for the liberating work of God. This indicates that some in the "great" category recognize the sovereignty of God and the deception, idolatry, exploitation, and brutality of the empire. By praising God, they commit themselves to be part of the journey to the Realm.

John's reference to the small and the great raises the issue of class. Congregations are often made up predominantly of one social class. What would it take for the congregation to reflect the community of the Realm by reaching farther towards both the small and great ends of the class spectrum? If a congregation is middle class, what can happen to help people with fewer—and more—material resources to become a genuine part of the community?

Revelation 19:6-8: The Lamb and the Church Come Together

19:6–7a. A multitude responds immediately to the command of 19:5. Scholars generally think this is an earthly crowd corresponding to the heavenly multitude of 19:1b–4. This choir raises its "Hallelujah" for two reasons: First, God is taking the next steps towards the final manifestation of God's reign and the coming of the new heaven and the new earth. Second, the marriage supper of the Lamb has come and the church is bedecked in fine linen, "the righteous deeds of the saints."

With regard to the first reason, apocalyptic theologians believed that God is always sovereign. Things take place either by God's direct initiation or by God's permission. The brokenness of the world—including the phenomenon of Empire—thus takes place under God's aegis. But, God had set a time by which to end the brokenness and to replace the old world with the new. That time has come. The defeat of Babylon (the two beasts) is the defeat of the most evident representative of Satan (the dragon), but the final defeat of Satan, while still to come, is guaranteed.

The core message of the book of Revelation can reduce to two words: "God rules." God has ultimate power. God is now using that power to bring all things into the kind of mutually supportive world God wants. Consequently, the multitude cries out in a voice like the sound of many waters and like great thunderpeals: "Hallelujah."[36]

19:7b-8. John moves to a marriage image that presages Revelation 21:1–22:5. The apocalyptic moment has come for the marriage of the Lamb

36. The geophysical phenomena intensify the experience. On loud waters and many thunders, see 14:1–5.

as bridegroom to the church as bride. John makes use of a tradition in Judaism that interprets marriage as a covenant and that applies this notion to God and Israel. God is the bridegroom and Israel the bride (e.g., Isa 54:1; Jer 2:2; 31; 32:32; Ezek 16:8; Hos 1:1–3:5).[37]

While the image of the bride is not as troubling with respect to gender as that of the great whore as the alluring, idolatrous city, the preacher still needs to call attention to its problematic character. As is well-known, women usually had secondary status in the social pyramid of antiquity. They were to be passive in arranging the marriage. Men negotiated the bride-price. The bride left her household and took up residence and the customs of the household of the bridegroom/husband. While women in the household had responsibilities and domains of power within the household, men usually determined the big life picture within which women operated. These dynamics assume a significant degree of passivity on the part of the woman, and, hence, the church. They discourage initiative and creativity. Even more troubling, the use of a traditional female-male role paradigm for speaking about God and the church reinforces the continuation of the hierarchical social pyramid in the relationship between women and men.

As in the case of language for the alluring, idolatrous city (17:1–6), I seek to minimize the damage of the bridegroom/bride metaphorical system by avoiding the language of bridegroom and bride and speaking more simply of God, Christ, and church. In a sermon on this passage, the preacher might follow a path similar to the one suggested at 17:1–6 by (1) explaining the function of the bridegroom bride language in antiquity, (2) reflecting critically on it, and (3) helping the congregation appropriate the liberating intent of the language while avoiding its hurtful aspects.

The alluring idolatrous city is clothed in purple, scarlet, with gold, jewels and pearls (all symbols of a decadent life) and holding "a golden cup full of abominations and the impurities of her fornication" (17:4). By contrast, John draws on metaphorical characterizations of Israel using dress to signal righteous living when John speaks not only of the church in "fine linen, pure and bright but also specifically saying that "the fine linen is the righteous deeds of the saints" (3:4; 6:11; 7:14; cf. Isa 51:1; 62:10; Zech 3:4).

On the one hand, a preacher can call attention to the covenantal commitment of Lamb and church. When churches today are accommodating to empire, the preacher could use aspects of this image to point the church toward choosing commitment to God and the Lamb, even while rejecting Empire.

37. Commentators habitually call attention to marriage themes in the Gospels and Letters, e.g., Mark 2:18–20; Matt 25:1–12; John 3:29; 2 Cor 11;2; Eph 5.

19:9a: A Beatitude

19:9a. The angel inserts a beatitude. "Blessed are those who are invited to the marriage supper of the lamb." Weddings of the time often included a marriage supper, as God would celebrate the transition of the ages with an eschatological banquet (sometimes called a "messianic banquet) (e.g., Isa 25:6–8; 35:5–7; Ezek 39:7–10; Zeph 1:9; 1 En. 62:14; esp. 2 Bar. 19:4–8; Mark 14:25; Matt 8:11–12; Luke 22:28–30). John uses the language of the marriage supper as a way of speaking of the eschatological banquet.

At one level, John indicates that this meal is soon to come and that the church will be part of it. At another level, this way of speaking interprets the meaning of the loaf and the cup (presuming John's community used these elements). When the community gathers for this sacred meal, the community proleptically experiences the new heaven and the new earth.

John's churches—like some others in antiquity—likely partook of the bread and cup in the context of a congregational meal. Such a common meal involving the great and small (per 19:5) would have been a dramatic contrast to the sumptuous banquets of the Roman upper classes where people ate to bursting. Yet, the former feeds a satisfaction that will go on forever in the new Jerusalem while the latter, for all its momentary filling, leads to eternal hunger.

My impression is that many congregations are undernourished when it comes to theology of the bread and cup. This focus on the sacred meal would be a welcome starting point for a sermon that could explain the theology of the Table at work here and bring that theology into conversation with other theologies of the supper, including comparison and contrast with the theology of the denomination or movement in which the congregation participates.

Revelation 19:9b-10. Worship God (and not the Angel)

Given the dynamics of John's historical situation—members of the church in danger of accommodating to empire which included toleration of idolatry, and perhaps even participation in it—Revelation 9b–10 is likely context-specific and polemical.

19:9b. The angel underlines the trustworthiness and authority of these things by saying, "These are true words of God." In a setting in which the empire uses its pomp and pageantry to cast a patina on its power, it could be hard for a person to believe the claim that an invisible God is bringing down the visible empire with its impressive idols. The words of the accommodationists are not trustworthy.

19:10. The depth of John's Jewishness shows when the prophet falls down to worship the angel, but the angel forbids it.[38] For the angel is a servant with John and with John's comrades "who hold the testimony of Jesus," that is, who continue to make faithful witness even when confronted by empire.

The angel admonishes John with the quintessential Jewish word to "Worship God." This directive contradicts those who would worship idols. Theologically appropriate guidance for the church ("the testimony of Jesus") comes through "the spirit of prophecy," that is, through prophets whose messages are consistent with the message of John.

This passage gives the preacher another opportunity to reflect on two continuous themes in connection with this book. One is the issue of authority. John could point to the word of the angel as the authority for accepting John's interpretation of the pathway to the new heaven and new earth. What reasons could the preacher today give for taking this interpretation seriously, even if one must reinterpret it for an early twenty-first century worldview? The other is the issue of ambiguity in history. Most readers of this book, I think, are compromised when it comes to empire and idolatry. We participate in, and or benefit from, aspects of empire and idolatry even as we object to them. What are the acceptable boundaries of participation and benefit?

---

38. Col 2:18 indicates that some in that congregation worshiped angels. This phenomenon may have been an issue in John's churches. On the presence of angel worship in that culture, see Aune, *Revelation 17–22*, 1036.

Revelation 19:11—20:15

Revealing the Final Judgment

This penultimate section of the book of Revelation tells a story with several parts. John introduces a rider on the white horse (19:11–16) who defeats the beast and its armies (19:17–21). The dragon, the power animating the beast, is still alive, so John describes God destroying the dragon and making the final judgment (20:1–15) which involves four sub-sections: God throws the dragon into a pit (20:1–3), initiates the millennial reign (20:4–6), after which God casts Satan into the lake of fire (20:6–10), and makes the final judgment with God consigning Death, Hades, and all whose names are not written in the book of Life, into the lake of fire (20:11–15).

These passages call for several comments. First, a preacher should address these materials, especially the notions of the final battle, the millennial reign, the final judgment, and the lake of fire. A lot of people today hear about these things but do not understand them in adequate historical, literary, and theological ways. Popular apocalypticism sometimes distorts these notions with unfortunate theological and ethical consequences.[1]

Second, the preacher needs to help the congregation recognize the relationship of time and events here. Some commentators so forcefully deny that John has a "literal" chronology in view, they do not give enough attention to the idea that John does anticipate an actual movement in history from the broken present through the defeat of evil to the Realm. John may not aim to predict specific events, but John does believe things will happen.

Third, the preacher can help the congregation understand that while the vision unfolds in a complicated way (especially in 20:1–15), the overarching point is simple: God will end the destructive power of the beast (the Empire) and Satan (the dragon) and will punish those who have collaborated with them. Congregations sometimes get mesmerized by the details and lose sight of the big picture and of the big theological questions at

---

1. Unfortunately, the Revised Common Lectionary does not assign these passages, so lectionary preachers need to find a time to preach from them.

stake. Keeping the big picture in mind, a preacher might use this material in the ways it functions in John's ecclesial world. (a) It encourages listeners to think seriously about the consequences of their present life orientation and behavior. To those accommodating to the Empire, this passage is the book's final and most desperate warning. John essentially says, "Your attitudes and behavior will lead to ultimate destruction." To those who testify to Jesus, the passage urges faithfulness. The suffering they face now or in the future is nothing compared to the eternal lake of fire. (b) It assures the congregation—especially those represented by the martyrs in 6:9–11, that God will enact justice in their behalf.

Fourth, the preacher might use the divisions of Revelation 19:11—20:15 as discussion openers to help the congregation reflect theologically on these ideas. To what degree does the congregation believe there will be a final battle? A millennium? A final judgment? An eternal lake of fire? Moreover, this material brings to mind the question of what it means to say that God enacts justice with respect to those who abuse others. Is the punishment (eternity in a lake of fire) proportional to the disobedience? Is such punishment necessary in the name of justice? This passage does not directly raise a question that surfaces in many conversations today: what are theologically appropriate ways for survivors of injustice to relate to the perpetrators of injustice?

Revelation 19:11–16: Flashback: The Rider on the White Horse Defeating the Beast

Revelation 19:11–16 is a flashback to show how the fall of 18:1—19:10 came about: the cosmic Christ returned from heaven to defeat the beast. Revelation 19:11–16 uses vivid symbols to explain the nature and purpose of the Christ while Revelation 19:17–21 offers an imagistic depiction of what happened. The vision in 19:11–16 recalls key elements of the multimedia image of Christ in 1:16–20. Isaiah 63:1–6 is also behind this passage.

Because 19:11—20:15 is complicated in and of itself, and because popular apocalypticism sometimes obfuscates the actual biblical narrative, the preacher may want to emphasize that Revelation 19:11–21 focuses only on the destruction of the beast and the false prophet (the Roman Empire and the imperial cult). When this battle ends, the dragon is still loose. Revelation 20:1–15 focuses on the defeat of the dragon.

19:11. Christ comes from heaven on a white horse. This white horse contrasts with the horse of the same color in 6:2 by coming from heaven whereas the earlier white horse emerged from a seal (a sign of judgment).

The name of the rider is Faithful (*pistos*) and True (*alēthinos*), designations explained more fully at 3:14 as trustworthy and as consistent with God's purposes (in dimetric opposition to the beast and the dragon).[2] The rider acts in righteousness (*dikaiosynē*) in accord with God's purposes, especially judging and making war. In accordance with the principle of being punished by the means whereby one sins, God will punish the beast by means of war since the beast's disobedience included making war on the saints (13:7).

19:12. The eyes of the rider are like flames of fire which, here, as in 1:14 and 2:18, signify that the rider comes as judge. Indeed, the lake of fire is just ahead (19:20; 20:9–10, 14–15). On the rider's head are many diadems, symbols of the use of power—here in faithful and true ways to move the world towards becoming a new Jerusalem, in contrast to the diadems on the heads of the dragon and the beast (12:3; 13:1) where the diadems represent the misuse of power in the service of idolatry, exploitation, injustice, and violence. Faithful and True power overcomes unfaithful and false power.

The rider's head is inscribed with a name that no one knows but the rider. At one level, this statement seems strange because John has named Christ many times.[3] At another level, a key principle related to name in antiquity is in the background. To know the name of a person was to have a measure of power over that person or entity. In some religious traditions, trans-human beings (such as gods and demons) had secret names. Some people in antiquity sought to tap into the power of such forces by calling out as many names as possible in the hope that at least one would allow them to manipulate the universe. While the many names for the rider in this book reveal many dimensions of the Rider's work, there is yet one more name that cannot be known. This name is altogether transcendent. Its secrecy means that no one can co-opt it for their own purposes.

19:13. The rider is clothed in a robe dripped in blood. Exegetes posit three possible sources for this blood: (1) the blood of the rider's enemies (2) the rider's own blood; (3) the blood of the martyrs (6:9–11). It seems likely that the blood came from the rider who, earlier, in the form of a Lamb, was slaughtered (5:6, 9; 12; 13:8). Many Christians see the blood as salvific, expiatory, even as substitutionary atonement; however, a better explanation put forward at 5:6 is that the blood reveals how far the beast and the dragon go to end the witness of the Lamb: they murder the Lamb, who is now the rider. The blood does not change the disposition of God towards the world.

2. On Faithful (*pistos*) and True (*alēthinos*), see 3:14.

3. For a list of twenty-four titles and names John uses for Jesus, see Reddish, *Revelation*, 370.

The preacher can call attention to the theological message that the blood on the rider's robe is a symbol of the failure of the greatest demonstration of force possible for the beast and Satan—putting people to death. Yet, God resurrected the Lamb who now returns to do battle as the rider who cannot die and who will be instrumental in establishing a new heaven and new earth where death is replaced by the tree of life. The preacher could see this phenomenon as a pattern for discerning divine activity in the present: the preacher could point to people, values, and movements that empire tried silence but who rebounded to continue to witness and who now lean towards the new heaven and new earth.

The beast and the dragon attempted to silence the martyrs in the same way. Their blood may also be on the robe, although John's language in this context does not overtly call the martyrs to mind.

The rider's name is Word of God. The expression "word of God" (*ho logos tou theou*) occurs five times in the book but only once (here) as a name. Elsewhere (1:2, 9; 6:9; 20:4) it refers to the revelation of the sovereignty and purposes of God, especially God's commitment to effect the new Jerusalem. The word of God contrasts with the propaganda of Caesar and the empire. Rome imprisoned John and murdered the martyrs because of their testimony to this word (1:2, 9; 6:9; 20:4). To say the rider's name is the Word of God is to say the power of God operates through Jesus as the agent through whom God is replacing the old Rome with the new Jerusalem.[4] The expression also reminds listeners that as God created by the word (Gen 1:1–2:4), so God can re-create by the same means.

19:14. The armies of heaven, dressed in white, pure, fine linen, follow on white horses. Who are these armies? They almost certainly include the 144,000 of 14:1–5 whom John described in the language reminiscent of an army (14:4). The reference to the fine linen, pure and white is similar to the fine linen of the church of 17:8 (pure and bright).[5] The 144,000 conquered while on earth through their righteous deeds (17:8), that is, they did not yield to the beast. Now, they join the rider for the final conquest.

Commentators almost universally point out that John does not directly say that the armies engage in physical combat. Indeed, they are not dressed for combat. They do not wear conventional battle gear but the fine linen of heaven and, particularly, of the eschatological banquet.

19:15. The sharp two-edged sword of 1:16 returns to strike down the nations. As we noted in connection with 1:16, this sword is not a first-century

---

4. Commentators often call attention to a parallel notion of the word in Wis 15–16 where the word acts as God's agent for judgment.

5. Apocalyptic literature often pictures a final battle involving myriads of angels as warrior. If John has such angels in mind, John left no direct clue in this text.

weapon but is akin to the name, the Word of God, in that it is a powerful life shaping word (Rev 2:12, 16, 12:15; 19:13, 15, 21; cf. Isa 49:2). Like the name "The Word of God," this expression reminds listeners that as God created by the word, so God can un-create and re-create by the word.

The fact that the rider conquers through the power of speaking calls the preacher's attention to the power of the spoken word. Preaching that names injustice and calls for repentance and justice does not magically bring about social transformation. But such preaching keeps the possibility of justice alive for those who are oppressed, empowers initiative for change, and confronts the empire with its disobedience.

The rider will rule the nations with a "rod of iron." As we observed at 2:27 and 12:5, the rod of iron symbolizes judgment and destruction (as in Psa 2:8–9 and Isa 11:4).

In language reminiscent of Isaiah 63:1–6, the rider "will tread the wine press of the fury of the wrath of God the Almighty." John has used similar language to make a similar point: the rider will be the agent of totalizing punishment (cf. 14:8, 10, esp. 19).

19:16. John introduced a slight variant on the title "King of kings and Lord of lords" at 17:14. At that point, we noted that the title stresses the rider is an instrument for manifesting the absolute sovereignty of God and for reminding the nations they are accountable to God. This name is on the rider's robe and "on his thigh." Although the meaning of the name on the thigh is debated, the simplest explanation derives from the custom of the soldier wearing a sword on the thigh. The name has such power that it is the rider's sword. The idea of the sword as a name coheres with the sword coming from the mouth of the rider and the life-shaping power of the Word of God.

Like many other passages in the book, this one raises the possibility of a sermon on the Christology of the book of elation, or a sermon that begins with the Christology of this book and broadens in a sermon (or series of sermons) on the diversity of pictures of Jesus in the Gospels and the Letters and in the much broader and deeper life of the church.

Many people are puzzled by Jesus as agent of punishment. Will Jesus really crush people like grapes in a wine press as an expression of the wrath of God? Even if Jesus accomplished this task by the word instead of by a physical sword, crushed is still crushed. Because this question is tied up with the larger concern for the degree to which the book of Revelation might envision God and Jesus annihilating a whole people in 19:17–21, I take it up in connection with that passage.

Revelation 19:17–21: Flashback: The Rider
on the White Horse Defeats the Beast

This passage continues the flashback of the actual battle that occurs when the rider returns from heaven to defeat the beast and its armies. Revelation 19:17–21 uses symbols to indicate how the defeat of the beast came about.

19:17–19. John begins with a counter-supper to the marriage supper of the lamb (19:9). The prophet takes up the memory of Ezekiel 39:17–20 to portray an angel who calls birds to prepare to feast on the flesh of rulers, military leaders, the mighty, and the regular soldiers and their riders. The birds come from mid-heaven, a place associated with judgment (8:13; 14:6). As the highest point in the sky, it affords a flawless view of what happens on earth and hence is an ideal location for judging. The birds are likely the same ones from 8:13 and 14:6. The flesh is multicultural: it come from all parts of the social pyramid—free and slave, small and great. John holds not only free and great accountable, but also the small and the slaves.

The great supper of the Lamb opens into a new Jerusalem. As Reddish points out, at the great supper for the empire, those who acceded to the claims of the empire are themselves the meal.[6]

The birds have a double effect. First, showing respect for the dead was a key value in antiquity and included burying the dead properly. Leaving the bodies to be eaten by birds was a particular indignity. The fact that the angel calls the birds to prepare for their feast of dead flesh indicates the seriousness of the crimes of the beast and its allies. They do not even deserve a decent burial. Second, the birds will clean up the space as quickly as possible so that it can be used for the purposes of mutual support that God intends.

19:19–20a. Many passages, images, and themes in the book of Revelation point to the final confrontation between God and the empire. The participants in the confrontation are the rider and the armies of heaven (see 19:14) and the beast (the empire) and its allies—client rulers, the ruling class, and others who have participated willingly in empire.

Revelation 19:19–20a is essentially a Twitter report in images on the occurrence of the battle of Harmagedon (16:14–16; cf. 17:14–16). However, when that confrontation comes, the prophet does not describe the battle itself but only reports, in only one-and-a-half verses: (1) the fact that it occurred and (2) its outcome. On the one hand, John has earlier painted such vivid, multi-sensory, painful images of this destruction that more hardly seems needed. Listeners know that the destruction is painful as when many people were pounded by one-hundred-pound hailstones (9:20–21). On the

6. Reddish, *Revelation*, 370.

other hand, the visionary's ultra-lean prose at this point bespeaks the truly awesome power of God and of the Lamb. Based on the nature of the rider's sword as the word of judgment (1:16; 2:12, 16, 12:15; 19:13:15), it is clear that God settled the issue with a word.

This part of the denouement of history ends as today's congregation might expect. The rider and the army of heaven capture the first beast (13:1–10) and the false prophet (the second beast, the imperial cult and others implicated with it, 13:11–18). The false prophet had performed signs (miracles) that seemed to demonstrate the prophet's power. Now, however, the false prophet can do nothing to prevent the warrior from defeating the empire with a word. This impotence is not surprising as the beast and the false prophet *deceived* "those who received the mark of the beast and who worshiped its image." Their deception is now fully and finally exposed.

19:20b–21. Someone from the rider's group throws the beast and the false prophet "into the lake of fire that burns with sulfur," the mention of sulfur (known for its stench) adds to the revolting character of the scene.[7]

The lake of fire is the popular apocalyptic picture of a place of fiery punishment for the unfaithful (e.g., 1 En. 10:6, 13; 48:8; 90:25–26; 2 Esd 7:26–38; Mark 9:43, 48; Matt 3:12; 5:22; 13:42, 50; 18:9; 23:15:15–33; 25:42; Luke 10:13–15; 16:23–28; cf. Isa 66:24). The beast and the false prophet will be in torment in the lake of fire forever (20:10).

The rider on the horse kills the rest of those who have cast their lot with the empire with the sword that came from the mouth of the rider—the powerful life-shaping/life-destroying word. This death is just the first. As noted earlier, John believes that many people will suffer two deaths—a first a temporary death at the end of their present lives, after which they exist as shades in Hades, a holding tank as they await final judgment. At the judgment, God will assign each person to a permanent state of being—the lake of fire, or the new heaven and the new earth (20:11–15). Those who go to the lake of fire experience a second death.

Because the themes in the book of Revelation are spiral in character, many observations about preaching from this passage (in conjunction with 19:11–16) have come up previously. The passage affirms God's desire to end empire as part of opening the path to a new Jerusalem. From John's point of view this is non-negotiable. The empire ruled through violence and it is now punished by the very means by which it ruled. The preacher could use this passage to assure the congregation that God has put empire on notice.

7. On fire as a symbol of judgment: see, e.g., 1:14; 8:5–8; 11:5; 17:16; 18:8: 20:9–10, 14–15. On fire and sulfur: 14:10.

While John speaks here in images of a climactic battle, he does not envision a singular event of face-to-face combat between the rider and the beast and their respective armies. John does not give direct details about the battle itself here or elsewhere. Indeed, in 19:19–20a, John does not *describe* the battle all. John only reports its occurrence and outcome: the defeat (capture) and punishment of the beast and the false prophet.

Throughout the book the prophet has indicated that social processes are already at work to cause the fall of the empire. Idolatry leads to a world built on false values and behaviors that cannot sustain a community. From outside of the empire, John imagines the Parthians moving against Rome. Alliances the imperial leadership made with client rulers and with the ruling classes will come apart. John uses the images in Revelation 19:19–20a to indict that such processes will reach their natural conclusion in the fall of the Roman Empire. God is the force behind those processes.

As we have indicated earlier, a preacher might explore with the congregation the degree to which such forces are at work in today's setting. One haunting possibility is that just as John perceived the forces of decay accelerating the end of the empire, so the early twenty-first century is a time of increasingly violent fragmentation along such lines as race, class, religion, and political ideology. Social tensions ratchet up ever higher. Such things point to coming cultural collapse if current directions continue without repentance.

What shall a preacher and congregation think theologically about the lake of fire, both here and in 20:10, 14–15? John's references to the lake are *images* of the consequences of disobedience. At one level, John places the beast and the false prophet in the lake of fire as a way of emphasizing that they suffer the pain they inflicted on others. At another level, the apocalyptic writers so widely portray fiery punishment for evildoers I am persuaded they believe in a literal place of eternal, fiery punishment. For reasons unfolded in the next paragraph, I do not share this conviction.

Many progressive preachers would likely be relieved to think that John does not have a singular doomsday scenario in mind, an actual battle of Harmegadon. Such preachers would also welcome the idea of judgment taking place through social process. As I have indicated earlier, I do not believe a God of unlimited love and unlimited power orchestrates such developments nor do I believe God actively seeks to condemn vast numbers of people to fire. However, the idea that human communities can bring judgment on themselves (and through the very means through which they sinned) accounts appropriately for communities facing and feeling the consequences of their disobedience without making God responsible for the suffering that results. In every situation—including seasons of collapse—I believe God offers possibilities for re-creation as those involved cooperate consciously or unconsciously with God.

Revelation 20:1–15: Defeat of Satan, Millennium, Final Judgment, and End of the Present Era

A preacher is hard-pressed to find a richer lode of passages than Revelation 20:1–15. While a preacher could treat this network of notions in one concise sermon, the preacher could also develop a short series around the functions of the three fascinating themes in this chapter—the double-defeat of Satan (imprisonment and final defeat, 20:1–3, 7–10), the millennium (20:4–6), and the final judgment (20:11–15).

At one level, the purpose of the defeat of Satan and the millennial reign is easy to state: these passages promise listeners that God will finally and fully defeat Satan. God will not only end the specific manifestation of Satan's dominion in the form contemporaneous with John (the empire), but God will render Satan irrevocably impotent. Never again will Satan be able to assume an incarnation in a historical entity (such as a later empire). God will punish Satan in the same way that Satan sinned. As Satan was a torment to the earth so Satan will be tormented forever.

John intends for this material to encourage faithful witness. Those who do not accommodate but continue to hold by the word of the God and the testimony to/of Jesus will enter the new heaven and the new earth without fear that Satan can distort the new world.

At other levels, many in the contemporary church are perplexed specifically about how to understand the defeat of the empire, the millennium, and the final judgment. Lay people continue to ask in Bible studies, "What does the millennium accomplish, really?" "Why doesn't God just finish off Satan in one fell swoop? Why incarceration and then defeat?" And when it comes to the final judgment, "Will one actually take place? If so, what do I need to do to prepare?"

Revelation 20:1–3: God Captures Satan

With the empire now eviscerated and its leaders in the lake of fire, John turns to Satan, the wizard behind the throne of empire. God captures Satan through an angel who comes down from heaven for judgment and seizes Satan, binding the Devil for a thousand years, thus demonstrating God's mastery of the Devil, the very soul of evil, and pointing to liberation for the faithful.

Revelation 20:1–3 and 20:7–10 brings the story of the dragon to a close. The dragon was cast out of heaven in 12:7–12. Believers have conquered the dragon by continuing to witness even when the dragon threatened them (12:11). The short time God allotted the dragon (12:12) is now ending.

20:1. The angel comes with the tools of a jailer—a key and a chain. In those days Roman prisons were typically underground (accessible by a hole in the surface). Jailers chained prisoners whom they especially wanted to hold. The jailer-angel uses the bottomless pit of 9:1–11 to incarcerate the devil. The bottomless pit was the domain of chaos in which Satan ruled, and from the locusts, Satan's agents of chaos, were released to terrorize the earth.

20:2. The power of God is so far reaching that God takes Satan's domain (the pit) and uses it as holding cell for Satan. God now transforms this hide-out of evil into the very prison for the chief of evil. The locusts who emerged from the abyss in 9:3 represent the nature and behavior of its inhabitants. When bound for a thousand years, Satan is presumably subject to the chaos in the abyss.

As part of evoking the ancient combat myth whereby God establishes and re-establishes order by defeating disobedient spirits, Isaiah 24:21–22 pictures such treatment of both angels and human beings by showing the punishment of disobedient angels and the incarceration of human beings. Other apocalyptic writers develop the motif of binding and imprisoning disobedient spirits until a final disposition (e.g.1 En. 10:4–14: 18:12–16; 21:1–10; 2 Bar. 40:1–4; cf. Jude 6; 2 Pet 2:4). John appears to be the first to designate a sentence of a thousand years which, scholars agree, is John's way of indicating a very long time under God's control.

20:3 By describing the angel throwing Satan into the pit and locking and sealing the entrance, John indicates that Satan is in a maximum-security site. Satan cannot escape. During this time, the dragon will no longer be able to engage in one of the quintessential means through which the dragon exercised power among the nations: deception.

Apocalyptic theology provides a historical answer to an aspect of this plot that many contemporary Christians find enigmatic. Why is Satan bound for a thousand years and then released for a second opportunity to deceive? The answer is revealed in 20:3c: the devil "*must* be let out for a little while." The expression, *dei*, is commonplace in such literature to indicate the plan that God had in place for how the transposition of the ages would take place. It had to be because God said it had to be.

A preacher might note that while the preceding explanation may have satisfied many people in the ancient world, the arbitrary nature of a pre-ordained plan by which to draw the present age to a close is not theologically adequate to many people today. For example, I believe God has a much more dynamic and responsive relationship with the world. I do not believe God has the power to effect such a plan.

Nevertheless, the underlying reason that apocalyptic theologians believed in such an approach connects with many congregations today. The idea that God is in control is intended to bolster confidence in God and to foster witness in the midst of difficult situations. John particularly aims for this idea to strengthen those whose refusal to collude with the empire will soon make their situations more difficult.

Frederick Murphy posits another reason for the two-stage defeat of Satan that has great possibility for preaching. "The author uses this opportunity to assert once again the resilience of Satan and the difficult and complicated process by which [Satan] is annihilated."[8] From this perspective, preachers can help congregations recognize the deep roots of so many personal and corporate distortions of life (e.g., alcoholism, racism, sexism, genderism, nationalism). The congregation needs to be prepared for long and difficult struggles away from such things and towards the new Jerusalem.

Revelation 20:4–6: The Millennial Reign

To use an imprecise image, the millennium is a limited preview of the new heaven and the new earth. Satan is imprisoned in the abyss. Most of those who have experienced the first death remain dead, awaiting the final judgment after which they will receive either the second death or a welcome into the new world.[9]

20:4. God has set some people on thrones (symbols of power). While scholars have debated the identity(ies) of those who sit on the thrones, a fairly wide consensus has emerged that sees them as the martyrs who had been beheaded (executed) because of their testimony to Jesus (6:9–11; cf. 16:6; 18:20, 24).[10] They did not worship the beast or its image and did not receive its mark (cf. 13:4, 13–17).[11]

---

8. Murphy, *Fallen is Babylon*, 396.

9. The first death is the end of this earthly life, at which point the self enters into an interim existence awaiting the final judgment which, for the condemned, will result in a second (and final) death (20:14). Cf. comments on 2:11; 21:8.

10. Beheading was but one Roman means of execution and functions here as a symbol for multiple forms of murder.

11. Scholars point out that the Greek of 20:4 could be translated to speak of two groups: "the souls of those who had been beheaded" and others who "had not worshiped the beast or its image." The expression "the souls" does not refer to the non-material part of the self but is a cipher for them as persons.

God gives them authority to "judge" (*krima*). Some commentators regard this "judging" not so much as rendering judgments and more as "reigning" according to the values and practices of the Realm of God. When John speaks of this group "reigning," the prophet uses a word that means just that, *basileuō*. The only other times John uses *krima* it refers to condemning those in league empire (18:20). This kind of judgment does not seem to occur during the millennium but does take place in 20:7–10. Other traditions in the gospels and letters envision faithful participating with God or Christ as a kind of panel of judges (my expression) (Matt 19:28; Luke 22;30; 1 Cor 6:2). Moreover, John has adapted this scene from Daniel 7:9–27 where a similar heavenly court sits in judgment on the fourth beast (Dan 7:26). While God vests the martyrs with authority to condemn, they will not participate in pronouncing final condemnation until the final judgment (20:7–10).

Several interpreters regard rule during the millennium as God's reward to the martyrs. Because they lost their lives in witness, God resurrects them to life in advance of the final resurrection. They get an extra thousand years of the experience of the qualities of the life of the new Jerusalem. During this time they participate with God in reigning (*basileuō*) that is, in bringing the values and practices of God to expression in the world.

20:5. Bringing the martyrs to life is "the first resurrection." As noted above, "the rest of the dead" are still in the grave awaiting the final judgment. This number includes the faithful who were not executed as well as the armies of the beast and others who made a pact with the empire, and others who survived Harmagedon (cf. 19:11). The idea that people die and exist in an interim state until the final resurrection (with accompanying judgment) is characteristic of some apocalyptic writings.

20:6. John now inserts the fifth of seven beatitudes into the book: "Blessed and holy are those who share in the first resurrection."[12] To be blessed in the apocalyptic worldview is to share in the presence and coming of the eschatological world. To be holy is to be defined by—and to participate only in—God's purposes.

The fear of the second death has no power over those who reign. As noted, the second death is a negative experience occurring after the final judgment. The second death results in punishment for those allied with the beast and Satan, while God welcomes the faithful into the new age.

When John refers to the people on the thrones as priests, John has in mind the kind of priesthood of Exodus 19:6 in which the life of the

12. On the form and function of beatitudes in the vision see comments on 1:3. Cf. 14:3; 16:15; 19:9; 22:7, 14. A preacher could develop a series of sermons on the beatitudes—one sermon on each beatitude.

community of Israel is priestly in the sense of representing God's presence and purposes. In the act of representing those purposes, which includes living according to them, the community experiences blessing. John has already pointed to this theme in 1:6 and 5:10.

Revelation 20:7–10. The Final Defeat of Satan

At the end of the millennium, God releases Satan from the abyss. The Devil emerges to take up the signature work of deceiving the nations "at the four corners of the earth," that is, on a worldwide basis (see 7:1).

While the beast, the Roman Empire, is no longer available for the dragon's purposes, there are other nations who can serve that role represented here by Gog and Magog. John takes these names from Ezekiel 38–39 but alters their identities and roles. In the earlier prophet, Gog is a person and Magog is a land; Gog rules the land of Magog. God puts Gog to death and incinerates Magog. The defeat of Gog and the destruction of Magog demonstrate the sovereignty of God (Ezek 39:7). John takes a slightly different tack by interpreting both Gog and Magog as nations that accept the deception offered by Satan.

John does not imply the specific ancient identities of Gog and Magog. Evidently they are peoples who were not bound together with the Roman Empire (which was destroyed in 19:17–21). They experienced the millennial reign, but when it ended and they could choose the possibility of life with God or life with Satan, they chose the latter. At one level, the image of Gog and Magog "as numerous as the sands of the sea," emphasizes the vast size of the enemy forces (as in Josh 11:4; Judg 7:12). At another level, the expression plays on the promise to Sarah and Abraham that their children would be similar in number (e.g., Gen 22:17; 32:12): Satan again engages in imitation.

Gog and Magog gather their forces from across the entire earth and they surround "the camp of the saints" which is also "the beloved city."[13] The language of "camp" recalls the people of Israel camping in the wilderness on the journey from slavery through the forty years of wandering to the promised land. From the outside looking in, this existence would seem to be tenuous, especially with the forces of God and Magog pressing in, but those in the camp experience the providence of God. The "beloved city" is Jerusalem which here refers not to the physical city itself but, figuratively, to the community of the faithful and true. The church—as community in the

13. Commentators point out that apocalyptic literature sometimes speaks of the forces of evil attacking Jerusalem and Israel at a climactic moment, e.g., Joel 3:2; Zech 11:1–9; 14:2–5; cf. Isa 5:16; Jer 25:32; 50:41; 1 En 56:7; 90:13–19; 2 Esd 13:5, 33–34.

interim between the millennium and the final judgment—is to point to the qualities of the new city, the new Jerusalem.

The preacher might pick up an important point in the dual images for the witnessing community—camp and city. Living in a camp in the wilderness was a tenuous existence, easily threatened by the elements, animals, and enemy forces. In antiquity, people sought security and safety in cities. However, testifying to the sovereignty of God in the face of Gog and Magog gives the life of the witnessing community the quality of living a camp-like existence even when in a city. The city is effectively a camp as it becomes a place of threat rather than of security and safety. The city is also a place where God proves provident, even as in the wilderness wanderings.

Preachers could help some early twenty-first century congregations understand that while they imagine themselves as city-like (figuratively speaking), their existence is, at the same time, camp-like (again, figuratively). Metaphorically speaking, the church today that begins to model the city that anticipates the qualities of Revelation 21:1—22:5 will find Gog and Magog setting siege. If the armies of empire seemed massive, so much more the threat of these latter disobedient nations.

As in the case of the destruction of the beast and its armies, John's description of what God does to Satan is spare. John does mention the means of destruction here—fire from heaven—but does not dwell on the gruesome details. John concentrates on the outcome: the defeat and the follow-through (eternal fire).

To the human eye, the reserves of evil may seem inexhaustible, but John calls upon Ezekiel 39:6 for the image of God sending fire down from heaven to consume the enemy of God as a paradigm for God sending fire on Gog and Magog.[14] This is another of John's ways of saying that God's reservoirs for punishment and redemption are limitless. For every powerful assertion of evil, God will make an even more powerful assertion of re-creative power.

This point is one at which some preachers in process perspective make a creative transformation of thought. Although God may not have limitless raw power to send fire from heaven (or to singularly recreate the world as a new Jerusalem), the invitation of God is limitless and appropriate to the possibilities for every situation. God invites all to join with God in deconstructing things that obscure God's purposes of community and to participate with God in reconstructing the world as new Jerusalem.

---

14. 2 Kgs 1:1–12 may also influence this passage. For destruction by fire, e.g., Zeph 1:18; 3:8; Sir 3:8; 2 Esd 13:8–11. Cf. Rev 8:5–8; 9:18; 11:5; 14:10, 18; 16:8; 17:16; 18:8; 20:14, 18; 21:8.

At 19:20, we commented on the nature and purpose of the lake of fire and sulfur, as well as on theological questions raised by this notion. God now condemns the devil to that lake. The detail that is new to John's narrative is that its inhabitants do not simply burn up. "They will be tormented day and night forever and ever."

Earlier we noted two likely purposes for this double defeat in the book of Revelation. One is that it is part of God's plan. The other is that it demonstrates the resilience of evil: evil has capacity to survive powerful efforts to destroy it. Individuals and communities need to be prepared for long and difficult struggles when seeking to turn away from attitudes and actions of Satan and to turn toward the world as God would remake it. Against this background, 20:7–10 speaks a definitive word: no matter how resurgent evil appears to be, the power of God runs deeper and longer and will eventually bring about what it promises.

Revelation 20:11–15: Final Judgment

The book of Revelation focuses on the judgment of four groups: (1) The beast, the false prophet, and those in the empire system (they are condemned) (19:11-21); (2) those executed by the empire (they are saved for the new Jerusalem); (3) Satan, the great deceiver (condemned) (20:1-3, 7-11); and (4) all others, including the many who have died (some condemned, and others saved) (20:11-15). The prophet has previously revealed God's verdicts on the first three groups and now explains the process of judgment on the fourth group.

20:11. In a manner similar to other judgment scenes in Jewish literature, John sees a great white throne (the same one as in 4:1-11) with God sitting on it as judge (e.g., Dan 7:9-27; Matt 25:31-46; 1 En. 62:1-16). John's description of the size of the throne emphasizes its power in comparison to earthly thrones. The color is the white of heaven. The scene solemnly portrays the ultimate authority of God.

Ancient apocalypticism envisioned two stages in cosmic transformation—destruction of the old and construction of the new. John invokes the first phrase of this process when saying that earth and heaven flee from the divine presence, "and no place was found for them" (20:11); John thus indicates that the present structures of existence disappear for both earth and heaven. As John says more clearly in 21:1, the first (present) heaven and the first (present) earth pass away, and the sea is no more. God will create a new heaven and a new earth. The end of the old assures the congregation that the threats and brokenness of the old will not recur.

A preacher can help a congregation recover a full-bodied sense of apocalyptic thinking. Apocalyptic themes in literature, movies, and other expressions today often end in destruction, whereas in full-bodied apocalypticism destruction is but one phrase of the end of history. The ultimate goal of apocalypticism is regeneration.

20:12–13. God brings all the dead back to life for judgment. By mentioning "great and small" the prophet emphasizes that everyone in the social pyramid will be judged, including those at the top of the social pyramid who were accustomed to controlling life in the old age. God brings the dead from Death and Hades for judgment. As we note at 1:18 and 6:8, Death is a power that rules over Hades, the abode of the dead. Although we today sometimes use "Hades" to refer to hell, in John's worldview it was not a place of punishment but was a somber, gray holding tank (so to speak) where the dead await this judgment. In 20:13 John reinforces the extent of the judgment by saying the sea gave up its dead—that is, sailors and others who died at sea and whose bodies were put to rest in the water. There is no place to hide. Every single person comes before this throne of judgment.

Two kinds of books are present. The first (and easier) set of books is a record of human deeds (e.g., Dan 7:10; Mal 3:16; 2 Esd 6:20; 1 En. 47:3; 81:1–4; 89:61–77; 90:17; 2 Bar. 24:1). The essential criterion of judgment is whether one has colluded with the beast and the false prophet (and, hence, with Satan, idolatry, exploitation, injustice, and violence) or whether one has witnessed to God and to the Lamb. These books contain the names of those who have colluded and those who have not.

The other document is the book of life (3:5; 13:8; 17:8). According to 13:8 and 17:8, the names in this book were written "from the foundation of the world." As we have noted earlier, many apocalyptic theologians believed that God preordained significant aspects of history, including those who would be part of the new Jerusalem.

Some contemporary interpreters see a tension between the notion of judgment on the basis of works and salvation on the basis of one's name being written in the book of life from the foundation of the world. However, there is no tension in John's mind. John operates out of classical Jewish thinking about covenant and community. From the prophet's perspective, God wrote the names of those who would be saved in the book of life as an act of sheer grace at the time of the creation of the world. God writes the names there without merit. However, a person whose name is in the book of life is responsible for living according to God's purposes for covenantal community. One's name remains in the book as a result of faithful witness. The prophet is clear in 3:5, that God will blot names of the unfaithful—those who have accommodated to the empire—out of the book of life.

This motif is yet another intended to encourage the congregations to whom John writes. Their names are in the book of life. They keep their names in the book by faithful and true witness. They can write themselves out of the book by being disobedient.

20:14–15. God throws Death and Hades into the lake of fire. In the coming world, there is no place for Death, with its opposition to God's purposes of life. There is no need for Hades as a repository of the dead in the next stage of history.

As noted earlier, the "first death" is the cessation of biological life. The self enters into an interim state awaiting resurrection and final judgment. John uses the expression "second death" for what happens to those who are not welcomed into the Realm of God but are consigned to punishment. John has earlier pointed out that those who testify to God and Jesus will not face this death (2:11; cf. 20:6).

Some interpreters argue that John uses the lake of fire as an image of separation from God. However, the notion of lake of fire is not just an absence of relationship but represents active punishment. Furthermore, as I mentioned previously, I think that John and other apocalyptic writers spoke of the lake of fire in a literal way.

John makes a categorical statement that "*Anyone* whose name was not found written in the book of life was thrown into the lake of fire." John has earlier noted that those condemned to the lake of fire "will be tormented day and night forever and ever" (20:10; cf. 14:10–11). This perspective prompts the preacher to consider a popular but misguided Christian perspective that the God of the first thirty-nine books of the Bible is angry and wrathful while the God of the last twenty-seven books is gracious and loving. In my mind, casting people into a lake of fire where they are tormented without any possibility of relief is worse than anything attributed to God in the Torah, Prophets, and Writings.

As said elsewhere, I do not believe a God of love actively causes people to suffer, even as a result of their disobedience. It follows that I cannot believe in a lake of fire, though I do believe in accountability and consequences for both individuals and communities. A deeper implication of this text is that enculturation with empire and the ways of Satan leads, ultimately, to tragic destruction of selves, relationships, and communities.

In this spirit, the text offers preachers the opportunity to help congregations with the distinction between authentic grace and the cheap grace that is characteristic of some Christian circles. Authentic grace offers assurance with expecting appropriate response, which may include repentance and certainly includes living out eschatological qualities of life. Cheap grace offers assurance without expectation of response. Under a truncated understanding of "unconditional grace" or "unconditional love," the church sometimes offers cheap grace. Without understanding real grace, or just wanting to feel better without emending their lives, people sometimes accept grace in the cheap way.

A preacher might help the congregation see that John's perspective is not "works righteousness" as Christians often think of it—the necessity of performing works that make one worthy of God's love. But John's point of view does mean that one's grace-given place in the community is conditional on obedience. Of course, the disobedient with names in the book of life have the opportunity to repent until the final judgment itself. At that point, from John's point of view, the chance to repent evaporates.

A preacher might rightly point out the idea that God wrote the names of the saved at the beginning of history is arbitrary with respect to those selected and unfair to those whose names are not written there.[15] Today's church should set out, as widely as possible, the invitation to repent and become part of the movement towards reconfiguring the world so that it will be more like the new heaven and new earth.

As I have indicated before, the issues about which I am most often asked when leading Bible studies in congregations include issues related to life beyond death. In my ecclesial circles there are not a lot of questions specifically about the final judgment per se, but a lot of people ask versions of the question, "What happens when I die?" which is often a way of asking, "What must I do to go to heaven?" Most people in my world seem to assume that the self is composed of two parts—the material body and the non-material soul—and that at death, the soul goes directly to the afterlife. Judgment, in this way of thinking, typically takes place at the moment of death.

A preacher could use the interest in life after death as an entre into a sermon that helps clarify John's point of view and its differences from the popular perspective on life after death. John's interest in resurrection and final judgment is not just in personal survival beyond death, but is in justice, multiplying blessing in community, and in God proving faithful, especially to those who suffered in witness. Moreover, John's viewpoint on the afterlife differs from the popular imagination today.

As indicated previously, I do not believe there will be a single, decisive moment of final judgment with the kinds of eternal destinies John describes. However, apart from that overlay, this passage like many others in this apocalypse stresses that we are accountable for what we do, and that

---

15. John spoke to established churches and not to those outside. Presumably, however, people outside the church could convert, which would then indicate that their names had been written in the book of life from the foundation of the world.

consequences come our way, both in deconstruction of our worlds (Rev 19:11—21:15), and in constructing new and better ones (Rev 22:1—22:5).[16]

John imagines the world dualistically. God or Satan. Good or evil. Faithful or unfaithful. My experience of the world is much more ambiguous. Moreover, I am never fully faithful (and when unfaithful, I am seldom *completely* so). But within this ambiguity, the book of Revelation reminds me to seek to be as faithful as possible, given the particularities of every context, recognizing that in every moment the opportunity to repent, repair, even restart is always present.

16. For an exceptional proposal on the afterlife that incorporates both universal grace and accountability, see Suchocki, *End of Evil.*

Revelation 21–22

Revealing the New Heaven
and the New Earth

A deep purpose of the book of Revelation is to strengthen those who are living faithfully towards the coming of the new heaven and new earth. For John's time, this involved both embodying the values and practices of the Realm and turning away from the empire and, thereby, risking the possibility of suffering. The prophet urges those in the church who are compromised with the Roman system to repent and to return to faithful life and, thereby, to avoid the lake of fire.

The climactic vision of the book, the new heaven and the new earth, offers listeners a powerful lure: by continuing to endure patiently, they can be part of the new world. Continuing the pattern of the book, John represents the qualities of the new Jerusalem in vivid symbols. As impressive as it is, the glory that was Rome is not even pale alongside the new Jerusalem.

When developing the sermon, the preacher might take a cue from John with respect to attitude. While the prophet is unflinchingly critical of the empire and warns those allied with Rome that they will share its punishment, John's final rhetorical appeal is based on the positive attraction of the new heaven and the new earth. Preachers today often find it easier to critique contemporary empires than to speak concretely about promising ways forward. Yet, many people are more motivated for long-term commitment by promise and possibility than by fear, threat, and anger. While the critique is important, preaching is often especially empowering when it aims towards a vision of the positively possible and toward helping people imagine how to get from there. Three simple questions are helpful to some preachers:

1. What of the new Jerusalem is possible for us?

2. How will it benefit our community and the larger families of humankind and nature?

3. What steps can our congregation take to get there?

Many people today assume that 21:9—22:5 is a blueprint of heaven. A preacher needs to help the congregation understand that the prophet is not simply broadcasting a news feed from the new world but uses word pictures to communicate its qualities.

John envisions the final and full manifestation of the new heaven and new earth as future, but many characteristics of the new Jerusalem can be manifest in the life of the church and world in the present. For the church is supposed to be a proto-eschatological community. A preacher can help the congregation reflect on the degree to which it embodies the qualities of the new heaven and the new earth, and how the congregation might move more fully in that direction.

This part of the book has a simple structure: a theological interpretation of the meaning of the new heaven and the new earth (21:1–8), a vision of symbols representing the new heaven and the new earth (21:9—22:5), and the closing of the book, including final instructions, beatitude, cautions, and benediction (22:6–21).

Revelation 21:1 8: Theological Interpretation of the New Heaven and the New Earth

Before unfolding the vision of the new heaven and the new earth itself, John narrates a brief commentary interpreting the new world. The elements of the narrative—things the prophet sees and hears—prepare listeners to understand the significance of the vision of 21:9–22:5.

21:1. Traditional prophetic eschatology envisioned the renewal of community taking place in the existing earth. Apocalyptic theologian came to believe that the world has become so ensnared in evil that world itself must be replaced (e.g., Isa 65:17; 66:22; 1 En. 45:4–5; 91:16; 2 Esd 7:75; 2 Bar. 32:6; cf. Mark 13:31; Rom 8:19–23; 2 Pet 3:10–13). In this spirit, John sees that the first heaven and the first earth have passed away and announces the coming of a new heaven and a new earth (cf. 20:11).

The first earth passed away since that earth was the domain in which the dragon gave birth to the beast and in which they ruled. A new earth is needed whose structures of existence do not allow the possibility of such misuse. The first heaven was a domain of conflict between the dragon and the forces of heaven (12:6–13). The structures of the first heaven must be replaced to eliminate the possibility of such confrontation. When the prophet

sees a new heaven and a new earth, the prophet sees new structures of existence to support life.

Even if the preacher does not expect a literal and total end of the present cosmos and the coming of a new one, some commentators point to a
hard truth here. Some things—e.g., institutions, communities, traditions,
values, practices—become so broken they cannot be repaired. They need to
be put on the shelf so that something else can take their places.

A preacher can easily identify such things in the larger culture, e.g.,
racism. Having benefitted in ways beyond measure from a place in the long-
established churches, I hesitate to say this, but many such congregations
need to make such transition or face the sad truth revealed in this last book
in the Bible: communities who do not become a part of the movement to the
new Jerusalem disintegrate in painful ways.

21:2. John uses the image of a city to represent the entire community.
To be holy is to use power in ways consistent with the purposes of God.
In contrast to Rome, a most unholy city (e.g.17:18; 18:10, 16, 18, 19), the
designation "holy city" indicates that the new city is shaped by God who
defines what it means to be holy (4:8; 6:10; 15:4; 16:5). The new city is an
eschatologically *new* Jerusalem.

The city comes down from heaven. The direction of the movement
(coming down) may surprise some people who think of going "up" to heav-
en for salvation. Here, the barrier vanishes between heaven and earth and
the qualities of the renewed world infuse the present.

Because the premillennialist hope for a "rapture" (in which believers
are elevated from the world as it endures the tribulation) is so widespread,
the preacher might note that the book of Revelation does not describe such
an event. Here in classic Jewish fashion, the movement embodies grace itself:
God takes the initiative to bring the holy city *down* from heaven. Preachers
might help the congregation look for signs of its appearance.

John uses the analogy for the holy city of "a bride adorned for her husband." On the one hand, this image uses the festivity of a Mediterranean
wedding to point to the joy that accompanies the coming of the new Jerusalem. It implies that covenantal commitment, the heart of marriage, is at the
heart of the new city. On the other hand, as I have pointed out in connection
with other feminine images in this book, the image has a troubling social
outcome. In the social pyramid of first-century culture, the woman was typically passive in the arrangement of a marriage. Imaging the new community
as a bride reinforces the idea that women are relatively passive while reinforcing hierarchical relationships in which men are the more determinative
members. Such relationships belong to the first earth that passes away.

A preacher should critique this aspect of the text. The preacher can point out that egalitarianism is an eschatological pattern of relationship in which opportunities are optimum for all to live in community marked by the qualities of the new heaven and the new earth.

The new world is important because in Jewish thinking, blessing encompasses the whole of life, including its material aspects which are associated with the earth. A full and free life requires soil, sun, water, and plants for food, clothing, and housing. Moreover, the earth is not just the stage on which human activity takes place. God intends for humankind and nature to be partners in mutual support (Gen 1:1—2:4).

As noted often in these pages, John sees a limited human role in bringing the new Jerusalem to expression. For churches today who believe that the human community has a significant part to play in transformation, the notion of a new earth includes witnessing to relationships between humankind and nature that can sustain the human family and the natural world and that honor the integrity of nature. In the first earth nature often pummeled humankind. But now the natural world becomes purely a source of blessing.

As a non-apocalyptic Christian, I do not anticipate a replacement earth. But I do believe God is attempting to renew the earth by encouraging humankind and nature to live together in covenant. Although God's lure is inexhaustible, some elements of nature are not. The church can join with others in stepping up the pace of sustainability.

21:3–4. The fact that the voice speaks from the throne underlines its authority. The voice is loud enough for everyone to hear. It expands on the meaning of what will happen in the new heaven and the new earth.

While John does not often use the word "covenant," the prophet frequently assumes a covenantal way of thinking, as in 21:3–4. God will dwell in the immediate presence of the human family in a way similar to the way God dwelled with Israel in the tabernacle during the wilderness wandering.[1] The tabernacle (and later the temple) were made out of the everyday materials of the lives of the community. Its architecture and liturgy were arranged to show how the presence and purposes of God gave life order and security (Exod 25:9; 26:1). The ordering, securing presence is now eschatologically eternal. Revelation 21:22 makes it clear that God's dwelling in the new world is not in a structure (tent or temple) but is in the community, as John had earlier indicated in 13:6.

---

1. The images are more vivid in the Greek than the NRSV suggests with the words "home" and "dwell." The Greek translated "home" is *skēnē*, "tent" or "tabernacle," and "dwell" is *skēnoō* meaning "to pitch a tent."

In covenantal language, the angel declares that the residents of the new Jerusalem will be God's peoples (e.g., Lev 26:11–12; Ps 95:7; Jer 31:33; esp. Ezek 37:27; Zech 2:11). God in God's own self "will be with them." As pointed out earlier, for God to "be with" the community is not simply to be present but is for God to actively seek to shape the life of the community in accord with the divine purposes.

The plural "peoples" (in contrast to the singular people) is significant. In much traditional expression, the singular predominates in reference to Israel as God's people in the sense of being the community through whom God chose to reveal God's nature and purposes in the world.[2] The plural suggests that some gentiles have repented and turned to the God of Israel and have become part of the community of witness.[3]

Earlier writers used language similar to that of 21:4 to encourage the people of God who had been bruised by the heels of earlier empires. Psalm 137:1, for instance, describes the exiles weeping by the waters of Babylon. Isaiah pictures God wiping away such tears and taking away the circumstances of exile (25:8; cf. 65:19; Jer 31:16). Some in John's community have shed tears similarly.

The description of tears, mourning, crying, pain, and death in 21:4 refers especially to conditions of life in the present for those whom the Empire punished because of their testimony to the word of God and to Jesus.[4] At another level, these things are qualities of life in the Roman Empire for those in the lower 97 percent of the social pyramid—daily lives that are accompanied by tears, awareness of the possibility of death, mourning, crying, and pain. At still another level, tears, mourning, crying, pain, and death belong generally to "the first things" that have passed away. They were characteristics of life in the world after the disobedience in the garden of

---

2. In an earlier stage in life, I was put off by the phrase "God's people" in reference to Israel and the church as I thought, "All people are God's people. God's people are not limited to the Jewish and Christian communities." To be sure, in the broad sense, all people are "God's people." However, in the Bible the network of expressions represented by the notion "God's people" often refers not to people in general (all of whom belong to God and for whom God seeks blessing) but functions as an almost technical expression for the community of witness.

3. Many ancient manuscripts contain the plural "peoples" but many the singular "people." According to the principle of textual criticism that the more difficult reading is to be preferred, it is more difficult to explain why a scribe would change the singular (which would have been the more expected usage) to the plural than to explain the reverse. It is easier to think that a scribe would change the unusual plural for God's people to the more typical singular.

4. The discussion of those who experience hunger, thirst, sun, and scorching heat at 7:16 is similar to this one.

Eden (Gen 3:1–23). To be human is to experience tears, mourning, crying, pain, and death.

Revelation 21:1—22:5 now shows God making good on God's promises. The unmediated presence of God dwelling with the community means transformation of all of life's personal and social circumstances.

The preacher can correlate with John's direct intent at the first level by passing the hand of this promise over those in the church today whom contemporary empire punishes because of prophetic witness. God is in solidarity with them to end tears, mourning, crying, pain, and death. The preacher can go beyond John to speak this promise to all whose daily lives are marked by tears, mourning, crying, pain, and death.

21:5. Again the issue of authority takes the microphone. God speaks directly only twice in the book of Revelation. In 1:8 God assures listeners that everything that happens in history takes place under God's aegis, for God is Alpha and Omega. The collapse of empire and the suffering of the faithful witness are not simply chaos but take place under divine control. Now God invokes that sense of sovereignty to affirm that God is, indeed, "making all things new." That may be hard to believe after the book has revealed so many things that make for mourning, crying, pain, and death. But here is the ultimate authority.

God directs the angel to "Write this, for these words are trustworthy and true." Commentators sometimes discuss whether "this" refers to writing the immediate promise or to the book of Revelation as a whole. While this discussion has merit, the difference in outcome is not great: the immediate promise is the goal of the book as a whole.

God stresses that the immediate promise, and the larger scenario of the book of Revelation, are trustworthy (faithful, *pistos*) and true (*alēthinos*). In covenant God promised faithfulness and blessing if the people lived in the way of blessing. The people promised to be faithful and were accountable for the degree to which they lived in the way of blessing. God was also accountable for keeping the divine end of the promise. The period of tribulation, and the empire's conflict with the witnessing community, seemed to belie God's faithfulness. However, John sees the coming of the new heaven and new earth as demonstrating God's promises to be true. This promise should add to the confidence of those who must struggle with empire because of their testimony.

22:6. At the time John received the vision, of course, the transitional process from first to last was still underway. During that difficult time, God declares "It is done," meaning that the outcome is guaranteed (as in 16:17) and that John is seeing the conclusion in the vision of the new heaven and the new earth. Per above, God reinforces the authority for this conclusion by recollecting the descriptive formula of 1:8, "I am the Alpha and the Omega," and adding for emphasis, "the beginning and the end," that is, the one who initially created the world and who is now re-creating it.

God engages in double entendre in promising to the thirsty that God will provide water "as a gift from the spring of the water of life." In the relatively dry eastern Mediterranean, people could often be thirsty. Moreover, Jewish literature sometimes uses the language of thirst to refer to the desire for the faithful to be aware of the divine presence (e.g., Ps 42:2: 63:1: 143:6), and for social restoration, for vindication and for the Realm (e.g., Isa 35:7; 41:17; Matt 5:6; cf.). Those in the great ordeal were thirsty, perhaps physically thirsty as a result of persecution, and certainly metaphorically thirsty for vindication (7:16).

Similarly, the gift of water speaks of both the physical liquid that is abundant and refreshing in the new Jerusalem, and as a figure for the new world. The sea—the water of threat—is no more. The image of the spring of the water of life taps into the deep Ancient Near Eastern mythological association of water with the power of life, such as God as fountain of life (Ps 39:6; cf. 68:26; Jer 17:13), the inexhaustible source of water. Water can be a figure for the eschatological world (Isa 49:10; 55:1; Zech 14:8) These ideas empower the image of the River of Life in 22:1–2.

This image is generative for preaching. To those who are thirsty for the new heaven and new earth, God provides the springs that give the water of life, that is the resources to satisfy that thirst by life in the new world. Where is this thirst manifest today? And what springs refresh those who have it?

21:7. God promises that "those who conquer will inherit these things, and I will be their God and they will be my children." Those who conquered, as we have noticed often, are those who resist accommodation to the empire, even when confronted with brutal punishment (2:7; 11, 17, 26, 3:5, 12, 21; 12:11; 15:2; cf. 5:5). In antiquity the familial household was a fundamental source of identity, vocation, community, and material resources for living. In a culture with little in the way of social support resembling our social security and pensions, the inheritance provided security from generation to generation. God announces that those who conquered (the faithful witnesses) are God's household and, consequently, God establishes the security of their future by giving them the divine inheritance which is the new heaven and the new earth.

People in many sectors of the early twenty-first century face uncertain futures. On the basis of divine omnipotence that would determine the next phase of history, John believed that the future was secure for the faithful. While I do believe that a secure future is *guaranteed*, a process hermeneutic comes away from conversation with John's perspective thinking that God provides the *resources* for better futures—if participants in those situations cooperate with the possibilities.

21:8. In Revelation 21:8, God states flatly that all are not welcome in the holy city. John lists eight categories of persons whose behaviors result not only in their disqualification from the holy city but in being assigned to the lake of fire. The prophet employs a common first-century literary/rhetorical device called a catalogue of vices that focuses less on the individual vices and more on the fractured way of life represented by the vices.[5] John mentions vices that relate directly to the life of the empire. The catalogue is representative, not exhaustive.

- Cowardly: those who are afraid to face the conflict with Rome.

- Faithless (*apistos*): those who do not have faith (*pistos*) or trust that the power of God is greater than that of Caesar and who collude with empire (contrast with the faithful: 2:10, 13; 17:14; cf. 1:5; 19:11; 21:5; 22:6).

- Polluted: those who are in league with the idolatrous, alluring community personified in 17:5–6; cf. 3:4; 21:27.

- Murderers: those who cooperate with putting the faithful to death (6:8; 9:15; 18: 20–21; 11:7; 13; 13:10, 15; 22:15).

- Fornicators: those who engage in theological adultery, so to speak, by relating inappropriately to Caesar (2:14, 20–21; 9:21; 14:8; 17:2–4; 18:3, 9; 19:2; 22:15).

- Sorcerers: those who help the empire deceive people by putting on impressive religious displays (9:21; 18:23; 22:15).

- Idolaters: those who worship the first beast (9:20; 13;1–10; 22:15), with a special eye on those who manage the imperial cult, facilitating this worship (13:11–18); cf. 2:14, 20.

- Liars: those who help Satan operate through Rome to deceive the world by presenting its values and practices as truth, as the real and reliable guide to highest quality of life possible (12:9; 13:14; 18:23; 19:20; 20:3; 20:8; contrast 14:5).

These and other vices create a social world that I think the visual aspect of the page would be improved if this line were followed by a blank line.

I have earlier contended that John believed it was no longer possible for the Roman Empire itself to repent. Condemnation was inevitable. Yet,

---

5. Examples of similar lists of vices: Rom 1:29–31; 1 Cor 5:9–11; 6:9–10; Gal 5:19–20; Eph 5:5; 1 Tim 1:9–10; Tit 1:10, 16.

members of the churches practice some of these vices. One purpose of the book of Revelation is to urge compromised church members to repent. Moreover, since John received this vision in advance of the events in the vision occurring, people within the beast in John's day still had time to repent.

A preacher might develop a series of eight sermons in which each sermon focuses on a different vice. The sermons would need more than word studies of the pertinent terms. Each sermon would need to consider the setting and purpose of the book of Revelation and the place of the concept in that setting, which might involve looking at multiple words and images. The sermon could consider particular texts and how they help the congregation understand the function of the concept in the book. The messages could consider how cowardice, faithlessness, pollution, complicity in murder, fornication, sorcery, idolatry, and lying compromise the church and corrupt the culture today. The sermons would not be complete without encouraging repentance, providing practical guidance in doing so, and helping the congregation envision how bravery, faithfulness, purity, giving life, honoring mutual commitment, honest religion, authentic worship, and truthfulness help the world become more like a new Jerusalem.

Revelation 21:9–22:5: Vision of the New Heaven and the New Earth

The vision of the new heaven and the new earth is the vision of a city. Although the long-established churches have found ways to relate to suburban and exurban settings, those churches have long struggled with how to witness with institutional vitality in urban settings. John does not provide a handbook for urban ministry, but the fact that John describes the new heaven and new earth as a city pushes the church today to think afresh about how to witness effectively in urban contexts and about how the image of the new Jerusalem can be life-giving for congregations across the social spectrum.

The prophet uses features of a city to symbolize qualities of life in the new heaven and the new earth. The complete manifestation of this community lies in the future but many of the characteristics represented in this picture can come to life in communities in the present—urban, suburban, exurban, or rural.

Befitting the theme of Satan and the Roman Empire imitating God and heaven, this final vision sets out an epic contrast between the qualities and destiny of the alluring, idolatrous city and its sponsor Satan in 17:1—19:10

and the qualities and destiny of the new heaven and earth and its sponsor God in 21:1–22:5.[6]

Revelation 21:9-27: The City with the Glory of God

21:9–11. One of the angels who poured the bowls of the seven last plagues shows John the new city. The message is that those who remain faithful during the devastation of the plagues will have a place in the new Jerusalem. John receives this vision "in the spirit," that is, in a state of religious ecstasy.

Before turning to the specific architectural theological symbols, the vision personifies the community as a bride, identifies its location, and describes its radiant glow. At 21:1 we reflected critically on the theological import of personifying the city as bride and wife. The positive side of this comparison is to see the new world as a community whose relationships are covenantal in the manner of the covenant of marriage, but in eschatological expression.

The prophet sees a great high mountain with "the holy city Jerusalem" coming down to it. For protection and defense, people in antiquity often built cities in elevated locations. Moreover, in Jewish life, mountains were often places of revelation. People went up the mountain to talk with God (Gen 22:1–14; Exod 3:1–12; 19:1; Deut 34:1–4; 1 Kgs 19:1–8; Ezek 40:2; Matt 5:1; 17:1–2; Mark 9:2–8; Luke 9:28–36). The location of the city on a mountain with God immediately present makes the city the ultimate safe space. The mountain directly contrasts with the wilderness, the location of the alluring, idolatrous city (17:1–3).

Resonant with 4:3 which uses jasper to bespeak God, this city has the "glory of God" compared to the radiance of a rare jewel, such as jasper. Ordinarily jasper is a pale green, but here (as in 4:3) it is "clear as crystal." This is the first of several times in 21:9—22:5 that John takes something valuable from the present world and indicates that it is transformed in the new Jerusalem. The glow of the city indicates that the city is valuable, but the transformation of jasper into something clear as crystal indicates that the jasper can no longer be the object of human greed or other human instincts that corrupt community.

This analogy is imprecise but catches the spirit of the image: the appearance of the city is similar to a disco ball on which the beam of a brilliant white spotlight shines. As the ball rotates slowly, the thousands of little mirrors

6. For an excellent table comparing the two cities, see Reddish, *Revelation*, 405. A preacher could who uses a big screen could project this table and use it as the visual outline of a sermon comparing the two cities.

reflect the light and turn a dark room into a wonderland of shimmering specks of light. The glow of the city has a similar awe-inspiring effect.

21:12–14. Like Ezekiel's temple and city (Ezek 40:5; 48:30–35), the city is surrounded by walls. The "great, high" walls are one hundred forty-four cubits (21:17), probably referring to a height that would make them approximately as tall as a twenty-story building. The walls are symbols of security. They protect the city from danger outside.

The preacher may join members of the congregation in asking, "Since the beast and Satan and their followers have been eliminated, why is a city wall here?" Moreover, although twenty stories sounds like a very high wall to a typical listener today, it is actually small in proportion to the size of the city (see 21:16).

This may be a case in which the symbol (the wall) gets in the way of its deeper significance (the new Jerusalem is a safe and secure community). However, the size of the wall—one hundred forty-four cubits—points to the nature of the wall itself. As noted multiple times, the number twelve is a symbol for community. In antiquity, the squaring of a number indicated intensification. The word "wall" in this instance is a way of speaking about community. The security of the city is in its nature as eschatological community in which God is present in an unmediated way.

During the period of walled cities, cities typically had a limited number of gates to both provide and limit access. The gates were closed at night. In comparison, the new Jerusalem has twelve gates—a large number that suggests open access. Having three gates on each of the four sides of the wall dramatizes the community's openness and sense of security.

Angels stand at the gates like gatekeepers (Isa 62:6). John has pictured angels as agents of both providence and judgment. Since the time of judgment has passed, these angels must represent the care and protection of God.

The names of the twelve tribes of Israel are inscribed on the gates, indicating that this community is in continuity with God's purposes in Israel. People enter this community through the gates of Israel (so to speak), that is, by embracing the God of Israel (over and against idols) and by living as God revealed to Israel (in covenantal community). Israel's purpose was to be "a light to the nations" (Isa 42:6).

This continuity is reinforced by the twelve foundations having "the twelve names of the twelve apostles of the Lamb." The work of God through Jesus is an eschatological extension of the work of God through Israel. Through the church, the light of Israel has drawn nations into community (e.g., 5:9; 7:9).

John's image suggests that real security in community comes less by keeping people out than by finding ways to be genuinely inclusive. Indeed,

John has earlier celebrated crowds gathered around the throne as people from "every tribe and language and people and nation" (5:9; 7:9).[7] Of course, while there are many gates always open, John indicates in 21:8 and 22:14–15 that there are boundaries: the city does not welcome community-destroying behavior.

21:15–18. The angel measures the city with a gold rod. The gold signals the value of the rod. The act of measuring, as in 11:1–2, means that God controls the entire city. God's protective hand is over all who enter through the gates and all who make up the community (the people represented by the number 144).

Many Christians grew up with the phrase "the city foursquare" in reference to heaven. Here is the origin of that expression: a city whose width and length are the same, thus indicating it is of God's design (Ezek 40:47; 41:21; 43:16; 45:2; 48:16, 20, 30–35). Even more, its height is the same as its width and length, making it a cube. The most significant cube in Israel was the Holy of Holies at the heart of the temple, the most set-apart piece of the community. The sense of holiness associated with the Holy of Holies now infuses the entire community. Later, John will say, explicitly, that the city has no temple. Why not? Because the life of city embodies the functions of a temple.

In one way, the NRSV gives the contemporary congregation a nice sense of the size of the new Jerusalem by saying it is 1,500 miles on a side, about equivalent to the United States from Canada to the Gulf of Mexico and from Washington, DC to Denver, Colorado. To a small community on Patmos, about 17 square miles, the size of the new Jerusalem takes one's breath away. In another way, the NRSV obscures the symbolism of the Greek which is "twelve thousand stadia." A stadia was a measurement of distance of approximately two hundred yards. The number "twelve" evokes community in God's way. Multiplying by a thousand intensifies so that twelve thousand stadia is a way of saying that the new heaven and the new earth is breathtakingly large—large enough to provide for the multitude too great to number (7:9) who honor the word of God and the testimony of Jesus. Though not referring to this biblical passage, the Jubilee Singers catch the spirit here, "There's room for many a more."[8]

The wall, which gives the city the radiant glow described in 21:9, is clear as glass, as is the "pure gold" of the city itself. Gold then as now was among the most valuable commodities. The amount of gold here—enough

---

7. As we have noted, this diversity alone is not an inherent good. Satan rules over a similar body (11:7; 13:7).

8. https://en.wikipedia.org/wiki/The_Gospel_Train. Accessed July 26, 2018.

to build a whole city—is unimaginable. The Roman Empire flaunted its wealth. But its wealth was nothing compared to a city which is pure gold. The gold here is a cipher for saying the importance and value of the community of the new heaven and the new earth are beyond measure.

21:19-21. The foundations of the wall are adorned with twelve jewels. The word "adorn" here occurred earlier to describe the jewels of the alluring, idolatrous city (17:4), thus showing again the empire's attempt to deceive. In Rome, material resources were controlled by the few. The new Jerusalem offers material abundance for all.

John's multilevel use of symbolism rises to a high tide with the list of jewels that adorn the city's foundations (21:19-20). At one level, John builds on Isaiah 54:11-12 which envisions a renewed Jerusalem with bejeweled foundation stones (cf. Tobit 13:16-17). These stones are quite similar to those on the breastplate of the high priest (Exod 28:17-21; 39:10-14). This association links the stones with priestly service—in line with Revelation 1:6; 5:10; 20:6—to suggest that the life of the entire city is priestly in representing the presences and purposes of God.[9] Since the high priest represented the representative community to itself, the holy city now enacts that role as community.

R.H. Charles points to an additional symbolic connection. The twelve stones were also associated with the signs of the zodiac. The first Babylon was noted for astrology—the attempt to understand and sometimes manipulate life by means of astral entities. The second Babylon (Rome) continued such emphasis. Given the fatalism of the Graeco-Roman era, many people turned to astrology to attempt make life more bearable.

According to Charles, the different foundation jewels are associated with the different signs of the zodiac. Moreover, Charles argues that John listed the stones in 21:19-21 in an order reverse to that in which they are typically found.[10] By placing the jewels in the new city, John indicates that real security comes not through astrology and astral deities but through God. The astral entities are not gods but created things that should serve God's purposes.[11] God is so powerful that God can take some of the most potent symbols of the Roman attempt to control life and transform them into the service of the priestly community.

9. The names of the apostles on the foundation stones (21:14) reinforces the notion that this community of Jesus is grafted into the priestly vocation.

10. Charles, *Revelation*, 2:167–69. Some scholars cast doubt on aspects of Charles' proposal because some of the evidence is missing. However, it should be noted that both Josephus (*Ant.* 3.7.5–7) and Philo (*Mos.* 2.124; *Spec.* 1.84–94) connect the stones in the breastplate of the high priest to the zodiac.

11. My oversimplification and adaptation of Caird, *Revelation*, 276–77.

A preacher might consider ways in which people directly interact with astrology today in seeking to control life. Beyond that, a sermon might explore analogies to the ancient use of the zodiac. How do people today try to manipulate life? A sermon going this direction should not only reflect critically on such efforts but should help the congregation consider how the movement of the community towards the new Jerusalem offers more hopeful and trustworthy perspectives.

John unintentionally gave history the phrase "pearly gates" to refer to the entrance to heaven by indicating that each of the twelve gates is made of a single gigantic pearl. Pearls were valuable in antiquity (e.g., Matt 13:45–46). The alluring, idolatrous city bedecked in pearls made inappropriate use of the jewel (17:4; cf. 18:12). God transforms the small pearls of the empire that contributed to its destruction into mammoth jewels as gates protecting the city.[12]

Here is another opportunity for the preacher to encourage the congregation to think about attractive things contemporary empires misuse. How can they be converted into things that build up mutually supportive community?

21:22–27. The new Jerusalem does not contain a temple because God and the Lamb have become the temple. Christians sometimes think the Jewish community believed that the temple was the only place God dwelled and, hence, the only place that God was accessible. At its best, however, Jewish theology recognized that God is universally present, with the temple serving as a symbol of that presence (e.g., 1 Kgs 8:27; Ps 139; Jer 23:22–23; Amos 9:2–5). The book of Revelation earlier used the figure of the temple in heaven as a heavenly prototype of the earthly temple and as a symbol of authority (7:15; 11:19; 14:15–17; 15:5–8; 16:1, 17). However, the new heaven and the new earth do not require a temple because the God and the Lamb are now so perceptibly present that an architectural reminder of that presence is no longer needed.

Christians sometimes view the temple through the anti-Jewish lens that sees the temple and its rites as outmoded, replaced by Jesus and the worship of the church. However, the new heaven and the new earth have no temple not because Jesus (and Christianity) supersede Judaism but because the eschatological world replaces "the first things."

John's reference to the absence of the sun and the moon, deriving in part from Isaiah 60:19–20, invokes two shades of meaning. One is from Genesis 11:14–19 when God made the sun and moon to give light in the

12. A later rabbinic tradition in the Talmud, drawing from Isa 54:11-12, foresees God creating gates for a new Jerusalem from massive pearls that are thirty cubits by thirty cubits (B. Bat. 75a).

first creation. These two heavenly bodies are part of the structure that supported a world in which disobedience distorted God's aim for people and
nature to live together in community. However, that world is displaced by
the new heaven and the new earth. Sun and moon are not needed in the new
Jerusalem. A second shade of meaning derives from the Roman proclivity to
regard the sun and moon as deities. These non-deities are not even present
in the reconfigured world. They no longer offer the temptation to idolatry.
The unmediated glory of God illuminates the new heaven and the new earth,
along with the lamplight of the presence of the Lamb.

The nations are gentiles who walk (live) in the city and who live by its
light. While God had sought to redeem the nations (12:5; 14:6; 15:4), many
nations opposed God and were punished (10:11; 11:2, 9, 18; 14:8; 16:19;
17:15; 18:3, 23; 19:11–20:15). Some people in the nations evidently came
out of Rome, that is, they repented and disengaged from the empire (5:6;
7:9). Moreover, these gentiles bring the glory and honor of the nations into
the city. The glory of the nations is their reverence for the God of Israel. In
the shame/honor culture of antiquity, honor centers in living according to
the expectations of the community which here means living according to
the principles of the Realm of God.

Most of John's direct references to the rulers of the earth presuppose
that the rulers of John's day were disobedient and subject to punishment.[13]
Yet John envisioned the day when some rulers would join a wider number of
repentant gentiles in coming out of Rome. The notion that the rulers of the
earth will bring their glory to the God of Israel is adapted from Isaiah 60:2–3
which anticipates a great eschatological reunion of Jewish and gentile peoples
as the nations bring their wealth to the God of Israel. While the rulers cannot
bring material wealth into the new heaven and new earth (since the world
is, by definition, materially super-abundant), they bring their glory into it,
that is, they no longer seek the self-serving control and acclaim characteristic
of the rulers of empires but they put their glory (and their wealth, i.e., their
material resources) at the service of the new Jerusalem.

A preacher might cautiously connect John's anticipation of the nations
and their rulers coming into the eschatological city with the yearning among
many communities for a multicultural world, that is, a world in which people
from various races, ethnicities and cultures live together in mutual respect.
As indicated in connection with 5:9 and 7:9, John gives no indication that
the people from the nations lose essential aspects of their identity when they
become a part of the new heaven and the new earth. They appear to enter in

13. Rev 1:5 emphasizes that Jesus has authority over the rulers of the earth and,
therefore, that all rulers are accountable to Jesus. Otherwise, John's references to the
rulers are negative: 6:15; 10:11; 16:12, 14; 17:2, 9, 12, 14, 18: 18:3, 9; 19:18–19.

their "nation-ness." Admittedly, this interpretive impulse runs the danger of anachronism. John does not deal with the issue in the same terms as people today who celebrate differences in communities.

John now adds that the gates are never closed in the day. A city would seldomly close its gates during the day except when attacked. This remark, then, re-emphasizes the security and openness of the holy city as the gates will *never* be closed by day.

Again, two shades of meaning are present in the short statement that there is no night there. For one, night belongs the structure of the old age of night and day following one another (Gen 1:4–5). This pattern of earlier earth-life passes away. The other shade comes from an association in Jewish literature between night and threat (e.g., Judg 20:5; Job 4:12–14. Ps 91:5; Jer 49:9; Mic 3:6). Zechariah 14:7 anticipates the eschatological time when God will end the threat symbolized by "night."

Revelation 21:27 is a small-scale reprise of the main theme of 21:8: people will not be part of the new heaven and the new earth if they retain attitudes and actions associated with the dragon and the beast, that is, those who are unclean and those who practice abomination and falsehood. The notion of the clean and the unclean referred not to physical cleanliness but to the degree to which someone manifested characteristics considered essential to order in community. Idolatry is an abomination that preoccupies the Revelation (17:4–5).[14] Falsehood refers to believing and acting on the deception offered by the beast and dragon. Such folk were condemned in 19:11–20:15, so, of course, are not present in the new world.

Revelation 22:1-5: The Climax of the Vision of the New Heaven and the New Earth

John turns to two places for the inspiration for the climax in 22:1–5: imagery from the garden of Eden (Gen 2:1–22) and from the final eschatological vision of Ezekiel (Ezek 47–48). Many apocalyptic theologians in antiquity anticipated that the end-times would be similar to the beginning times. The end-time would be a return to paradise. A significant difference between Eden and the new Jerusalem is that disobedience was possible in the first garden, but not in the new city.

22:1–2a. In the semi-arid world of the Mediterranean basin, a source of potable water was essential for things to live—plant, animal, and human. Rivers were particularly prized, for their flow of water tended to be reliable. In the parts of North America that are forested and fertile, and in the towns

14. On abomination and idolatry, see Dan 9:27; 11:31; 12:11.

and cities where water flows freely from the tap, we are not always aware of the significance of the statement in Genesis 2 that a *river* flowed through the garden (Gen 2:10). John's river flows from the throne of God, the ultimately reliable source, and it is "bright as crystal," that is, remarkably clear and pure, in contrast to some of the water in urban settings in the empire where water was sometimes unpotable.[15] Beyond that, a river was a symbol of the things necessary to sustain life: God provides those things.

While John has the ultimate eschatological future in view, that future bleeds into the present in such a way that the preacher can offer the congregation the possibility that what happens in the flow of the river can happen in the congregation and in the wider community. The river begins at the throne and following Ezekiel 47:1–12 splashes out of the temple and the city and through the desert until it reaches the Dead Sea. As it flows the soil becomes moist and vegetation appears, including trees. The Dead Sea becomes fresh—except for swamps and marshes that provide salt necessary for life. The river—the flow of the power of God through community—can soften hard, arid places and help them bring forth vegetation and restore dead waters.

The river of life flows through the middle of the city so the water is available to all. Water is not distributed according to one's place in the social pyramid.

There is no indication that John has baptism in mind. But being in a church that practices the immersion of believers, I am theologically compelled to say that the prophet's picture of the flow of the river can be a paradigm for what happens in immersion.

22:2b. Scholars have posited various possibilities for the unusual statement that the tree of life (singular) grows on both sides of the river. The best explanation is that while Genesis 2:9 pictures one tree of life, Ezekiel 47:12 has expanded this one tree into a forest growing on both sides of the river, evidently running from the temple to the Dead Sea.

The tree of life—a figure found in many cultures in the Ancient Near East—is a symbol of the power of life itself. As it grows it provides food for the immediate generation and seeds for trees for subsequent generations. After the first couple disobeyed, God excommunicated the couple from the

---

15. Although the Tiber River flowed in the city of Rome, and the seven hills had some springs, by the time of John these had become unreliable sources of clean water, so that the Romans eventually built nine aqueducts to carry water to the city. The aqueducts experienced lengthy breakdowns. Water—especially clean water—was often hard to come by. The upper class had private sources of water, but most people got their water from public fountains. The hygiene situation was compromised by people dumping chamber pots onto the streets.

garden so they could not eat of the tree of life and, hence, become immortal (Gen 3:22–24). God graciously continued to provide the things necessary for human existence, but as punishment, God expulsed them from the garden and made death a reality for every human being.

In the new Jerusalem, the power represented by the tree is greatly multiplied by the number of trees in the city. Since God and the Lamb do not restrict access to the tree, those who eat of it live forever (as specified in 22:5b). Both 22:14 and 19 reinforce this view.

The prophet underscores the life-sustaining power of the tree of life by saying it gives fruit each month (Ezek 47:12). Every moment is generative. The city never faces a shortage of food or other resources necessary for a secure existence. God thus keeps the promise made in Revelation 2:7.

Another image enlarged from Ezekiel 47:12 is especially provocative for our time, "The leaves of the tree are for the healing of the nations." In Bible studies in congregations, I am often asked, "How do the leaves of the tree heal the nations?" In those days, people made some medicines from tree leaves: the leaves of the tree contain medicine that heals the nations.

The sickness of the nations (so to speak) is idolatry. The symptoms: they worship the beast and the dragon (false gods), collude with these enemies of God, and, hence, deserve punishment. The medicine is the worldview of the book of Revelation. God offers the nations the opportunity for healing (being part of the new Jerusalem) through repentance and living towards mutually supportive community.

John's reference to the nations has three functions, any or all of which could become a tree on which to hang the leaves of a sermon. (1) This part of the vision confirms for people from the nations that they are in full standing in the community on the way to Realm. (2) It reminds the present community that God intends for the eschatological world to be multi-ethnic. This function may challenge some in the present congregation to enlarge their sense of who is welcome. (3) While John communicates this vision before the actual end-time it describes, the vision implicitly invites people from the nations to take the medicine that God graciously offers in the present so that the healing can begin.

With respect to the sermon, the early twenty-first century is a season in which relationships among the nations—broadly conceived as the peoples of the world—need healing. Multiple forms of contentiousness along such lines of race, sex, gender, economic class, ethnic identity, religious practice, geographical location, political philosophy, and national identity are often like multiple cancers causing a body excruciating pain as it withers and loses functions. The preacher can point to the leaves of the tree as promising the possibility of healing.

Preachers who cannot, because of theological integrity, ask other peoples to give up their own religious (and other) commitments and to repent and come to the God of Israel, can nonetheless help the church encourage community-building and life-giving relationships across lines of difference. When true community is not forthcoming, the church can call for mutual respect. If that does not evolve, the church can seek tolerance in order to give community-building possibilities time to develop.

22.3a. Nothing accursed will be in the city. After the first couple ate the forbidden fruit, God cursed the world (Gen 3:14–19). The effects of this general curse will not pertain in the city (Zech 14:11). Moreover, in covenantal thinking, God curses (punishes) those who disobey the guidelines for living in covenant. John has chronicled multiple forms of disobedience in the empire ranging from idolatry to the murder of those who hold to the word of God. There are no conditions of curse here. The new Jerusalem is a punishment-free zone. Furthermore, the community in the new heaven and new earth does not face temptation as the first couple did. Satan is not present to try to deceive them.

22:3b–4. The throne of God and the Lamb will be in the new city which means that the authority of God will shape life for everlasting blessing. God's servants will worship the living God. The imperial cult, which legitimized idolatry through the worship of both Caesar and Satan, was destroyed (20:11–15).

After being expelled from the garden, people had only indirect, mediated access to God (except for Exod 33:18–23; cf. Deut 34:10). Now the people in his holy city see God's face. They have direct, unmediated access to God. They will no longer have to ask the kind of question posed by the martyrs in 6:9–11, "How long?" They will be fully aware of the divine presence and purposes.

God's name will be on their foreheads. As we noted earlier, the mark on the forehead, while physically invisible, is like a cattle brand (7:3; 9:4; 14:1, 9). Moreover, as the high priest had the name of God on the priest's forehead (Exod 28:36–38) so does this high priestly community.[16] The mark identifies the person as belonging in this city, and contrasts with the mark which the beast placed on its followers (13:6; 17:4).

The hearers in John's church had been marked in this way. The mark had two effects. First, it assured them they have a place in the new Jerusalem. Secondly, it reminded them to continue to witness faithfully.

---

16. On the high priestly nature of the community, see 21:19-20. On the priestly character of the community see 1:5; 5:10.

22:5. At 21:23–24, we noted the absence of night means an absence of threat and the absence of the inability to see what they need to see. We also noted that the unmediated presence of God becomes their light and gives them the capacity to perceive clearly. The sun and the lamp belong to the structures of the old age and are no longer needed. The population now has a complete view of God and of their fellow citizens in the new Jerusalem and of the values and practices that characterize the life of this community. As we might say today, they can now fully see God 24/7. And, they now have an uninterrupted view of the deception associated with the dragon, the beast, and the false prophet.

We said earlier that John borrowed an idea already in apocalyptic literature that the faithful will join God in reigning in the coming age and that John gave that notion a distinctive twist: the martyrs would rule during the millennium as a reward for their endurance to death (5:9; 20:4, 6). Now it seems that all the faithful will worship God (22:3b) and will "reign" with Christ. In worship the community serves God through the symbolism of liturgy as a way of indicating the readiness of the community to serve God in the rest of life. To reign with God is to serve God's community building purposes "forever and ever."

We have noted before that John sees the new Jerusalem as if it is an accomplished fact in heaven though awaiting final realization in John's present world. In this context, these images have a double function. First, they assure John's congregations that they are, indeed, in the community on the way to the Realm. Second, they remind the community that they need to remain faithful and true in the eschatological tension they experience now, and in the intensification that John anticipates ahead.

A preacher might point to some contemporary situations in which aspects of the new heaven and new earth are already coming to expression, though always imperfectly. An example: for almost forty years I have lived in an area of a city with an urban feel. For a long time, many businesses were abandoned and houses run down. There were several vacant lots, mostly overgrown with piles of trash, and even occasional rusted automobiles. But over the last ten years the area has slowly changed. Business have opened. Houses have been fixed up. Yards are mowed in the summer and walks shoveled in the winter. And most recently, urban farms and community gardens have reclaimed the vacant lots.

Yet this renewal bears significant marks of the old Jerusalem. Many of the people who lived in this area for years have essentially been forced to relocate several miles to parts of the city that are farther from their places of work and have fewer public services. Moreover, the housing in their new neighborhoods is not as well constructed. One of the reasons we moved to this area was its racial, ethnic, and cultural diversity. Not surprisingly the refurbishing takes place hand-in-hand with gentrification which here means rising percentages of middle class Eurocentric young families and smaller percentages of everyone else.

A preacher in this neighborhood can find a limited analogy to John's promise of a new Jerusalem. But, like John, the preacher must also stress that the movement towards the realization of the promise is still underway. Those who catch the vision of the truly inclusive community must, like John's first-century congregations, move forward with patient endurance.

Revelation 22:6–21: Appeal to the Congregations to Commit

Preachers today often end sermons in ways designed to encourage the congregation to do something consistent with the purpose of the sermon—e.g., to take an action such as marching against a particular social injustice. In my congregation, the sermon typically ends with an invitation to make a confession of faith to be followed by immersion, to transfer membership to the congregation, or to rededicate oneself to Christian life and witness.

Commentators in earlier eras often regarded 21:6–21 as a collection of independent expressions strung together in seemingly random fashion. Recent interpreters acknowledge that while John uses elements of the closing of the Greek letter, Revelation 21:6–21 does not formally conform to an ancient rhetorical convention. This part of the letter functions similarly to the endings of sermons today in that this section is designed to help listeners say "Yes" to the message of the book.

John uses the voices of an angel, Jesus and God, and a variety of literary approaches to encourage the congregation to commit itself to being faithful and true. John does not introduce new theological considerations but deftly invokes the power of things that came before .The prophet seeks to evoke commitment by recurring to four related themes: (1) the message of the book of Revelation is trustworthy; (2) the center of the message is that Jesus is coming soon; (3) God will soon reward the faithful and punish the unfaithful; (4) consequently, listeners need to move into the future with the patient endurance necessary to continue to witness in the teeth of opposition.[17] A preacher might organize a sermon with parts along the lines of these themes.

22:6. In language reminiscent of earlier passages John reminds listeners that the words of the book of Revelation are trustworthy and true (cf. 21:5) because God—who guides the spirits of the prophets—sent an angel

17. This summary is adapted from Murphey, *Fallen is Babylon*, 433.

to show God's servants (the witnessing community) what must soon take place (cf. 1:1–2). This statement underlines the authority of the book.

22:7. Jesus announces, "I am coming soon." While commentators often rightly insist that John does not set out a specific timeline for the return of Jesus, the book nevertheless expects the return of Jesus to take place soon enough that the congregation needs to engage full-force in witness.

Apocalyptic writers sometimes insert expostulations into the narrative, as John does when quoting a beatitude of Jesus. The seventh beatitude in the book declares that those who are blessed—to be blessed means to be part of the community of the new heaven and new earth—are those who "keep the words of the prophecy of this book." To blessed in this eschatological sense is to believe what the book says and to make a witness that is faithful and true even when encountering hostility from the empire.

22:8a. The prophet adds eyewitness authority to the book. "I, John, am the one who heard and saw these things." "These things," of course, are the message in vision of the book of Revelation.

22:8b. John ushers the preacher into an interpretive space for a sermon by repeating John's theological mistake of 19:10, where a fuller discussion occurs. John falls down to worship at the feet of the angel who had conveyed the vision. However, the angel becomes John's theological instructor in reminding the prophet that God alone is worthy of worship. All others are servants—angel, prophets, and others who "keep the words of the Book."

22:10. John significantly adapts the traditional element in apocalypticism that held that God had long ago planned the outcome of history, written it down, and placed it in hiding where it would remain until the present age was nearing its end, at which time the plan would be revealed. God joined Daniel, for instance, to seal up the words of Daniel's prophecy until the right time (Dan 7:26; 10:14; cf. 12:4; 1 En. 1:2). By contrast John believes the time until the transformative events is so near that there is no point in sealing the prophecy. Leaving the prophecy unsealed should help motivate John's congregations to continue to witness as history thickens.

22:11. As we have often noted, John thinks the time has passed for the Roman Empire to repent. That idea is at work in 22:11 refracted through Daniel 12:10: while many would be in the process of being "purified, cleansed, and refined," the wicked "would continue their behavior. "None of the wicked shall understand, but those who are wise shall understand" (Dan 12:10). Those engaged in evil and filth will continue doing so and will not grasp that time is running out, while the righteous and holy will accurately grasp the eschatological quality of the era and live faithfully. To be sure, the possibility of repentance is open to the churches (e.g., 2:5, 16, 21–22; 3:3, 19) and, presumably individuals in the empire, but history is moving inexorably towards the final judgment. John writes to help those in the congregations understand the denouement of history through which they are living and to respond appropriately.

As noted repeatedly, while I respect the intent of the approach of 22:10—to communicate to congregations in situations of uncertainty that God is in control so they will witness boldly—I cannot believe God has the power or mindset to pre-plan history except to set out the broad goal of ever offering the lure to the new Jerusalem in ways appropriate to the unfolding contexts of history. Not do I believe that the possibilities of repentance for the evildoers and the filthy are foreclosed. A preacher can deconstruct these notions on the way to offering constructive rationales for bold calls to repentance.

22:12–13. This short section ramps up intensity and authority. Hearing Jesus state again, "I am coming soon," is designed to redouble the hearers' sense of the urgency: Jesus comes with the reward that will repay all people according to their deeds, i.e., according to the degree that they have come out of Rome and have witnessed forcefully. Some will be welcomed into the new heaven and new earth but others will be consigned to the lake of fire.[18]

John has Jesus self-describe in the same way as God: Alpha and Omega, first and last, beginning and end. This designation indicates that Jesus is an utterly reliable authority. He joined God as Alpha and Omega.[19] He is first and last, and beginning and end.[20] As we have observed elsewhere, Christology is a significant matter of discussion in the contemporary church. While John does not resolve this issue for contemporary constructive/systematic theology, a sermon could make an inroad into this discussion by beginning with John's approach.

22:14–15. John continues to emphasize the importance of enduring faithfully by setting the final beatitude in the book alongside the fate of those who align with the empire. To be blessed, in this apocalyptic context as we noted most recently at 22:7 (and at 1:3; 14:3; 16:15; 19:9; 20:6) is to have a place in the new world. Using the figure of a robe for the deeds of a life, John indicates that those who "wash their robes" of filth (per 22:11) and who witness faithfully in the present will eat of the tree of life (cf. 7:9, 13–14; 3:5, 18; 6:11; cf. 1:13; 15:6). They enter the new Jerusalem by the gates (see 21:12–13; 21; 22:2).

John employs a brief catalogue of vices to characterize those who are not on the path to the new city: dogs, fornicators, murderers, idolaters, and

18. On the nature of this separation see discussion at 20:11–15.

19. On these descriptions of God, see discussion at 1:8; 21:6.

20. On first and last, see discussion at 1:17; 2:8. On beginning and end, see discussion at 21:6.

all who love and practice falsehood—qualities we have identified with those who accommodate to the empire.[21] They are dogs. This is the only use of "dogs" in the last book of the Bible. In the ancient world, the epithet "dog" was degrading as dogs were often associated with wild behavior and with eating dead flesh (e.g., 1 Kgs 14:11; 2 Kgs 9:10; Prov 26:11).

In the midst of the rhetorically overcharged ethos of the early twenty-first century, a preacher might turn to John's derogatory use of the term "dogs" as a negative pole for what is needed today. The preacher might reflect on the ways in which name-calling (such as referring to someone as a "dog") contributes to social polarization in the very time that civil discourse should begin with understanding the perspectives of others and engaging them respectfully, even when disagreeing.

22:16. John takes another step on the road of authority by citing Jesus yet again as the source of the vision and by specifying what Jesus does. As at 5:5, the designation of root and descendent of David recollects Isaiah 11:1–10, the first Isaiah's vision of the peaceful dominion. According to Isaiah 11:10, the establishment of that domain is a signal to "the nations" to "inquire," that is, they would go up to the mountain of God so that God could teach them the divine ways (Isa 2:1–4). John's emphasis on the rulers of the earth (21:24, 26) and the "nations" (22:3; cf. 5:9; 7:9; 12:5 15:4) in the new Jerusalem means that day has arrived. Moreover, Jesus is "the bright morning star," an image derived from Numbers 24:17 where the star refers to one who will conquer the enemies of Israel (cf. 2:28). While John calls attention to Jesus as God's agent in these things, the larger picture is the coming of the new world as the means whereby God keeps the promises made through Isaiah and Numbers.

The congregation then and now can take the risk of faithfulness because they can count on a promise-keeping God. A challenge for the preacher is to help the congregation today discern believable signs that the promise is still good.

22:17. John's capacity to speak at multiple levels again shines at 22:17. For these sentences pray simultaneously for Christ to come back and complete the eschatological transformation of the cosmos and for Christ to appear in a proto-eschatological fashion in the sacred meal.

Christians struggle with the identity of those invited to "Come" in 22:17. Many preachers would like to see the invitation directed to the human family generally. The preacher can then use all four lines of the text to invite everyone who is not on the road to the new Jerusalem to come. Although this invitation would resonate with John's plea for the unrepentant in the

---

21. E.g. sorcerers: 9:21; 18:3; 21:8; fornication: 2:14, 20–21; 9:21; 14:8; 17:2–4; 18:3; 19:2; 21:8; murder: 9:21; 21:8; idolaters: 21:8; falsehood: 2:2; 16:13; 19:20; 20:10; 21:27. See especially comparable lists of vices at 9:21; 21:8.

church to "Come out" of Babylon (18:4), this expansive audience seems
unlikely to me because the prophet does not directly issue such invitations
to the empire (even while inviting disobedient members of the church to
repent, and recognizing that some members of the empire may do so: 2:5,
16, 21–22; 3:3, 19). As noted several times (most recently at 22:10–11), the
time for the empire itself to repent is past.

Most scholars see the first two lines directed to Jesus and the second
two lines directed at people. The Spirit (i.e., the Holy Spirit), the bride (i.e.,
the church), and all who hear (i.e., those who hear the book of Revelation)
pray for Jesus to return and complete the transformation of history. This
thinking is consistent with the main themes in 22:6–21, especially the intense expectation that Jesus is coming soon.

The last two lines, then, are directed to people. A majority of interpreters think the two sentences are directed to people in the world at large to
repent and obey and join the movement towards the new heaven and new
earth. As just noted, however, John does not directly issue such invitations.
Indeed, the book of Revelation is directed to the church, an insider audience. It seems truer to the exegetical context to hear the appeal to the thirsty
and the offer of the water of life in light of references to thirst and water in
the book. In 7:17, John envisions the Lamb guiding the martyrs to "springs
of the water of life." In 21:7, God promises to give "water as a gift from the
spring of life" to those in the church who are thirsty for the Realm of God.
John thus reiterates the invitation to the unfaithful in the church to take the
steps that will enable them to become part of the holy city: repent, obey, and
witness.[22] This perspective is consistent with the book as a whole.

Preachers with conversational theologies who want to call not only
the unrepentant church but the larger world to repent can do so by going beyond the viewpoint in 22:17. Indeed, the process theology to which
I subscribe often encourages a preacher to see beyond the church to God's
hopes for the world. The preacher simply needs to be clear about the points
at which the sermon goes beyond the text.

I join several scholars in hearing concurrent echoes of the eschatological meal in this passage.[23] Revelation 22:20 sets out a brief prayer, "Come,
Lord Jesus" (*erchou, kurie iēsou*) that is very similar to the prayer that comes
at the climax of the sacred meal in many first century congregations: "Our
Lord, come" (*marana tha*) (1 Cor 16:22; Did. 10:6).[24] From this perspective, the prayer to "Come" is a prayer for the cosmic Christ (as pictured in

22. Adapted from Beale, *Book of Revelation*, 1149.

23. Since I am a member of a church that partakes of the loaf and the cup every
week, I am predisposed to favor this interpretive possibility.

24. This prayer likely originated in Aramaic from which comes the well-known
transliteration, *marana tha*, that is, "Our Lord" (*marana*) "come" (*tha*).

1:12–16) to be present and transform the everyday bread and cup into an anticipation of the eschatological victory meal of 19:9. Hearing this allusion makes sense in view of the fact that John anticipated the book being performed in services of worship (1:3–4, 10) and that such services often climaxed with the sacred meal. In view of antiquity's perception of life as a communal fabric, the emphasis is not just on the person (Jesus) being present at the supper but is also on the event itself (the supper as a proto-eschatological experience of the new heaven and the new earth) occurring as the congregations partake.

Ideally, preaching on this text should take place when the congregation eats the bread and drinks the cup. The worship team could plan the entire service around these motifs. In many congregations, the preacher could help the congregation expand its understanding of the Lord's Supper from a time of feeling close to Jesus to the larger social awareness of the proto-eschatological world.

22:18–19. Seminary students often have good-natured humor around the warning of 22:18–19. "What," they ask, "does it mean to add to the prophecy of the book or to take away from it?" More broadly, some Christians think John's directive applies to the Bible as a whole. In such settings, a preacher can help a congregation recognize that, from a historical-critical point of view, John has only the book of Revelation in mind.

John's admonition derives from the fact that those who performed the book out loud could easily change the texts they performed. Furthermore, in the centuries before standardized printing, copyists could also easily make such changes. Consequently, several documents in the ancient world contain warnings such as 22:18–19. The Deuteronomic Moses, for instance, forbids the audience from taking away or adding to anything in the book of Deuteronomy (4:2). The Letter of Aristeas 310–11 pronounces a curse on anyone who changes Scripture (the Torah, Prophets, and Writings).

The curses in 22:18–19 are toxic. God will visit all the plagues in the book on the person who adds to "the words of the prophecy of this book." God will deny eternal life in the holy to those who take away any part of the vision.

From this text, a preacher might launch a sermon designed to help the congregation clarify its perspectives on interpreting the Bible. John stresses the importance of not changing the words of the vision. Very few in the church today propose changing the wording of biblical texts.[25] But going beyond that issue, the preacher could use this text as a figure for multiple perspectives in the church on the nature of the Bible and how to interpret it,

25. The discipline of textual criticism seeks to establish the most likely wording of the biblical text in the light of differences in wording in ancient manuscripts. I have in mind adding new words, taking away words, or changing words.

ranging from those on one end of the interpretive spectrum who think the church needs simply to repeat the message of the Bible, to those who think the church needs to clarify and apply the message of the Bible, to those who think that the church can reject the authority of some biblical texts and can offer alternative theological viewpoints. A congregation that is clear about its own interpretive perspective is in a good position not only to interpret texts but also to distinguish the congregation's interpretive lens from the lenses of other congregations, and to assess the strengths and weaknesses of the various lenses at play, including its own.

22:20. The prophet quotes Jesus as the author of "these things," i.e. the vision of the book. John reiterates yet again the imminence of Jesus return yet again to reinforce the importance of faithful witness and to deepen hope in the difficult periods at hand and ahead when he has Jesus say, "Surely I am coming soon."

John then responds to this heightened awareness with the cry "Amen. Come, Lord Jesus." As we note when discussing 22:17, the cry "Come, Lord Jesus" interprets the well-known Aramaic expression *marana tha*, "Our Lord, Come." This expression continues the central idea in Jesus' affirmation, "I am coming soon."

22:21. Just as John began the book of Revelation as a Greek letter (1:1-2, 4-6), so John ends the book with a benediction format adopted by letter writers in the early churches. As we note 1:4—the only other point at which the word "grace" (*charis*) appears in the book—the notion of grace includes not only unmerited favor (as in much Christian theology) but also the covenantal faithfulness associated with *chesed*.[26] John assures the saints facing the tensions of the final transformation that Jesus, the cosmic savior of 1:12-16, can sustain them in the struggle.

---

26. Several times the Septuagint (the translation of the Hebrew Bible into Greek) renders *chesed* with *charis*.

Bibliography

Achtemeier, Paul, ed. "The Book of Revelation." *Interpretation* 40 (1986) 227–301.

Allen, O. Wesley, Jr. *The Homiletic of All Believers: A Conversational Approach to Proclamation and Preaching*. Louisville: Westminster John Knox, 2005.

Allen, Ronald J. "Preaching as Conversation among Proposals." In *Handbook of Process Theology*, edited by Jay McDaniel and Donna Bowman, 78–90. St. Louis: Chalice, 2006.

————. "Preaching as Mutual Critical Correlation through Conversation." In *Purposes of Preaching*, edited by Jana Childers, 1–22. St. Louis: Chalice, 2004.

————. *Thinking Theologically: The Preacher as Theologian*. Elements of Preaching. Minneapolis: Fortress, 2008.

Allen, Ronald J., ed. *Patterns of Preaching: A Sermon Sampler*. St. Louis: Chalice, 1998.

Allen, Ronald J., and O. Wesley Allen Jr. *The Sermon without End: A Conversational Approach to Preaching*. Nashville: Abingdon, 2015.

Aune, David E. *Revelation 1–5*. Word Biblical Commentary 52A. Waco, TX: Word, 1997.

————. *Revelation 6–16*. Word Biblical Commentary 52B. Waco, TX: Word, 1997.

————. *Revelation 17–22*. Word Biblical Commentary 52C. Waco, TX: Word, 1997.

Balmer, Randall. *The Making of Evangelicalism: From Revivalism to Politics and Beyond*. Waco, TX: Baylor University Press, 2010.

Barr, David L. *The Reality of the Apocalypse: Rhetoric and Politics in the Book of Revelation*. Symposium Series 39. Atlanta: Society of Biblical Literature, 2006.

————. *Tales of the End: A Narrative Commentary on the Book of Revelation*. The Storyteller's Bible 1. Santa Rosa, CA: Polebridge, 1998.

Bauckham, Richard. *The Theology of the Book of Revelation*. New Testament Theology. Cambridge: Cambridge University Press, 1993.

Beale, G. K. *The Book of Revelation*. The New International Greek Testament Commentary. Grand Rapids: Eerdmans, 1999.

Beasley-Murray, George R. *The Book of Revelation*. New Century Bible Commentary. New York: Harper Collins, 1974.

Blount, Brian K. *Can I Get a Witness: Reading the Book of Revelation through African American Culture*. Louisville: Westminster John Knox, 2005.

————. *Invasion of the Dead: Preaching Resurrection*. Louisville: Westminster John Knox, 2014.

————. *Revelation: A Commentary*. New Testament Library. Louisville: Westminster John Knox, 2009.

Bock, Darrell, ed. *Three Views on the Millennium and Beyond.* Grand Rapids: Zondervan, 1999.

Boesak, Allan A. *Comfort and Protest: Reflections on the Apocalypse of John of Patmos.* Philadelphia: Westminster, 1987.

Boring, M. Eugene. *Revelation.* Interpretation: A Bible Commentary for Teaching and Preaching. Louisville: Westminster John Knox, 1989.

Boring, M. Eugene, and Fred B. Craddock. *The People's New Testament Commentary.* Louisville: Westminster John Knox, 2004.

Brownlee, William H. *Ezekiel 1–19.* Word Biblical Commentary 28. Waco, TX: Word, 1986.

Caird, G. B. *The Revelation of St. John the Divine.* Harper's New Testament Commentaries. New York: Harper & Row, 1966.

Carey, Greg. "Teaching and Preaching the Book of Revelation in the Church." *Review and Expositor* 98.1 (2001) 87–100.

———. *Ultimate Things: An Introduction to Jewish and Christian Apocalyptic Literature.* St. Louis: Chalice, 2005.

Carey, Greg, and Gregory L. Bloomquist, eds. *Vision and Persuasion: Rhetorical Dimensions of Apocalyptic Discourse.* St. Louis: Chalice, 1999.

Carter, Warren. *The Roman Empire and the New Testament: An Essential Guide.* Abingdon Essential Guides. Nashville: Abingdon, 2006.

———. *What Does Revelation Reveal? Unlocking the Mystery.* Nashville: Abingdon, 2011.

Charles R. H. *A Critical and Exegetical Commentary on the Revelation of St. John.* International Critical Commentary 44. 2 vols. Edinburgh; T. & T. Clark, 1920.

Collins, Adela Yarbro. *Christ and Catharsis: The Power of the Apocalypse.* Philadelphia: Westminster, 1984.

———. *The Combat Myth in the Book of Revelation.* Harvard Dissertations in Religion 9. Missoula, MT: Scholars, 1976.

———. "The Political Perspective of the Revelation to John." *Journal of Biblical Literature* 96.2 (1977) 241–56.

———. "What the Spirit Says to the Churches: Preaching the Apocalypse." *Quarterly Review* 4.3 (1984) 69–84.

Collins, John J. *Apocalypse, Prophecy, and Pseudepigraphy: On Jewish Apocalyptic Literature.* Grand Rapids: Eerdmans, 2015.

———. *The Apocalyptic Imagination: An Introduction to the Jewish Matrix of Christianity.* New York: Crossroad, 1987.

———. *Daniel with an Introduction to Apocalyptic Literature.* Forms of Old Testament Literature 20. Grand Rapids: Eerdmans, 1984.

Consultation on Common Texts. *The Revised Common Lectionary.* Nashville: Abingdon, 1992.

Craddock, Fred B. "Preaching the Book of Revelation." *Interpretation* 40.3 (1986) 270–82.

de Silva, David. *Seeing Things John's Way: The Rhetoric of the Book of Revelation.* Louisville: Westminster John Knox, 2009.

Dodds, E. R. *Pagan and Christian in an Age of Anxiety: Some Aspects of Religious Experience from Marcus Aurelius to Constantine.* Cambridge: Cambridge University Press, 1965.

Efird, James M. *Left Behind? What the Bible Really Says about the End Times.* Macon, Ga: Smith & Helwys, 2006.

Ellul, Jacques. *Apocalypse: The Book of Revelation.* New York: Seabury, 1977.

Farley, Edward. "Preaching the Bible and Preaching the Gospel." In *Practicing the Gospel: Unconventional Thoughts on the Church's Ministry,* 71–82. Louisville: Westminster John Knox, 2003.

Farmer, Ronald L. *Revelation.* Chalice Commentaries for Today. St. Louis: Chalice, 2005.

Frilingos, Christopher A. *Spectacles of Empire: Monsters, Martyrs, and the Book of Revelation.* Philadelphia: University of Pennsylvania Press, 2004.

Glabach, Wilfried E. *Reclaiming the Book of Revelation: A Suggestion of New Readings in the Local Church.* American University Studies. New York: Lang, 2007.

Gorman, Michael J. *Reading Revelation Responsibly: Uncivil Worship and Witness. Following the Lamb into the New Age.* Eugene, OR: Cascade, 2010.

Grenz, Stanley J. *The Millennial Maze: Sorting Out Evangelical Options.* Downers Grove, IL: InterVarsity, 1992.

Gundry, Robert H. *Church and the Tribulation: A Biblical Examination of Posttribulationism.* Grand Rapids: Zondervan, 2010.

Gunsalus, Katherine, and Justo L. González. *Vision at Patmos: Study of the Book of Revelation.* Abingdon Lay Bible Studies. Nashville: Abingdon, 1991.

Handel, George F. "George Frederic Handel: *Hallelujah!* Lyrics." http://lyrics.wikia. com/wiki/George_Frideric_Handel:Hallelujah!.

Hays, Richard B., and Stefan Alkier, eds. *Revelation and the Politics of Apocalyptic Interpretation.* Waco, TX: Baylor University Press, 2012.

Heber, Reginald. "Holy, Holy, Holy." In *The Chalice Hymnal,* edited by Daniel B. Merrick, 4. St. Louis: Chalice, 1995.

Hoffman, Elisha. "Are You Washed in the Blood?" In *Baptist Hymnal,* 229. Nashville: Lifeway Resources, 2008.

Horsley, Richard, ed. *In the Shadow of Empire: Reclaiming the Bible as a History of Faithful Resistance.* Louisville: Westminster John Knox, 2008.

Howe, Julia Ward. "Mine Eyes Have Seen the Glory." In *The Chalice Hymnal,* edited by Daniel B. Merrick, 705. St. Louis: Chalice, 1995.

Jacobsen, David Schnasa. *Preaching in the New Creation: The Promise of New Testament Apocalyptic Texts.* Louisville: Westminster John Knox, 1999.

Jensen, Robert. *We Are All Apocalyptic Now: On the Responsibilities of Teaching, Preaching, Reporting, Writing, and Speaking Out.* Austin: Monkeywrench, 2013.

Jonaitis, Dorothy. *Unmasking Apocalyptic Texts: A Guide to Preaching and Teaching.* New York: Paulist, 2005.

Jones, Larry Paul, and Jerry L. Sumney. *Preaching Apocalyptic Texts.* Preaching Classic Texts. St. Louis: Chalice, 1999.

Keller, Catherine. *Apocalypse Now and Then: A Feminist Guide to the End of the World.* Minneapolis: Fortress, 2005.

———. *God and Power: Counter-Apocalyptic Journeys.* Minneapolis: Fortress, 2005.

Koester, Craig R. *Revelation and the End of All Things.* Grand Rapids: Eerdmans, 2001.

Kraybill, J. Nelson. *Apocalypse and Allegiance: Worship, Devotion, and Politics in the Book of Revelation.* Grand Rapids: Brazos, 2010.

Krodel, Gerhard. *Revelation.* Augsburg Commentary on the New Testament. Minneapolis: Augsburg, 1989.

Ladd, George Eldon. *A Commentary on the Revelation to John.* Grand Rapids: Eerdmans, 1972.

LaHaye, Tim. *Revelation Unveiled.* Left Behind. Grand Rapids: Zondervan, 1999.

Lindsay, Hal. *The Late Great Planet Earth.* Grand Rapids: Zondervan, 1970.

Malina, Bruce J., and John J. Pilch. *Social-Science Commentary on the Book of Revelation.* Minneapolis: Fortress, 2000.

Minear, Paul S. *I Saw a New Earth: An Introduction to the Visions of the Apocalypse.* Washington, DC: Corpus, 1968.

Moore, Stephen D. *Untold Tales from the Book of Revelation: Sex, Gender, Empire, and Ecology.* Resources for Biblical Study. Atlanta: Society of Biblical Literature, 2014.

Murphy, Frederick J. *Fallen is Babylon: The Revelation to John.* The New Testament in Context. Valley Forge: Trinity Press International, 1998.

O'Day, Gail R. "Teaching and Preaching the Book of Revelation." *Word and World* 25.3 (2005) 246–54.

Otto, Rudolph. *The Idea of the Holy: An Inquiry into the Non-rational Factor in the Idea of the Divine and Its Relation to the Rational.* Translated by John W. Harvey. London: Oxford University Press, 1923.

Pagels, Elaine. *Revelations: Visions, Prophecy, and Politics in the Book of Revelation.* New York: Viking, 2012.

Pippin, Tina. "The Heroine and the Whore." In *From Every People and Nation: The Book of Revelation in Intercultural Perspective,* edited by David Rhoads, 127–45. Minneapolis: Fortress, 2005.

Powery, Luke A. "Painful Praise: Exploring the Public Proclamation of the Hymns of Revelation." *Theology Today* 70.1 (2013) 69–78.

Reddish, Mitchell. *Revelation.* Smith and Helwys Bible Commentary. Macon, GA: Smith & Helwys, 2001.

Rhoads, David M., ed. *From Every People and Nation: The Book of Revelation in Intercultural Perspective.* Minneapolis: Fortress, 2005.

Rice, Grantland. "The Four Horsemen." *New York Herald Tribune,* October 18, 1924. http://archives.nd.edu/research/texts/rice.htm.

Richard, Pablo. *Apocalypse: A People's Commentary on the Book of Revelation.* Bible and Liberation. Maryknoll, NY: Orbis, 1995.

Rogers, Cornish R. "Images of Christian Victory: Notes for Preaching from the Book of Revelation." *Quarterly Review* 10.3 (1990) 69–78.

Rogers, Cornish R., and Joseph R. Jeter, eds. *Preaching Through the Apocalypse: Sermons from Revelation.* St. Louis: Chalice, 1992.

Rossing, Barbara. *The Rapture Exposed: The Message of Hope in the Book of Revelation.* New York: Basic Books, 2004.

Rowland, Christopher C. "The Book of Revelation." *The New Interpreter's Bible,* edited by Leander Keck et al., 12:501–743. Nashville: Abingdon, 1998.

———. *The Open Heaven: A Study of Apocalyptic in Judaism and Early Christianity.* London: SPCK, 1982.

Schüssler Fiorenza, Elisabeth. *Book of Revelation: Justice and Judgment.* Philadelphia: Fortress, 1985.

———. *Invitation to the Book of Revelation: A Commentary on the Apocalypse with Complete Text from the Jerusalem Bible.* Garden City, NY: Image, 1981.

———. *Revelation: Vision of a Just World.* Edinburgh: T. & T. Clark, 1993.

Steinbeck, John. *The Grapes of Wrath.* New York: Viking, 2014.

Stowers, Stanley K. *A Rereading of Romans: Justice, Jews, and Gentiles.* New Haven, CT: Yale University Press, 1994

Suchocki, Marjorie. *The End of Evil: Process Eschatology in Historical Context.* SUNY Series in Philosophy. Eugene, OR: Wipf & Stock, 2005.

———. *Fall to Violence: Original Sin in Relational Theology.* New York: Continuum, 1995.

Sweet, J. P. M. *Revelation.* Westminster Pelican Commentaries. Philadelphia: Westminster, 1979.

Talbert, Charles H. *The Apocalypse: A Reading of the Revelation of John.* Louisville: Westminster John Knox, 1994.

Thompson, Leonard L. *The Book of Revelation: Apocalypse and Empire.* New York: Oxford University Press, 1990.

———. *Revelation.* Abingdon New Testament Commentaries. Nashville: Abingdon, 1998.

Travis, Hannibal. "The Cultural and Intellectual Property Interests of the Indigenous Peoples of Turkey and Iraq." *Texas Wesleyan Law Review* 15 (2009) 601–80.

Williams, Michael E., ed. *Daniel and Revelation.* The Storyteller's Companion to the Bible 8. Nashville: Abingdon, 2009.

Williamson, Clark M. *A Mutual Witness: Towards Critical Solidarity Between Jews and Christians.* St. Louis: Chalice Press, 1992.

———. *Way of Blessing, Way of Life: A Christian Theology.* St. Louis: Chalice, 1999.

Witherington, Ben, III. *Revelation.* The New Cambridge Bible Commentary. New York: Cambridge University Press, 2003.

Yen, Leah. "Revelation 20:7–15: The Final Defeat of Evil." Student Paper. Christian Theological Seminary, 2018.